Illinois Studies in Communications

Illinois Studies in Communications

Senior Editors
Sandra Braman, James W. Carey, Clifford G. Christians,
Lawrence Grossberg, Thomas H. Guback, James W. Hay, John C. Nerone,
Ellen A. Wartella, and D. Charles Whitney.

Books in the Series

Fifties Television: The Industry and Its Critics
William F. Boddy

Hollywood and Broadcasting: From Radio to Cable
Michele Hilmes

The American Radio Industry and Its Latin American Activities
James Schwoch

Hollywood
and Broadcasting

FROM RADIO TO CABLE

Michele Hilmes

University of Illinois Press
Urbana and Chicago

© 1990 by the Board of Trustees of the University of Illinois
Manufactured in the United States of America
C   5   4   3   2   1

This book is printed on acid-free paper.

Library of Congress Cataloging-in-Publication Data

Hilmes, Michele, 1953–
    Hollywood and broadcasting: from radio to cable / Michele Hilmes.
        p.   cm.
    Revision of the author's thesis (Ph.D.)—New York University.
    Includes bibliographical references.
    ISBN 0-252-01709-9 (alk. paper)
    1. Broadcasting—United States—History.   2. Motion picture indus-
try—California—Los Angeles—Influence.   3. Motion picture studios—
California—Los Angeles—Influence.   4. Hollywood (Los Angeles, Calif.)—Industries.   I. Title.
PN1990.6.U5H5   1990
384′.0973—dc20   89-20423
                                                                          CIP

To Bruce and Amanda

Contents

Acknowledgments

This book stems from doctoral research done at New York University in the Department of Cinema Studies. I would like to thank all the faculty members who contributed, directly or indirectly, to its genesis and development there, especially Brian Winston, Robert Sklar, Janet Staiger, Robert Stam, William Simon, Jay Leyda, and William Everson, as well as the members of the fall 1982 Dissertation Seminar, whose interest and commiseration helped the process along. At Spring Hill College, I owe special thanks to Tom Loehr, David Sauer, Dottie Hempfleng, Bettie Hudgens, Stuart Bullion, Jerry Scott, Linda Lankewicz, and Glen Bell, among others, for their encouragement and support, whether moral, pragmatic, or connected in some way with computers.

At the University of Illinois Press, it was Lawrence Malley who first saw potential in the dissertation manuscript and provided cheerful and friendly guidance through the revision process. Thanks to Richard Wentworth for his help at a later stage, and to James Carey for his interest and approval. Above all, I am indebted to Robert C. Allen, whose criticism, advice, encouragement, and unstinting generosity with his time contributed greatly to the development of this project beyond the dissertation stage and helped me to clarify and extend its scope, especially in the writing of the chapter on the "Lux Radio Theatre."

Introduction

This study examines the interrelationship of two major American institutions, the film and broadcasting industries, over a historical period that stretches from the days before network radio to the present. Its central purpose is to document the considerable, although neglected, influence that Hollywood exerted—and continues to exert—over the development of the broadcast medium. My primary assertion is that the film industry played a central role in the evolution of economic structures, program forms, and patterns of distribution in broadcasting, because Hollywood has functioned since the early 1920s as broadcasting's alter ego, its main rival and contributor, the only other force unified and powerful enough to present a viable alternative definition to the uses made of the medium by established broadcast interests, yet a necessary contributor to broadcasting's growth and success. The ongoing process of conflict, compromise, and accommodation between the two has shaped the economic and expressive structures of both media. This book begins with the period of radio, as film and broadcasting interests struggled over the right to define and control the possibilities opened up by the new technology. Later chapters examine the period of television's introduction and the changes made in the film-broadcasting relationship by new technologies such as cable, satellite distribution, and pay television.

The first chapter, which deals with the development of the regulatory framework from which network radio emerged, argues that radio technology brought with it special problems of definition, control, and support. Distrust of government monopoly power over radio, countered by equally strong fears of private monopoly over the airwaves, led to

radio's compromise between private ownership and government regulation. However, the unwillingness of government agencies to exert
strong control over the medium left an open field to radio manufacturing
interests, backed by a seemingly ancillary but in fact vitally involved
nonbroadcast concern, the American Telephone and Telegraph Company. The resulting network-based, advertising-supported oligopoly,
unforeseen by early regulators, would dominate broadcasting for the
next sixty years.

Chapter 2 examines the film industry's initial forays into radio,
placing Hollywood's growing interest in broadcasting in the context of
intraindustry conflict. Tension between film exhibitors and producers
was an integral component of the movie business, leading at various
points in its history to technological and formal innovations designed
to enhance the control of producers over their product. Radio played
a similar role for the Hollywood studios, as early ownership of radio
stations led studios to various forms of experimentation, including
attempts to form radio broadcasting networks. However, a combination
of internal oppositon from exhibitors, resistance by broadcasting interests, inability to gain access to land lines, and regulatory difficulties
prevented these plans from succeeding.

Blocked in their initial attempts to enter broadcasting at the level of
network operation and ownership, the studios turned their attention
to programming in the 1930s (chapter 3). The growth of the two major
radio networks is traced, as radio's economic system and programming
forms began to take shape. With the relaxation of advertising restrictions
in the early 1930s, sponsored programs came to dominate the airwaves,
and Hollywood became an important component of radio advertising
strategy. As the studios became more involved with radio production,
the complaints of exhibitors intensified, leading to a brief crisis in
1932—however, the idea that the studios placed a "ban" on radio in
1932, a piece of received history that dominates many references to
film-radio relations, is erroneous. In fact, Hollywood's involvement
with radio programming intensified in the 1930s, and the studios played
a key role in the development of several of radio's most enduring
program genres. Again, the actions of AT&T affected the structure of
broadcasting in the 1930s; the federal government's 1936 investigation
of telephone rate structures finally removed barriers to West Coast
production, and Hollywood became a major broadcast production center
as the new technology of television waited in the wings.

In chapter 4, one aspect of the process of competition and cooperation
is discussed in detail. Throughout this book, an implicit link has been
made between the economic and regulatory forces that shaped the

network structure and the programs ultimately produced for those networks. This link becomes explicit as one particular radio program, the "Lux Radio Theatre," is used as a case study of the evolution of one of radio's characteristic program forms. Drawing on a theoretical orientation often associated with the British "cultural studies" perspective, particularly with the work of Stuart Hall, I argue in this chapter that the encoding process at work in the production of radio programs reflects the interests of the major economic forces involved in it, in specific ways that affect the formal and signifying structures of the program.[1]

These forces are identified as first, the commercial sponsor and the advertising agency through which the sponsor's interests are activated; second, the networks and stations that distribute the program; and third, in the case of "Lux," the Hollywood studios whose stars and film properties provided the material adapted for radio exhibition. These conflicting and cooperating forces operate in tension to produce the characteristic structure of the radio program, whose most dominant trait consisted precisely of this constant and precarious balancing of the interests of sponsor, network, and studio. The type of discourse thus produced—segmented, permeable, marked by frequent interruptions and a relatively shallow diegesis—differentiates the broadcast program from the theatrical film, yet draws on many of its narrative and signifying conventions. Most of radio's economic structures and program forms would carry over into network television, including the characteristic broadcast discourse, although the shift to a visual medium would again upset the balance between Hollywood and the networks developed during the 1930s and 1940s. Chapter 4 concludes with a discussion of some of the reasons for the failure of the video version of "Lux," as the era of television began.

With the introduction of television, a new period of struggle ensued between Hollywood and broadcasting forces. At first, as with radio, the studios attempted to gain an ownership foothold in the new medium but found this avenue largely blocked by regulatory restrictions. The studios responded to limited opportunities for station ownership by proposing or backing new ideas that would extend the direct-sale economics of the box office to the technology of television. Chapter 5 traces the development of two alternative uses developed by film interests, theater television and subscription TV. Again, powerful opposition by film exhibitors, combined with regulatory actions of the federal government backed by broadcasters, resulted in the defeat of both of these alternatives.

Chapter 6 details the system of accommodations made by the networks and studios during broadcast television's "Golden Age." Beginning with the networks' endorsement of "live TV," the utility of which in early television economics is discussed, the gradual shift to filmed programming produced by Hollywood studios followed the same pattern as that established in chapter 3. It parallels the transition from sponsor-controlled programs to the "magazine format" system of spot advertising the networks developed in the late 1950s. Both in direct production for television and in the sale of films to the networks, Hollywood once again became a significant force in broadcast economics. In addition to growing network dependency, syndicated theatrical films provided an alternative source of programming to both independent and affiliated stations, thus again challenging network hegemony.

Although Hollywood and the networks may have reached a comfortable arrangement of mutual benefit by the mid 1960s, other pressures at work, many of them brought on by built-up contradictions in the history of broadcast regulation, soon combined to upset the balance of power. Cable television's entry into the broadcast-film relationship in the 1970s, made inevitable by FCC restrictions on alternative services over the airwaves, opened new opportunities both for Hollywood and for a new set of players, the cable companies. The emergence of satellite-distributed pay television in 1975 provoked a third attempt by the major studios to gain a position of control in a television-related technology. Although their initial effort failed, the 1980s witnessed an increasing involvement of Hollywood interests in the business of cable, pay television, videocassette distribution, and other new channels, as well as continued production for network and syndication. As the economic base of traditional broadcast networks erodes, film producers—with the major studios still in the dominant position—find themselves with expanding opportunities and a heavy demand for their product. However, the merging of formerly separate interests in the 1980s may also point to the disappearance of "Hollywood" and "broadcasting" as we know them, as the various facets of the entertainment media merge and become more diversified.

Overall, then, we need to examine the relationship of the film and broadcasting industries in a new light. For various reasons having to do both with differentiation in product and organization maintained by the institutions themselves, and with the reception accorded them in the academic institution, film and broadcasting have been traditionally regarded as inherently separate, having little to do with each other except in discrete and unusual circumstances. Most accepted historical accounts on both sides of the topic routinely ignore any overlap between the two industries, particularly during the early period of network radio. As Richard Jewell remarks in one of the few published works to acknowledge their relationship, "Relying on the stardard texts, one would conclude that each medium developed in its own hermetically sealed vacuum tube, without knowledge of or interaction with the other."[2] To revise this version of history, it has been necessary to go back to primary materials—government records, trade periodicals, and industry publications—and in some cases to "discover" or reinterpret secondary materials, whose neglect rests not on their nonexistence or unavailability, but on a concept of institutional history that has simply overlooked their presence and effect. Drawing on a model of historical narrative that focuses on process rather than outcome, on conflict rather than consensus, some of the forces that presented alternatives or opposition to those that came out on top can be worked into this account, enriching our understanding of the patterns and structures that ultimately emerged.[3] And by regarding economics and industry structures as an inseparable component of the texts they produce, a greater depth of understanding can be brought both to the interpretation and analysis of texts, and to the study of their reception processes.[4]

As central a role as the institutions of film and television play in our culture, it is vital that we understand some of the forces and processes that shaped them. The tension between the two industries occurs across some of the major fault lines, or structural oppositions, that shape our society: public interest versus private profits, government regulation versus laissez-faire economics, free audience choice versus audience manipulation, the "marketplace of ideas" versus the power of vested interests. If the materials we encounter every day on television and in movie theaters is the product of long-ago—as well as current— decisions and compromises made among large institutions and governing bodies, we must take these interests into account in assessing the product. This book may open a small window onto the assessment process.

NOTES

1. See, for example, Stuart Hall, "Encoding and Decoding in the Television Discourse," Occasional Papers, Centre for Contemporary Cultural Studies, University of Birmingham, 1973; and Stuart Hall, "The Toad in the Garden: Thatcherism among the Theorists," in *Marxism and the Interpretation of Culture*, ed. Cary Nelson and Lawrence Grossberg (Urbana: University of Illinois Press, 1988), pp. 35–58.

2. Richard B. Jewell, "Hollywood and Radio: Competition and Partnership in the 1930's," *Historical Journal of Film, Radio, and Television* 4, no. 2 (1984): 125–41.

3. Raymond Williams is a cultural historian whose work develops this model; see Raymond Williams, *Television: Technology and Cultural Form* (New York: Schocken Books, 1977). Colin McArthur presents a critique of traditional historical method in *Television and History* (London: British Film Institute, 1978).

4. Critical works employing this perspective include Robert C. Allen, *Speaking of Soap Operas* (Chapel Hill: University of North Carolina Press, 1985); Janet Staiger, "Mass-Produced Photoplays: Economic and Signifying Practices in the First Years of Hollywood," in *Movies and Methods,* vol. 2, ed. Bill Nichols (Berkeley: University of California Press, 1985), pp. 144–61; Douglas Gomery, "The Coming of Sound to American Cinema," Ph.D. diss., University of Wisconsin-Madison, 1975; and Robert Vianello, "The Power Politics of 'Live' Television," *Journal of Film and Video* 7 (Summer 1985): 226–40.

1

Hollywood and the
Broadcasting Industry

THE FORMATIVE YEARS

Any attempt to explore the interrelationship of the film and television industries must begin with, or at least take into account, the period of interaction between the two industries that began in the early days of radio. Radio's economic base and regulatory structure emerged during these years, as did the film industry's initial forays into broadcasting that were to determine its later relationship to television. Little critical or historical attention has been given this period, however. Most studies begin only in the 1930s, and even such an influential and respected writer as Erik Barnouw has stated categorically that "At the start of the decade [the 1930s] relations between radio and the Hollywood world had been minimal...Hollywood strategy for the moment was to ignore radio."[1]

Film historians have spoken even less frequently of any sort of connection between film and radio, either echoing Barnouw or referring to radio only in terms of its "threat" or "challenge" to the film. William Everson, although one of the few writers to discuss any interaction at all in the early 1920s, limits his analysis to the influence of radio's new popularity on film form, as writers discussing the effects of television only deal with technical changes in the film such as CinemaScope and 3-D.[2] This historical blind spot becomes a serious problem when later writers attempt to address the film-television relationship, leading to histories predicated on the "tunnel vision of the studios"; the "complacency" of the studios rooted in the view that "television [was] a form of 'visual radio' and not "movies in the home,"[3] or in drawing false parallels between radio and television such as the contention that,

"Having rebutted radio, the movie moguls were confident that they could blunt the challenge of TV."[4]

In fact, Hollywood maintained a lively and innovative interest in radio from the early 1920s until the introduction of television in the late 1940s. By an examination of primary materials of the period—trade journals, the business press, popular periodicals, and government reports and publications—a new picture emerges of Hollywood as an active experimenter with the new technology, presenting a serious challenge to the established broadcasting interests by proposing an alternate economic base for the medium. A closer look at this period also reveals some of the reasons behind Hollywood's failure to make substantial inroads into the radio business, based in part on two factors that would impede its later expansion into television: federal regulation of broadcasting and the ever-present threat of antitrust litigation. To understand the first factor, broadcast regulation, we must begin with the evolution of the regulatory concepts determining radio's later legislative and economic conditions. These in turn would have a decisive effect on the film industry's ability to enter that field.

Broadcasting Regulation: Laws and Loopholes

The peculiar blend of private enterprise and government regulation that characterizes the American system of broadcasting did not arise full blown in the Communications Act of 1934, nor did it emerge as a clear response over the years to obvious technical and social needs. Between 1912 and the writing of the influential Radio Act of 1927, several different proposals for the economic and regulatory structure of radio appeared. Each reflected the governing interests of one or more powerful public or private entities—corporations, government branches or offices, citizen groups—all with different and often competing plans for the shape this new medium was to take, different definitions of the basic "nature" or appropriate use of the new technology. Although none were adopted in their pure form, each contributed, in concept or statute, to the growing body of thought on the radio question. The lasting perception of radio as a scarce "natural monopoly," as properly belonging in the public domain, and as a mysterious technology somehow requiring unprecedented legal status, underlies present regulation and influences our thinking in contemporary debates over television and cable regulation.

Also recurring, and linked to such ideas, is the conflict between government domination of this important communication medium, on the one hand, and private monopoly power on the other. These ideas and conflicts culminated in the Radio Act of 1927, which reflects an uneasy but lasting compromise. The many contradictions and loopholes in these competing conceptions would have a decisive effect on the structure of commercial broadcasting and the later ability of the film industry to gain a foothold in the radio business.

Mysterious Technology

It is hard for those of us living in the latter half of the twentieth century to comprehend the fantastic, almost magical qualities attributed to the idea of radio waves in its first decades. Earliest responses to the coming era of "wireless" communication combined head-shaking mysticism with ecstatic predictions of a new utopia.[5] The presentation of radio as a mysterious technology, a wonder machine calling up voices from the void, allowed technological bedazzlement to overshadow potential social and economic implications, even among those assigned to the task of harnessing and regulating this new phenomenon. Very early in the history of broadcast regulation, as one analyst suggests, "an economic problem was mistakenly diagnosed as a technical one,"[6] sowing the seeds of future confusion which could be exploited by those in a position to do so.

Indeed, a reluctance to legislate in areas deemed so technologically complicated as to be beyond the grasp of the nonscientist, and hence to be mediated by industry-trained experts, persists throughout the history of broadcasting. William Howard Taft, chief justice of the Supreme Court from 1921 to 1930, is reported to have said, "I have always dodged this radio question...interpreting the law on this subject is like trying to interpret the law of the occult. It seems like dealing with something supernatural. I want to put it off as long as possible in the hope that it becomes more understandable before the court passes on the question involved."[7]

In a 1927 address following the formation of the Federal Radio Commission, Senator James Watson, whose position as head of the powerful Interstate Commerce Committee (under whose jurisdiction radio regulation fell) had certainly brought him into frequent contact with radio, developed this theme in a poetic manner and touched a religious note: "Nor shall I attempt to portray the mysteries of this force which has been projected through 500 feet of firm rock and a dozen feet of solid lead, a force by means of which the voice of the orator and of the prima donna may be heard across the continent swifter than the coming light. Certainly it is renewed evidence of the sublime fact that 'God moves in a mysterious way his wonders to perform'."[8]

Watson's address was heard throughout the country over the NBC network. This almost willful insistence on radio's inscrutability, although perhaps exaggerated by the rhetorical style of the day, had some very real and serious results. The early radio conferences relied heavily on testimony from outside experts, respectfully regarded as the only ones able to express a valid opinion on such matters—and where better to find expertise than in the research departments of those corporations that invented the receiving and transmitting devices? As Robert H. Stern, writing about the early regulatory decision affecting the development of television in the 1920s and 1930s, has observed, too often in the history of broadcasting the only source of informed opinion about the complex issues confronting legislators was the broadcasters themselves, whose presentation of the facts "might not be altogether free from self-regarding coloration."[9] This situation would greatly affect the development of radio regulation, and would eventually work against the film industry's involvement in broadcasting. But definition of the nature of broadcasting of, for, and by the engineering departments of major corporations merely reflects the larger struggle affecting regulation during the period. To whom did this invisible, intangible resource belong? Who should control it, and how should it be supported?

The Public Resource

One of the most basic premises underlying traditional American thinking about the broadcasting medium is the concept of public ownership of the airwaves. Whether referred to as the "ether" as in early writings, or later as the electromagnetic spectrum, the peculiar properties of the invisible, intangible resource somehow mark it as properly belonging in the public sphere. This perception of broadcasting draws its precedents from the "transportation" model established to regulate railroads by the Interstate Commerce Act of 1887, but its applicability to broadcasting stimulated debate from radio's inception. In 1924, it was believed to be necessary to introduce a Senate resolution proclaiming that "The ether and the use thereof for the transmission of signals, words, energy and other purposes...is hereby reaffirmed to be the inalienable possession of the people of the United States and their Government."[10]

It is an assumption rarely challenged outright, although inroads on the spirit of the law, such as the imminent corporate monopoly envisioned by legislators in 1924, occasionally give rise to the reaffirmation of the principle. Although private alternatives to this definition of ownership of the airwaves have been proposed, no coherent presentation of the idea appeared until 1951, when Leo Herzel published a controversial article in the *University of Chicago Law Review.* It is significant that this idea gains serious consideration not in the early days of radio, when the basic economics of the broadcasting venture had not yet been worked out, but in 1951 as the advent of television raised the stakes, and broadcasting promised to become an extraordinarily profitable field.

Herzel suggests, as an alternative to the complicated system of spectrum allocation employed by the FCC, a standard pricing mechanism approach: channels should be leased to the highest bidder. However, the idea of the broadcast spectrum as private property contrasts strongly with the regulatory structures of the Federal Communications Commission as they originally were intended.[11]

Writing in 1969, Nicholas Johnson of the Federal Communications Commission analyses past spectrum allocation policies of the commission and evaluates various proposed alternatives, including a modification of the market pricing strategy based on the leasing of spectrum space by the government to private enterprise. This system, although advocated by other critics of past and present FCC policies, suffers in Johnson's view from the difficulty of assigning fair value to use of the spectrum, and from the resulting loss of all public control over broadcasting content that would ensue. Johnson defends the conceptual basis of current regulation—although deploring its enforcement—and links public interest/public ownership to economic concerns in a manner implied, although unstated, in earlier legislation.

> The theory of the Communications Act was that the inherently oligopolistic structure of radio use necessitated a system of licenses for a limited term with no property rights accruing to the licensee. The radio spectrum was meant to be a resource owned and retained by the people. Their representatives—the Congress, and its delegated agency, the FCC—were to manage it. Private interests could use the spectrum as proxies for the public, but in return for the right to its use for private gain *they were to "pay" by performance in the "public interest".*...Congress clearly saw that the use of the spectrum without monetary payment might procure large returns for the private users. But Congress contemplated that the spectrum users, in exchange for the spectrum, would not simply profit-maximize as do other businesses. The concept was that *operation in the public interest would preclude profit maximization by the spectrum user, and that the difference between a public-service operating level of profits and a theoretical level of maximum profits would be the price exacted for the use of the spectrum.* It was thought that this system would produce benefits to the public in excess of the money that the public could have received from a sale of spectrum to a user with no public obligation.[12]

Indeed, the earliest years of broadcasting, from the formation of NBC in 1926 until the rise of commercial advertising in the 1930s, show an adherence to this conception of radio's proper function. Sustaining, or network-funded, programs outnumbered commercially sponsored shows in prime hours until the mid 1930s. During the same period, the sale of radio receiving sets rose sharply to near saturation point, representing a strong source of profits for the networks' parent companies.

However, the reasons behind the adoption of current regulatory structures as formulated in the Communications Act of 1934 cannot be understood in terms of simple economics but must be situated in the events preceding the writing of the act—events engendered by the economic, political, and perceptual circumstances of the time, including the dominant attitudes and opinions surrounding the new technology. Prevalent among these was the struggle over government control of radio broadcasting versus the dangers of private monopoly that occurred as an aftermath of World War I.

Rejection of the Government-Controlled System

Before World War I, the Marconi Wireless Telegraph Company of America dominated commercial radio communication in the United States, while thousands of amateurs across the country transmitted on home-built sets. As early as 1905, the U.S. Navy pressed for some regulation of ship-to-shore communications, but not until 1910 were powers authorizing mandatory radio communications aboard ship given to the secretary of commerce. In 1912, the first Radio Act introduced the concept of frequency assignments, but limited the scope of regulatory control to this simple function. Although the Commerce Department, through deputation to the Bureau of Navigation, attempted to settle frequency and air time disputes between early broadcast stations, their jurisdiction extended only to making recommendations under the justification of "public interest." As an ultimate penalty, broadcasters violating time and wavelength agreements could find their assigned wavelength revoked.[13] The onset of the war brought a temporary halt to the multiplying voices in the air when, for reasons of national security, the government instituted a freeze on radio broadcasting and the Navy assumed the operation of all private stations. Wartime exigencies also led to a pooling of patents under Navy supervision, resulting in unimpeded technological progress during the war years.[14]

In the period immediately following the war, the idea of permanent governmental control of radio, analogous to that of the BBC in Great Britain, emerged at the urging of its longtime guardian, the Navy. In

1917 and 1918, congressional hearings were held on "Government Control of Radio Communication," a significant development because it is in the proposals for Navy control of radio that the concept of broadcasting as a "natural monopoly" first occurs.

Both in 1917 and in 1918, bills appeared before the House suggesting that complete control over broadcasting be ceded to the Department of the Navy. Other rivals for such control included the Post Office and the Interstate Commerce Commission, but it was the Navy, thanks to its wartime experience, that most strongly urged its own case. Josephus Daniels, secretary of the Navy, introduced as a basis for his claim the idea of the "limited ether"—later, the "scarcity" concept of spectrum space—which must be apportioned and regulated by a central force in order to avoid interference. "There is a certain amount of ether, and you cannot divide it up among people as they choose to use it; one hand must control it . . . my judgment is that in this particular method of communication the government ought to have a monopoly, just like it has with the mails—and even more so because other people could carry the mails on trains without interference, but they cannot use the air without interference."

Commander Stanford C. Hooper, an advisor to Secretary Daniels speaking later in the hearings, spelled the issue out clearly: "radio, by virtue of the interferences, is a natural monopoly; either the government must exercise that monopoly by owning the stations, or it must place the ownership of these stations in the hands of one concern and let the government keep out of it."[15] However, the war years also brought about a strengthening of private interests involved in radio.

In 1919, prompted by the attempt of the American Marconi Company, at that time owned by the Marconi Wireless Telegraph Company Ltd., to acquire rights by purchase over certain essential General Electric patents, the federal government took over the assets of American Marconi. In October of that year, working under governmental approval that may have extended as high as President Woodrow Wilson, the corporate officers of the General Electric Company, who had worked closely with the Navy and the War Department during the war years, met to form a new company to take management control over American Marconi. This new corporation was the Radio Corporation of America.[16] The original participants in RCA were General Electric with 25 percent of the shares; Westinghouse with 20 percent; and the American Telephone and Telegraph Company with 4 percent; the rest was held by 1,800 persons who held small amounts of American Marconi shares. The major shareholders' participation was based on the number and importance of patents controlled.

As a result of this merging of governmental and big business interests, American broadcasting would never again be as accessible to individuals or to small business concerns. Government management consolidated power and technical development in the hands of the major prewar players. Westinghouse and General Electric emerged from the war years with huge manufacturing capacities that, with the military market gone, required an outlet. As Sidney Head has stated, "The pre-war era had been dominated by the inventor-entrepreneur. Now began the era of big business."[17]

Not surprisingly, the owners and managers of these businesses felt that they had much at stake in the apportioning and control of the "ether" they had discovered and were poised to exploit. In fact, the 1924 Senate resolution proclaiming the spectrum to be the "inalienable possession" of the public points as much to the very real threat posed by these powerful corporations as to the clear altruistic intentions of the legislators. However, having rejected the idea of private ownership of the airwaves, a new question emerged. Given that the government would "own" the airwaves but was not prepared to dominate, or, more important, to *fund* their use, and that neither were companies such as RCA, GE, and AT&T to be allowed to buy them outright, what was to be this thing called broadcasting, and how would it support itself?

The Beginnings of the Commercial System

The subject of advertising on radio was much discussed in the popular press as early as 1919, when pioneer station KDKA in Pittsburgh began broadcasting musical programs giving on-air credit to the local music store that supplied the recordings. In 1924, *Radio Broadcast* magazine sponsored an essay competition on the increasingly pressing subject of the future economic basis of radio, asking its readers what they thought about this precedent, and in this context to propose "a workable plan which shall take into account the problems in present radio broadcasting and propose a practical solution."[18] The result was somewhat surprising in light of future developments, but its assumptions are more telling than its conclusions.

In the winning essay, H. D. Kellogg suggested a one-time tax on radio receivers to be paid by the radio owner at the time of purchase. This tax would be adjusted according to the cost and power of the receiver, with owners of the most powerful sets paying the largest amount. Kellogg suggested that the most expedient way of estimating power would be by counting the number of tubes, or crystals, built into the set. He then designated the federal government as the logical administrator of the plan, and pointed out that "the tremendous value to the government of having broadcast stations continuously under its control in times of emergency, or even in ordinary times, to crystallize and direct public opinion and thought, cannot be overemphasized." As a control to possible abuse of this system, Kellogg made the rather mystifying statement that "the work of administering a national broadcasting service is not particularly susceptible to political corruption" and suggested that the public would be the daily judge of the quality of the government's entertainment.[19]

How it happened that an essay promoting government control of radio in such a totalitarian form came to win a national contest is hard to understand, but another reference by the author provides a clue. It is, Kellogg wrote, "inconceivable to require manufacturers and producers of tubes and crystals to collect a stamp tax and turn it in at a pool or fund held as a monopoly for private interests...if run by private interests [it] would require the granting of dangerous monopolistic power." There, the fear of domination by rapacious private corporations lead to the espousal of an extreme degree of government control.

An alternative to the award-winning essay appeared in the following issue of *Radio Broadcast,* this time written by one of the contest judges, Zeh Bouck, a frequent contributor to broadcasting journals of the day. His plan retained the idea of tax on receivers, perhaps supplemented by the sale of printed programs and giant public fund-raising drives to set up a permanent endowment for the broadcasting service. The fees would be collected by a trade organization, which, through methods somehow agreeable to private interest but not regulated by the government, would allocate the funds equitably. Bouck did not indicate how equitable allocation should be achieved, instead quoting Herbert Hoover, then secretary of commerce: "If we are agreed that broadcasting has a mission, it follows that it must and will work out its own financial basis." Current proponents of deregulation would seem to agree.[20]

The fear of *private* monopoly runs as a persistent subcurrent through all the debate and later legislation on radio. It is a fear well founded, as history shows, but the strength and volume of rhetoric directed against it—similar to the rhetoric against advertising during the same period—seems remarkable in the face of the eventual establishment of just such a system. The fact that the form and content of later federal regulation, although designed expressly to guard against private monopoly control, allowed this control to emerge almost before the congressional ink had dried attests to the power of existing private interests over the ostensible efforts of the public and its protectors.

In fact, as is so often the case, the force of rhetoric seems to act as a measure of its lack of effect. While declaring its intention to protect the public from a private broadcasting monopoly, the early efforts of the Federal Radio Commission in effect ensured the eventual triumph of just such a situation, largely by error of omission, as we shall see. Government and private interests, horns locked over authority in the airwaves, produced a vacuum of direction in which monopoly, advertising, and and an inefficient system of indirect government control were allowed to grow. But as of 1922, the question of radio's economic base, along with other such basic questions as its ownership, content, and purpose, had not yet been determined. It is with the convention of a series of four conferences on radio, leading up to the Radio Act of 1927 from which later legislation directly derived, that all these ideas, pressures, and interests converged.

Federal Radio Conferences 1922–27

The first radio conference assembled on February 27, 1922, at the behest of President Warren G. Harding, via Secretary of Commerce and Labor Herbert Hoover. This first conference was marked chiefly by the hostility between amateur and commercial forces over allocation of broadcasting frequencies, the amateurs fearing that their interests could not compete with the powerful manufacturing contingent. Although Secretary Hoover spoke out warmly on behalf of the amateurs and recommended creating more amateur airspace by clearing the air of "advertising chatter" and commercial messages, the division of the conference into three committees—amateur, technical, and legislative— in effect removed the amateurs from the important areas of debate, which at this time were defined as purely "technical." Technical expertise, not surprisingly, was drawn for the most part from research departments of the large manufacturing firms: RCA, AT&T, Westinghouse, and General Electric. However, legislation recommended by the technical group failed to pass in Congress because of the ongoing debate over the rights and powers government could exert over radio.[21]

The second radio conference, held on March 20, 1923, met only to consider interim measures to relieve the interference problem before enacting new permanent legislation. Here the thorny copyright problem, which was to plague early broadcasting, arose as the American Society of Composers, Artists, and Performers (ASCAP) for the first time insisted on royalties for the broadcast of music. Here also the concept of broadcasting as a *local* phenomenon, requiring local control and local financing, emerged, as well as a regional system of distribution of frequencies. The conference produced a radio control bill, H.R. 7537, which again failed to emerge from committee.[22]

The third radio conference of October 1924 introduced what was to become the one controlling factor behind the development of broadcasting, although it was not yet perceived as such: the wired or shortwave interconnection of broadcast stations. All the previously discussed conceptions of broadcasting and its nature came together to form a kind of smokescreen around the soon-to-be-felt radical effects of this seemingly ancillary innovation. The mysterious technology of broadcasting, requiring unprecedented governmental legislation to ensure its operation in the public interest, would eventually, as interconnection led to the beginnings of network broadcasting, become a regulated technology held captive by technology belonging to the protected private monopoly of the American Telephone and Telegraph Company.

But in 1924, Secretary Hoover, although still decrying the possibility of private monopoly and stressing the importance of local broadcasting, could nevertheless throw his weight behind the potential for an "organized national system of station interconnection." In the eighteen months between the second and third conferences, much experimentation had taken place in the area of interconnection, both by AT&T with its wired system and by RCA using shortwave. In view of subsequent events, one particular controversy reported by Edward F. Sarno takes on special significance: "In answer to a deluge of telegrams received in opposition to a broadcast monopoly, Secretary Hoover added that no present monopoly existed and *with several alternative methods of interconnection available,* no monopoly would be allowed in the future."[23]

The conference ended on October 10 with several recommendations, one of which resolved to promote the development of wired interconnection, while another condemned monopolistic practices in the radio industry and demanded government control of such practices. The presence of these conflicting resolutions in the same document begins to explain the inability of the emergent Federal Radio Commission (FRC) to control, or even to recognize, the hidden loophole already in place that would make the 1927 Radio Act obsolete almost before it was written. Secretary Hoover's references to the "several alternative methods of interconnection available" in retrospect seem naively optimistic, given the history of the telephone industry and its regulation up to that point.

Here, it becomes necessary to discuss a powerful interest group not usually examined in the context of the history of broadcasting. The American Telephone and Telegraph Company has been closely linked with the broadcasting industry in this country, often playing a decisive role in industry structure and economics. The monopoly AT&T possessed over the long-distance land lines necessary for the formation of networks in effect provided an "escape clause" from full compliance with the spirit of broadcast regulation. The FRC, first, and later the FCC, would assert its control over the spectrum space needed for local broadcasting stations to reach receivers in their areas, but the wires that linked them were regarded as a private business, and did not fall under the jurisdiction of broadcast regulations. To this day the FCC can legislate network practices only indirectly, through the license-holding stations that subscribe to them. The fact that, moreover, AT&T possessed a government-sanctioned monopoly over telephone lines allowed it to exert a restraining function in the broadcast business, and the fact that very early on a convenient set of agreements were reached between AT&T and the largest radio manufacturer, RCA, produced a kind of monopoly in the airwaves all the more dangerous for its official nonexistence.

American Telephone and Telegraph

The American Telephone and Telegraph Company, by virtue of an 1879 patent settlement with Western Union Telegraph Company as well as ruthless competition with smaller firms, had by the early 1920s achieved complete domination over the field of telephone service. Telegraph companies led by the two second largest firms, Western Union and the Postal Telegraph Company, continued to compete with the telephone giant, but as early as 1905 its extensive unified network transmitted nearly forty times the number of messages handled by all the other telegraph companies combined. The early relationship of the telephone and radio broadcasting industries began as an openly competitive one, with both RCA and AT&T holding important patents central to transmission and reception technology. But patent agreements concluded in 1922 gave AT&T sole rights over the manufacture and sale of radio transmission equipment; RCA claimed control over receiving apparatus technology. No one disputed AT&T's rights to land-line connections, which were soon to play such a decisive role in the development of broadcasting.[24]

In 1923 the AT&T-owned station WEAF in New York City began its novel experiment with toll-broadcasting, asserting its rights under the heading of radio-telephony, or the provision of a "common carrier" service over the air. WEAF quickly expanded its audience by inter-connection via AT&T land lines, beginning with Bell-owned WCAP in Washington, D.C. and soon extending to fifteen stations on the East Coast. RCA, meanwhile, also experimented with interconnection but was limited in its attempts by restriction to the technologically inferior lines provided by Western Union and the Postal Telegraph Company.[25]

In February 1923 at a meeting of AT&T executives from across the country, A. H. Griswold, vice president for broadcasting activities, spoke bluntly: "We have been very careful, up to the present time, not to state to the public in any way, through the press or in any of our talks, the idea that the Bell System desires to monopolize broadcasting; but the fact remains that it is a telephone job, that we are telephone people, that we can do it better than anybody else, and it seems to me that the clear, logical conclusion that must be reached is that, sooner or later, in one form or another, we have got to do the job."[26]

After the 1923 meeting, AT&T began to formulate policies regarding the furnishing of lines to non-AT&T broadcasters, which reflected its larger goals in the field. Even though non-Bell stations might be licensed by AT&T to operate transmission facilities (i.e., broadcasting stations), these stations would not be allowed to compete with Bell-owned stations in access to wires. "Such service might be furnished to government stations, to stations licensed under [AT&T's] patents, and to Bell System stations. Stations licensed by the American Co. [AT&T] which operated in the same area as a Bell System station were, in general, to be denied wire facilities."[27]

Although these restrictions were eased somewhat in 1924 to allow licensed but competing stations (i.e., those who paid AT&T a fee of $4 per watt for the use of its transmission patents) to use AT&T wires, nonlicensed stations were denied access until 1928, despite the 1926 rearrangement of patents and rights with RCA. The 1926 agreements between RCA and AT&T redefined each company's areas of operation and provided for a mutually beneficial long-term relationship. AT&T sold WEAF to RCA and agreed to stay out of the ownership and operation of broadcast stations in return for RCA's pledge to keep out of wire transmission. RCA specifically agreed to build no wire networks of its own; to utilize only Bell System wires unless the telephone company, after a lengthy notification process, was unable to provide the facilities; and that even in the event that broadcasters were forced to lease lines elsewhere, this arrangement would end as soon as AT&T lines were made available. In exchange for guaranteed access to lines, RCA agreed to pay AT&T a minimum annual fee of $1 million for ten years—no inconsiderable sum, considering that radio's money-making capabilities remained uncertain.[28]

As for non-RCA stations' access to telephone land lines, the experience of CBS is an interesting one. Arthur Judson, one of the founders of the fledgling network which would, after 1929, provide the only existing competition to NBC's Red and Blue networks, recalls:

> We now had the stations, but before we could operate we had to have telephone lines. We held a good many rather hectic meetings to discuss the question of getting them. We applied to the telephone company and were informed that all of their lines were in use and that it would be impossible to furnish lines for at least three years. We argued but got nowhere.
>
> Finally Coats [George A. Coats, another CBS founder], who was from Indiana, said, "I think I'll go down to Washington. I know some Indiana people in Washington."
>
> He came back and said, "There's a friend of mine down there." I said, "Who is he?" "Well," he said, "he's just a man about Washington who fixes things. He has contacts."
>
> Coats went down to Washington again, came back and said: "If you give him two checks, one for $1,000 and the other for $10,000, he will guarantee that you will get the wires."[29]

The "Indiana people" to whom Judson refers may well have included the Hoosier Senator James E. Watson, head of the Interstate Commerce Committee and an influential voice in the history of broadcast regulation. By this time, too, complaints by citizens and other would-be broadcasters had reached the point that it behooved RCA/NBC to be able to point to the existence of at least one viable competitor in order to head off antimonopoly legislation. What better choice than the haphazard and relatively powerless group of entrepreneurs headed by Judson and J. Andrew White, and later backed up by William Paley, the very young scion of a Philadelphia cigar manufacturer? They certainly would not represent competition in the area of radio receiver sales, and in fact seemed unlikely to stay in business at all for the first several years.

But the primary tool AT&T used to restrict competition in the provision of wires to broadcasters was the problem of system interconnection. Claiming patent superiority that made it undesirable to hook up Bell-system plant and wires with non-Bell station transmitting equipment (much like subsidiary Electronic Research Products's strictures against RCA sound film technology at a later date), AT&T maintained a policy of refusing lines to stations using any other kind of long distance or local transmission. As broadcasters were later to learn, even where land lines could be leased over major interstate routes from the telegraph companies, local loops in and out of any given community must necessarily be obtained from AT&T, which often refused this sort of interconnection.[30]

Telephone communications, like radio broadcasting, fell under the jurisdiction of the powerful Interstate Commerce Committee until the founding of a separate Federal Communications Commission by the Communications Act of 1934. However, the same problems that arose in connection with the regulation of radio—technical mystification, competing demands of private business and government, and the concept of "natural monopoly"—also applied to the regulation of the telephone industry. Senator Clarence C. Dill, one of the principal supporters of the 1934 Communications Act, called regulation of the telephone monopoly "really nothing effective" for most of its early history. Other analysts agree that the ICC concerned itself primarily with railroad regulation, another extremely active area under its jurisdiction at the time, thus giving its communication responsibilities short shrift.[31]

In addition, as stated in the 1939 FCC Investigation of the telephone company: "Prior to the Communications Act of 1934 the Bell System successfully avoided any commitment that the furnishing of wire services to broadcasters was a part of its public service undertaking." Thus even such regulations that existed to protect consumers did not apply, in the eyes of AT&T, to its transactions with the broadcasting industry.[32]

The Fourth Radio Conference

By the time of the fourth radio conference of 1925, the issue of wired interconnection of broadcasting stations no longer appeared on the agenda. Again the conference submitted the point that "no monopoly in radio communication shall be permitted," but did not elaborate on how this could be avoided. Indeed, in 1924 the central problem for the conference was that of interference; an enormous increase in the number of stations on the air, licensed and unlicensed, and the ensuing overlap of signals made almost unimaginable the emergence of one dominant network that would occur within the next three years. Clearly, the conference participants believed, a licensing system must be devised to restrict the number of stations on the air and fix their frequencies.[33]

Thus the concept of "public interest" was extended and used for the first time as a basis for the granting of licenses. Secretary Hoover in particular espoused the philosophy that "the ether is a public medium and must be used for public benefit"; he then went on to state that "There is no proper line of conflict between the broadcaster and the listener. *Their interests are mutual,* for without the one the other could not exist."[34]

Again, this ingenuously optimistic assumption was to have a decisive effect on the future structure of broadcasting. The denial of conflict between the interests of the broadcasting industry—in particular its almost sole investiture in the hands of RCA—and the best interest of the general public gave an unrecognized but powerful carte blanche to the industry.

Failure to recognize that the commercial basis of broadcasting must eventually lead to some conflict between the desire for profit and the best interest of consumers can be most easily recognized in the history of broadcast advertising. What happened to change the opinions of those who, like Herbert Hoover in 1922, felt that "It is inconceivable that we should allow so great a possibility for service to be drowned in advertising chatter" to the prevalent attitude of 1924—"The radio can be used for indirect advertising, but that is all...the radio audience will certainly never stand for direct advertising...it would kill the radio industry as quickly as anything you can thing of"—to the de facto acceptance of just such direct advertising by 1932? Barnouw analyzes this and other inconsistencies in Hoover's policy toward broadcasting: "Secretary Hoover provided...admonitions—against monopoly, vested interests, excessive advertising—but continued to give dominant groups virtually what they asked for."[35]

But most of all, the confusion and contradiction surrounding the concept of the "public interest," along with a fundamental misconception of the direction this new medium was soon to take, led to a regulatory structure that ignored the two chief factors that would determine the American system of broadcasting: interconnection (or "chain broadcasting," the formation of networks), which effectively bypassed legislative efforts through a powerful combination of private business interests, and the eventual dominance of commercial advertising, which rose to fill the void created by the lack of any other provisions for radio's support. From these two elements the novel forms of commercial broadcasting would arise, already indissolubly linked to the dominance of network economics and the interests of commercial advertisers. The American system of broadcasting would eventually spread across the world, coming slowly to dominate even those broadcasting systems originally formed along quite a different model.[36]

The fourth radio conference provided the last formal hearing of views on radio. Its resolutions went before Congress in the form of a bill (H. R. 5589) in December 1925. Although two more years of administrative and technical turbulence followed, marked by a 1926 court case that invalidated almost all existing federal powers over radio, the resolutions of the fourth conference would essentially determine the shape of the Radio Act of 1927. That, in turn, would pass nearly unchanged, as far as basic concepts, structures, and areas of authority were concerned, into the Communications Act of 1934. The next chapter will examine the actions of the film industry in regard to radio and the effects of the emerging regulatory structure on the film industry's ability to gain a foothold in the new field.[37]

NOTES

1. Erik Barnouw, *The Golden Web* (New York: Oxford University Press, 1968), p. 103.

2. William Everson, *The American Silent Film* (New York: Oxford University Press, 1978).

3. Garth Jowett, *Film: The Democratic Art* (Boston: Little, Brown, 1976), p. 348.

4. Lewis Jacobs, *The Rise of the American Film* (New York: Columbia University Press, 1939), p. 186; see also Christopher Sterling and John Kitross, *Stay Tuned* (Belmont, Calif.: Wadsworth, 1978), pp. 309-10); and Arthur Knight, *The Liveliest Art* (New York: Macmillan, 1957), pp. 297-98.

5. Daniel J. Czitrom discusses popular reaction to radio and other new technologies in *Media and the American Mind: From Morse to McLuhan* (Chapel Hill: University of North Carolina Press, 1982).

6. W. H. Meckling, "Foreword," in Arthur DeVaney et al., *A Property Systems Approach to the Electromagnetic Spectrum* (San Francisco: Cato Institute, 1979), p. xiii.

7. R. H. Coase, "The Federal Communications Commission," *Journal of Law and Economics* 7 (October 1959): 40.

8. *Congressional Record,* November 5, 1927, p. 1792.

9. Robert H. Stern, "Regulatory Influences upon Television's Development: Early Years under the FRC," *The American Journal of Economics and Sociology* 2, no. 3 (1963): 349.

10. U.S. Senate, "Senate Resolution No. 2930," *Congressional Record,* Record no. 5735, 65th Cong., 2d sess., 1924; Mary Mander, "The Public Debate about Broadcasting in the Twenties: An Interpretative History," *Journal of Broadcasting* 28 (Spring 1984): 167-85.

11. Charles A. Siepmann, "An Excerpt from an Interview with Former Senator Clarence Dill," transcribed from the television series "Communications and Society," Fall 1968; Leo Herzel, "'Public Interest' and the Market in Color Television Regulation," *University of Chicago Law Review* no. 18 (1951): 802-26; Coase, "The Federal Communications Commission," p. 379; DeVany et al., *A Property Systems Approach to the Electromagnetic Spectrum,* p. 14.

12. Nicholas Johnson, "Towers of Babel: The Chaos in Radio Spectrum Utilization and Allocation," *Law and Contemporary Problems* 34 (Summer 1969): 533, emphasis added. See also Harvey J. Levin, "New Technology and the Old Regulation in Radio Spectrum Management," *American Economic Review* 56 (May 1966): 339-49; Glen O. Robinson, "Radio Spectrum Regulation:

The Administrative Process and the Problems of Institutional Reform," *Minnesota Law Review* 53 (June 1969): 1179.

13. Lawrence W. Lichty and Malachi C. Topping, *American Broadcasting: A Sourcebook on the History of Radio and Television* (New York: Hastings House, 1975) pp. 527–33; Erik Barnouw, *A Tower in Babel* (New York: Oxford University Press, 1966); Gleason L. Archer, *A History of Broadcasting to 1926* (New York: New York Historical Society, 1938); Sidney W. Head, *Broadcasting in America* (Boston: Houghton Mifflin, 1956).

14. David A. Cook, "The Birth of the Network," *Quarterly Review of Film Studies* 8 (Summer 1983): 3.

15. U.S. Congress, House Merchant Marine and Fisheries Committee, *Hearings on Governmental Control of Radio Communications* (Washington, D.C.: Government Printing Office, 1919); Coase, "The Federal Communications Commission," pp. 3–4; U.S. Congress, House Merchant Marine and Fisheries Committee, *A Bill to Further Regulate Radio Communications, Hearings on H.R. 13159,* 65th Cong., 2d sess. (Washington, D.C.: Government Printing Office, 1918).

16. Gleason Archer has detailed the negotiations among American Marconi, General Electric, and the U.S. government that led to RCA's birth in *A History of Broadcasting to 1926.*

17. Head, *Broadcasting in America,* pp. 112–13.

18. Westinghouse Broadcasting Company, Public Relations Department, "History of Broadcasting and KDKA Radio," news release, no date, in *American Broadcasting,* ed. Lichty and Topping, pp. 102–10; *Radio Broadcast,* May 1924 (advertisement), ibid., p. 207.

19. *Radio Broadcast,* March 1925, in *American Broadcasting,* ed. Lichty and Topping, p. 209.

20. Zeh Bouck, "Can We Solve the Broadcast Riddle?," *Radio Broadcast,* April 1925.

21. Edward F. Sarno, Jr., "The National Radio Conferences," *Journal of Broadcasting* 13 (Spring 1969): 192.

22. Robert B. Horwitz, "The Regulation/Deregulation of American Broadcasting," *Quarterly Review of Film Studies* 8 (Summer 1983): 25–38; Sarno, "National Radio Conferences," p. 193.

23. Sarno, "National Radio Conferences," pp. 195, 196, emphasis added.

24. Walter B. Emery, *Broadcasting and Government* (East Lansing: Michigan State University Press, 1971), p. 17.

25. W. P. Banning, *Commercial Broadcasting Pioneer: The WEAF Experiment, 1922–1926* (Cambridge: Harvard University Press, 1946), p. 156.

26. Federal Communications Commission, *Report of the FCC on the Investigation of the Telephone Industry in the U.S.,* House Document no. 340, 76th Cong., 1st sess., (Washington, D.C.: Goverment Printing Office, 1939), p. 389.

27. Ibid., pp. 389–90.

28. Ibid., p. 390; Eugene Lyons, *David Sarnoff* (New York: Harper and Row, 1966).

29. Arthur Judson, "How CBS Got Its Start," *American Heritage,* August 1955, p. 80.

30. Federal Communications Commission, 1939, passim.

31. U.S. Congress, *Congressional Record* 1934, vol. 78, p. 8822; Emery, *Broadcasting and Government,* p. 31; N. R. Danelian, *AT&T: The Story of Industrial Conquest* (New York: Vanguard, 1939).

32. Federal Communications Commission, 1939, p. 399.

33. L. F. Schmeckbier, *The Federal Radio Commission* (Washington, D.C.: Brookings Institution, 1932).

34. Fourth National Radio Conference, *Proceedings and Recommendations for the Regulation of Radio,* November 9–11, 1925 (Washington, D.C.: Government Printing Office, 1925), p. 6, emphasis added.

35. John W. Spalding, "1928: Radio Becomes a Mass Advertising Medium," in *American Broadcasting,* ed. Lichty and Topping, pp. 219–28; Samuel L. Rothafel and Raymond F. Yates, *Broadcasting: Its New Day* (New York: Century, 1925), p. 10; Barnouw, *A Tower in Babel,* pp. 177–79.

36. Michele Mattelart, "Can Industrialized Culture Be a Culture of Difference?: A Reflection on France's Confrontation with the U.S. Model of Serialized Cultural Production," in *Marxism and the Interpretation of Culture,* ed. Carey Nelson and Lawrence Grossberg (Urbana: University of Illinois Press, 1988).

37. Sarno, "National Radio Conferences," p. 202; Frank J. Kahn, ed., *Documents in American Broadcasting* (New York: Appleton-Century-Crofts, 1968), pp. 21–31.

2

Radio Broadcasting
and the Film Industry

THE UNINVITED GUEST

Throughout the period of regulatory turbulence and reconstruction, the film industry remained, on the surface, an aloof and disinterested spectator. No delegates from the film industry appear in the lists of participants at the radio hearings; very seldom is reference made to a linking of film industry interests and those of the struggling evanescent medium of radio. But just as the factors that would later dominate commercial broadcasting entered the scene through the back door, so to speak, unnoticed at first and unremarked, so the involvement of the film industry in radio grew slowly but steadily through the early years, reaching a peak in 1927.

By 1927, however, the structures of radio had hardened to such an extent that significant competition with the existing radio powers was already almost impossible, due once again to two factors: the bottleneck new entrants encountered in the radio network business, jointly controlled and jealously guarded by the AT&T and RCA alliance; and the public-service rhetoric of broadcasting's early days, designed to screen and offset its growing dependence on commercial sponsorship. Both of these factors operated to the disadvantage of the movie industry.

To begin with the latter point, the early history of the movie business shows a continuing struggle between the forces of "high culture" and moral authority, on the one hand, and the somehow low-brow and morally suspect nature of the movies as entertainment on the other. From its popularity in storefront nickelodeons, where it appealed to an audience of immigrants and workers, to the shocking behavior of some of Hollywood's emerging stars, the film industry retained a somewhat disreputable image, even in the mid-1920s as film magnates' efforts to raise the tone of the industry began to take effect.

To make the conjunction of film and radio even worse to contemplate, the pre-1927 chaos in the broadcasting field brought many of the same accusations to radio's door. Because virtually anyone able to buy, borrow, or lease transmission equipment could go on the air relatively unhindered, small stations sprang up all over the country broadcasting the extremely mediocre talents of amateurs, spurious advice shows, and the then-suspect jazz music, often from recordings. This proliferation created interference and reception problems and outraged many listeners' tastes and sensibilities, as the following 1925 review of WEAF's programs shows:

> The much-discussed question of having a few very high-powered stations in this country that would ultimately control all the broadcasting has met with violent opposition from the hundreds of stations conducted for the purpose of advertising the products of the business firms operating them. The majority of these stations are far below any commendable standard so far as their programs and the manner in which they are presented is concerned. Will this new development in radio which is bringing the best in radio music to far distant points, in time put these stations out of business? There would be nothing lost and a good deal gained for the public were this to come to pass.[1]

The writer then cites statistics given by AT&T, showing that the preference of "radio fans" for jazz music had fallen from 75 percent in January 1923 to only 5 percent two years later. As the author concluded, "Radio music, having had this upward trend, can never again sink to the low level that has so widely obtained."

These concerns led, eventually, to some little-known and later dropped provisions in the regulatory policies of the Federal Radio Commission, which acted against the ability of the film industry to appear as a serious and public-minded entrant in the radio field. In its first annual report published in 1928, the FRC stated that, "In view of the paucity of channels, the Commission is of the opinion that the limited facilities for broadcasting should not be shared with stations which give the sort of service which is readily available to the public in another form." The commission specifically cited phonograph records as an example of this discouraged activity; stations broadcasting live entertainment would be given precedence in the allocation of air space because that material presumably remained unavailable in any other form. Although the report does not develop this ruling's applicability to the rebroadcasting of motion picture material, the notion of nonduplication, combined with the service guidelines which came out the next year, may well have discouraged film industry attempts at programming.[2]

The *Third Annual Report* of the FRC, covering the period of October 1, 1928 to November 1, 1929, spelled out several points and restrictions that would later affect the film industry. In seeking to define the concept of "public interest," the commission stated that it would give priority in spectrum allocation to those groups meeting certain qualifications. First, no attempt could be made to limit service to one selected group of listeners, as in the efforts toward instituting a "subscription radio" service. (Although Hollywood was not involved in subscription radio, this very early provision would come back to haunt it during the subscription television conflict.) Second, emphasis was to be placed on a "well rounded" broadcasting schedule, "in which entertainment, consisting of music of both classical and lighter grades, religion, education and instruction, important public events, discussion of public questions, weather, market reports, and news, and matters of interest to all members of the family find a place." Third, the commission stated that "In such a scheme there is not room for the operation of broadcasting stations exclusively by or in the private interests of individuals or groups so far as the nature of the programs is concerned." Were Hollywood to attempt to enter the broadcasting field under these conditions, a considerable expansion of its normal areas of concern, as well as an extensive public-service image-improvement campaign, lay ahead.[3]

As for early entry into television, similar rules applied. Also in the 1928 report, a brief by Alfred N. Goldsmith, a consultant to RCA as well as the FRC's chief technical advisor, states bluntly that "In the interest of both the vision and the television of the public, only an experienced and responsible organization such as the Radio Corporation of America, should be granted licenses to broadcast television material, for only such organizations can be depended upon to uphold high ideals of service."[4]

After a further two-and-one-half pages of technical specifications and discussion, Goldsmith concludes, "The Radio Corporation of America can be depended upon to broadcast television material with high technical and program quality." Thus the formation of NBC and CBS and the efforts of some of the larger manufacturing firms in radio and television were couched in terms of public service, the social responsibilities of broadcasters, and serious technical research and development. None of these qualities could be applied as well to the interests of the film producers, whose products had in 1916 been ruled to be the result of "a business pure and simple," not protected even by First

Amendment privileges. In addition, the business practices of the film industry at the time and throughout its history had excited considerable negative publicity, further confirming the disreputable habits and tendencies of Hollywood in the eyes of the nation. The alleged unfair and monopolistic practices prevalent in the industry reached a peak of attention in 1927, just as Hollywood interest in radio took a form that would never again be duplicated.

Finally, the control exercised by AT&T over long distance and local interconnection worked to the studios' disadvantage. The experience of CBS, as discussed in chapter 1, was not atypical. As the conversion to sound film threatened to enforce a dependency on one or the other of the broadcasting giants, the prospects dimmed for serious efforts at entry into network broadcasting on the part of the film industry. But despite these obstacles, Hollywood experimentation with radio took many and diverse forms in the mid-1920s, for reasons that have more to do with the internal dynamics of the industry itself than with external pressures or impediments.

Dynamics of Conflict: Production, Distribution, Exhibition

For the film industry, the onset of World War I meant a further tightening in the supply foreign films to the United States. An expanding marketplace both at home and abroad, as the war took its course and European movie production slowed to a trickle, prompted the expansion of the American movie business. A myriad of producers and exhibitors sprang up, increasing with the breakup of the Motion Picture Patents Company in 1914. A wave of theater building hit the country, and as the number and power of exhibitors grew, so tension within the industry among producers, distributors, and exhibitors led to the integration of all three arms of the business into what would become the major movie studios.

The Early Years: Conflict and Signification

May Huettig, in an analysis of the motion picture industry, has likened the relationship between the production-distribution and exhibition arms of the business to "a chronically quarrelsome but firmly married couple," pointing to the essential interdependence of the two despite conflicts of interest in specific situations. But these conflicts are deep and can be traced to the earliest days of the film industry. Several historians and theorists have pointed to the ways in which these economic and structural tensions affected the evolution of specific film techniques and practices. Janet Staiger links the conflict between the need for standardization of film product and the equal demand for differentiation of one product from the other to such widespread film techniques as the use of dissolves over double exposures, spatial unity of action, the evolution of art titles, and several other dominant features of early silent films. Focussing specifically on the production-exhibition tension, Charles Musser analyzes the development of longer narrative film, beginning with such early works as Porter's *Jack and the Beanstalk,* in terms of effort by the producer-cameraman to gain control over the circumstances of exhibition. According to Musser, earlier films were organized as a series of individual scenes, with self-contained narratives or meaning, that were not dependent on any particular ordering but could be shown in the sequence desired by the exhibitor. The exhibitor thus became an important part of the early films' "meaning" structure, functioning as an additional "author." With films like *Jack and the Beanstalk,* constructed as interlinked shots, the film exhibitor's role was reduced in importance.[5]

By linking scenes through repetition of spatial elements, Porter and subsequent filmmakers could create a continuous story that needed no connective explanation by the exhibitor-narrator and resisted being broken apart and reassembled at the exhibitor's discretion. The longer films could also be marketed more efficiently, leading to a more standardized product, which smoothed the course of both distributors and exhibitors. As the film took form, power shifted from the distributor-exhibitor axis to the production company. "This kind of filmic construction could be achieved only by the producer/cameraman. It thus signaled a decisive shift in editorial control. . . . In the process, creative control became centralized primarily in the production companies."[6]

The rising popularity of the new feature films sparked a period of conflict and growth in the industry as exhibitors struggled to secure a continuous supply of quality films to their theaters, while producers gained strength by the increased demand for their product. Moviemakers began to realize that the producer's profits could be maximized by integrating the production-distribution functions. Instead of leaving a considerable percentage of a film's profits in the hands of a special distribution organization, an integrated company could participate in profits down the line. In 1916, Famous Players-Lasky formed, with Paramount Pictures Corporation, a nationwide distribution corporation, as a subsidiary. Relying on the box-office draw of the impressive array of stars under contract, Famous Players' head Adolph Zukor delayed integrating the ownership of theaters into his empire until First National Exhibitors Circuit formed in 1917 and began to finance their own productions, winning Mary Pickford away from Paramount in 1918.[7]

In 1919, Zukor obtained financing from the investment banking house Kuhn Loeb and Company, and over the next seven years aggressively purchased more than a thousand theaters across the country. He was not alone, however, in the trend. In addition to First National, Metro-Goldwyn-Mayer soon formed under the direction of Marcus Loew, and the Fox Theaters Corporation ventured into production, as it built more than thirty new first-run theaters across the nation. Thus the dynamics of intraindustry conflict were internalized but not eliminated.[8]

Canned Vaudeville: The Introduction of Sound

In order to continue the history of intraindustry conflict and to show the place that broadcasting held in it, it is necessary to jump ahead a few years to the period 1925-27, when the technology of recording sound on film first began to revolutionize the industry. Douglas Gomery discusses the reasons behind the role Warner Brothers Studios played in the innovation and diffusion of sound film, not in terms of the last-ditch attempt of struggling studio to compete, but as a calculated attempt to break away from distributor-exhibitor financing and thus gain control over these functions as well. But, as Gomery points out, this process cannot be understood simply by enumerating and describing the feature-length sound films that followed *The Jazz Singer* (1927). The process of adaptation to sound began much earlier, under circumstances that help to make sense of the sudden revolution in film form as well as broadcasting's attraction for Hollywood.[9]

By 1925, the theater ownership expansion discussed previously had already created four major players in the film business, and those who had not yet integrated operations saw that they must gain a foothold in the exhibition business or slowly be squeezed out. Warner Brothers, one of the smaller of the existing "majors," was one of the last to do this, hampered by a cumbersome "states-rights" distribution system. This method of financing production, popular in films' early days, involved sale of distribution rights on a regional basis, usually with the distributor retaining a 60-75 percent share of the film's eventual profits. Very often these regional distributors were the owners of large theater chains within their regions.

In Warners' case the burden placed on the producers by this system was even more onerous. The twenty-eight Warner states-rights franchise holders, one franchisee per zone, each advanced Warner Brothers Studios money toward production of a set number of films in exchange for exclusive distribution in his zone. The studio was then required to pay interest on the sums thus advanced, as well as foregoing a share of profits above production costs. But besides placing the producer in a dependent position and limiting his percentage of profit, control of exhibition in 1925 brought other powers in its train.[10]

In the mid-1920s, exhibition of a single feature film, by itself, with no preliminaries or other type of entertainment, would have been enough to send customers streaming into the street in disbelief. Indeed, although the development of motion pictures has been blamed for vaudeville's demise, up until 1927 or 1928, the cinema provided steady employment for thousands of performers and musicians in prologues and accompaniment to silent films. Not only did each silent film, long or short, demand live musical accompaniment ranging from a single piano player in small theaters to complete orchestras in the larger ones, but also live acts ranging from a few simple skits to the Broadway-like "prologues" of the 1920s and 1930s were regarded as part of the evening's entertainment in the first-run houses.

All of these "extras," which also included an orchestral overture, a newsreel, and a short, were selected and arranged at the discretion of the exhibitor. Indeed, exhibitors sometimes went so far as to cut down the length of the scheduled feature in order to fit the entire program into the standard two-hour format. Booking of orchestras and vaudeville acts became in many cases a more profitable part of the business than that of the films. The larger theater chains soon attempted to schedule these presentations more efficiently by centralizing production, with live shows created in New York traveling to a network of theaters across the country. This allowed Paramount and some of the other major chains such as Loew's and later Fox to spread the costs of high-quality, big-name productions over a number of theaters—and also placed the controls over the quality and length of the pre-film materials in the hands of the central offices of the integrated studios. But outside of the first-run circuit, exhibitors still ran the show according to their own best interests.[11]

In February 1925, Warner Brothers distribution franchise holders rebelled against the negotiations that Harry Warner had begun with the banking firm of Goldman-Sachs to finance the purchase of the Vitagraph Corporation, a failing group of fifty film exchanges. For the franchise holders, the states-rights system had been an extremely profitable low-risk investment. Financial backing flowing into production from Wall Street rendered their comfortable arrangement unnecessary. By the fall of 1925, Wall Street funds made the purchase of ten first-run theaters possible, and Warners joined the ranks of vertically integrated companies.

In order to compete in the uncontrolled orchestra and vaudeville booking business, in which not only live theaters and the bigger movie companies but also radio competed, Warners took advantage of prior contacts in the radio business by pioneering sound-on-film recording technology. By producing sound recordings of orchestral film scores, as well as vaudeville shorts complete with dialogue and music, Warners could afford to pay higher prices for its talent, who could make a single recording rather than nightly appearances or months of road shows. The films and scores could then be reproduced photographically and electronically and sent out to dozens of theaters at once. Not only did recording promote economics of scale, but it also further cemented control in the hands of the vertically integrated film companies, removing even from the first-run independents and smaller chains the need to schedule their own acts.

Thus, Gomery concludes, Warners' innovation of sound rested not on "a desperate effort to ward off bankruptcy," but on the well-planned strategy of an expanding company to break free of the economic influence of powerful exhibitors. This strategy also led Warners to experiment with a technology emanating from the same source as Vitaphone: radio broadcasting.[12]

During the period 1919 to 1927, radio broadcasting grew from the disorganized experimentation of its earlier days into a thriving entertainment industry controlled by some of the largest and most powerful corporations in America. Given the fact that, until the introduction of sound film, the art of the film revolved around "silent" dramatics whereas radio relied only on unrecorded sound, it would not be surprising if the two industries had little or nothing to do with each other, or if the movie industry in particular, with the heyday of the silent film upon it, should have regarded the squabbling, squealing business of broadcasting as an irrelevant noise. Yet a closer look at the numerous points of contact between the two industries in the 1920s shows that as early as 1925 a few far-sighted companies on both sides of the fence had begun to explore some of Hollywood's potential for radio endorsements, talent, and sponsorship, and broadcasting's potential for Hollywood publicity and, possibly, for profit.

Early Innovators: Warner Brothers and "Roxy"

Hollywood's awareness of radio's potential as a medium for film publicity grew rapidly in the late 1920s, and Warner Brothers led the way. Sam Warner, whose interest in radio's technological strides during the early 1920s put him in contact with Western Electric's regional manager Nathan Levinson, purchased Western Electric radio transmitting apparatus and set up station KFWB in Los Angeles in March of 1925. Warner Brothers used this station to promote the current Warner Brothers line-up of films and stars, borrowing techniques from an even earlier radio innovator, Samuel Rothapfel of New York's Capitol Theater. "Roxy," as he was known, pioneered in live broadcasts from his first-run theater, one of the Balaban and Katz chain, beginning in 1923. "Roxy and His Gang" featured vaudeville and solo performers then appearing at the Capital Theater's pre-film presentations, but soon expanded into material created expressly for the Sunday morning broadcasts over the WEAF chain. This series would continue into the 1930s as the "Capital Theater Family" under the direction of Rothapfel's successor, Major Edward Bowes.[13]

In 1925 Rothapfel published a book, *Broadcasting: Its New Day,* dealing with his radio experiences and speculating on the future of the medium. He sounded a theme that was frequently to be heard from those in the movie business interested in radio: a broadcasting system built on direct, nonentertainment advertising was an imposition to which the American public would never submit. "In the opinion of this writer advertising by radio does not offer solution to the problem of making broadcasting self-supporting on the scale that is necessary for national success. Its intangible aspects and the danger to broadcasting that would attend its wide-spread application, place it in the position of a new phase of advertising with limited possibilities."[14] He then quoted Herbert Hoover as interviewed by the *New York World*: "People will gladly listen to some hotel's orchestra broadcasting music...but if you try to sell them some brand of shoes or anything else over the radio you'll have no radio audience."[15]

In other words, Rothapfel and the film business in general promoted the kind of "indirect" advertising so often referred to in radio's early days: publicity generated by radio performances for another related entertainment product. The distinction may seem a vague one, particularly in light of radio's subsequent history, but it does represent a lingering attempt at an alternative to the economic base that eventually developed. And of all potential backers for this kind of system, the movie industry represented the largest organized force with the financial means to support the indirect publicity idea.

In 1925, the plan seemed workable. Harry Warner went so far as to propose that year that the industry as a whole set up a radio "network," to be used by all the major studios to publicize their products.

> I am in favor of the motion picture industry, after the wave-length situation has been adjusted (as it will be)—building and maintaining its own

broadcasting stations in New York and Los Angeles, and possibly in the
Middle West. Through these sources... programs could be devised to be
broadcast before and after show hours, tending to create interest in all
meritorious pictures being released or playing at that time. Nights could
be assigned to various companies, calling attention to their releases and
advising where they were playing in that particular locality. Artists could
talk into the microphone and reach directly millions of people who have
seen them on the screen but never came in contact with them personally
or heard their voices. Such programs would serve to whet the appetites
of the radio audience and make it want to see the persons they have
heard and the pictures they are appearing in.[16]

These programs would be financed, not by selling advertising time to
outsiders, but by the enhanced receipts from the industry itself at the
box office.

Unlike the radio manufacturers, who in order to support radio receiver
sales had originally proposed a similar scheme, the movie industry had
at its disposal the talent and material to provide the content for such
a service at very little extra cost. The radio powers took advantage of
performers' desire for publicity by building early radio programs on
donated talent, but as performers raised the issue of payment for
performances, and songwriters and playwrights demanded copyright
protection for their works, additional support from sponsored advertising
became necessary to meet the cost of talent and make the stations
profitable. The movie industry, on the other hand, already had under
contract some of the biggest names in show business, and thus may
well have been able to support such a scheme.

The Warners themselves were pleased enough with the effectiveness
of their first station, KFWB, to open another in 1926, this time in
New York City. WBPI, headquartered at the Warners' Theater, continued the same kind of dramatic publicity provided by KFWB on the
West Coast. In the summer of 1926, Sam Warner took a portable
transmitting device and "studio" on a cross-country tour, broadcasting
on KFWB's bandwidth from theaters showing Warner films.[17]

But 1925 brought radio experimentation from other quarters of the
industry as well. First National, another integrated company, in April
of 1925 advocated theater support of radio on the local level. Richard
A. Rowland, general manager of First National Pictures, made some
recommendations for easier producer-exhibitor relations in this area.
"One way that suggests itself is to give radio programs all the big
stars they want—but restrict their relations to hours that do not conflict
with theater hours. The contrast will react to the benefit of the theater. ..."[18] In Chicago, Balaban and Katz created an in-house "radio

department" for house orchestra and organ concerts over four local stations owned by Chicago newspapers. Every night from 6:00 to 6:30, Jesse Crawford played "the big organ" from the Chicago Theater over WMA, owned by the Chicago *Daily News*, which also aired every Saturday from 9:00 to 10:00 P.M. a "special radio review" of films currently playing. On Sundays, Chicago listeners were treated to similar concerts from 11:45 to 12:45 over WGN, owned by the Chicago *Tribune*, and the Chicago *American* contributed a midnight show every Wednesday and Friday night over KWY from the McVickers Theater. The *Evening Post*, not to be outdone, soon initiated a half-hour program four nights a week over its station WEBH from the Riviera Theater.[19]

In January of that year Pathé News also announced a radio tie-in with its semiweekly newsreel service, consisting of "an interesting radio talk based on the current Pathe News release and human interest phases of the news reel service broadcast twice a week...to every city, town, and village of the United States." Although "every village" may have been an exaggeration, Pathé boasted of an impressive line-up of stations for its broadcasts, including WEEI Boston, WHK Cleveland, WWHO Des Moines, WCK St. Louis, WLW Cincinnati, WKY Oklahoma City, WCBE New Orleans, KFRC San Francisco, KFO Seattle, and WCAY Milwaukee.[20]

1927: Experimentation and Resistance

The year 1927 marked the high point of film industry attempts to expand into radio broadcasting. Although the 1930s and 1940s would bring heavy Hollywood involvement in production for the radio networks, after 1927-28, Hollywood potential for actual "control" of the medium diminished rapidly. The reasons for this are intricately bound up in both the internal dynamics of the film industry itself and in the anomalies of the broadcasting industry's economic and regulatory structure as it solidified. In the meantime, Hollywood and radio audiences were treated to some experiences that would never again be duplicated.

The year began with heightened interest in the possibilities for actual transmission of pictures over radio waves: in a word, television. The *New York Times* carried a front page article on January 11, "Radiomovies in Home Forecast by Expert." The "expert," H. E. Alexanderson, a consulting engineer for both RCA and General Electric, "aroused enthusiastic applause from his audience...when to show toward what he is working he put on his drum for transmitting photographs a strip of motion picture film....As the picture was transmitted...the movements of the hands and heads of the men in the film were reproduced.

It was crude reproduction, but it moved." At the same time, experiments were taking place in London and in Berlin involving the radio transmission of black and white photographs, whose tones made for a sharper contrast on the receiving end than "live" transmission of real scenes.[21]

The movie industry, although not as yet involved in the technical development of television, watched closely from the sidelines and was among the first to participate in experiments with some of television's related technologies. For example, on October 2, 1927, Carl Laemmle would make news worldwide by using the newly installed "radiophone" link between New York and London to negotiate the purchase of rights to a Broadway play. Transmission of the contract for signatures via "photoradio" from Laemmle in London, to the theatrical entrepreneurs in New York, and back again to Laemmle for the final signature, took just under six hours. No demonstration of the technology for transmitting pictures over the airwaves was complete without representatives from the movie business confirming the wonder of the event with an assertion that the movies would not change too soon.[22]

Whether or not farsighted speculation over the imminence of television prompted film industry interest in radio, a more pressing motive was simply that of publicity. By 1927, radio broadcasting had become an important feature of everyday American life—perhaps even as important as the twice-weekly visit to the Bijou. In 1926, RCA announced the purchase of WEAF from AT&T and the subsequent formation of National Broadcasting Company (NBC), in order "to provide the best programs available for broadcasting in the United States." Toward that end, the new company would seek "to provide machinery which will insure a national distribution of national programs, and a wider distribution of programs of the highest quality." The age of network broadcasting now began in earnest, with NBC unrivaled in its field. Although many alternatives for the economic support of radio had been discussed in the preceding years, the emergence of the radio "chains" linked together by AT&T wires made certain the eventual triumph of advertising as the foundation of broadcasting. With the purchase of WEAF, RCA tacitly abandoned its proposed "super power station" approach to broadcasting in favor of the wired network.[23]

Also in 1927, a network emerged that was to become NBC's only real competitor in the years to come. On January 27, three independent agents and promoters, Arthur Judson, Edward Ervin, and George A. Coats, formed United Independent Broadcasters "to contract for radio station time, to sell time to advertisers, and to furnish programs for broadcasting." In April 1927, Columbia Phonograph Company agreed to invest in the fledgling operation, but heavy losses caused the recording company to withdraw the following October, leaving only its name behind. Although continuing to operate with a chain of sixteen stations, the network stumbled through its first year of operation; not until the purchase of 50.3 percent of its stock by William Paley in September 1928 did CBS begin to function, if not in the black, at least in a manner that promised future growth. But the main factor allowing CBS to exist as a network—its luck in obtaining lines from AT&T—has already been described in chapter 1. Not all aspiring broadcasters were so fortunate or well connected.[24]

The Paramount Network

Executives at Paramount Pictures had also watched the progress of the new medium. Paramount approached the issue of broadcasting not piecemeal and short term, as with the Warners' use of temporary stations for publicity, but structurally, with a proposal to compete in the broadcasting business on the level at which the power would soon clearly concentrate: that of the networks. On May 24, 1927, the *New York Times* announced that Paramount-Famous-Lasky Corporation planned to originate a new radio chain, "for dramatizing and advertising first-run motion pictures." This new "Keystone Chain" would consist of "at least a dozen stations," and among those mentioned specifically were KMOX St. Louis, WHT Chicago, and WMAK of Lockport, N.Y. More interesting are the names associated with the project. The *Times* mentions both Senator James E. Watson and Clarence McKay of the Postal Telegraph Company, both of whom had connections and past interests that made them likely participants in a ventures undertaking to defy the RCA-AT&T axis.[25]

Watson, an influential figure in Washington as chairman of the powerful Senate Interstate Commerce Committee (under whose jurisdiction lay appointments to the newly established Federal Radio Commission) was considered a potential presidential candidate for the 1928 election, and as such a rival to Herbert Hoover. An alliance with Watson could be a powerful tool for a radio venture, and in particular for one that promised to challenge the Hoover-supported dominance of the RCA-AT&T arrangement. Another area under Watson's jurisdiction was that of radio frequency allocations as the 1927 Radio Act ushered in a massive wave of reassignments. Indeed, some evidence exists that Watson's involvement in the Keystone plan centered around the battle for a favorable frequency between two big New York radio stations, WGL "atop the Hotel Majestic," and WOR, which eventually became the originating station for the UIB (CBS) chain. The *Times* of June 6, 1927, announced "Lasky Chain Linked to Radio Contest" (referring to the allocation "contest" between the two stations) and quoted WGL's manager as saying "Negotiations between WGL and the new network have been under way for the past three months." In a later report, Watson is said to have been active on the part of the proposed chain "in order that the stations proposed for the new chain might fare well in the distribution of wave lengths."[26]

The name of Clarence McKay also indicates something of the nature of the new enterprise. McKay, head of the Postal Telegraph Company, "mentioned as among those interested in the project," represented a longstanding opposing force to the powers of AT&T, having resisted AT&T's monopoly of the telegraph business since 1885. When stations unlicensed by AT&T needed wires to interconnect for broadcasts, Western Union or Postal Telegraph provided the only alternative. Although their wires, never intended for voice transmission, remained technically inferior to those of the telephone company, an arrangement with a new network along the lines of NBC's with AT&T could have spawned a second communications giant with wires stretching across the country.[27]

However, the May announcement of the Keystone Chain proved premature. In June, new reports circulated about Paramount's plans for a radio chain, this time linking Zukor's interests to the UIB venture, along with Columbia Phonograph. September 4 was set as the opening day for the new chain, to originate from WOR-Newark and spread to nine cities. Its purpose: "the dramatizing of first-run motion pictures and the exploitation of phonograph records on the radio." Once again, though, the Paramount connection failed to materalize, and the UIB plan fell upon hard times. After Columbia Phonograph's defection, CBS had to fall back on the personal contributions of two individual investors, Mrs. Christian Holmes of Cincinnati and later Jerome Loucheim of Philadelphia, to eke out a bare existence until William Paley purchased the company in 1928.[28]

The reasons for Paramount's withdrawal from the plan—reversing itself in 1929 when Zukor finally completed a stock trade with Paley— have been attributed to several different causes. Barnouw claims that Zukor's offer rested on the renaming of the company to the Paramount Broadcasting System. "There was talk of studios in the Paramount Theater on Times Square—Possibly, it was thought, Times Square could be renamed Paramount Plaza,"—an idea at which CBS balked. Arthur Judson remembers that Paramount requested a thirty-day option, and that CBS's urgent financial plight made them unable to wait even that long: "We were very brave and refused. It was not that we wouldn't have liked to wait but we couldn't." A look at the larger situation in the film industry in 1927 reveals some other possible reasons for Zukor's withdrawal.[29]

Internal Conflicts

On July 10, 1927, Paramount made front-page news as the Federal Trade Commission released a sweeping indictment of film industry practices, with specific charges and a sixty-day order to desist directed at the Famous Players-Lasky Corporation. Based on an investigation in progress since mid-1926, the report ordered Famous Players immediately to cease several "unfair methods of competition," naming three points specifically: (1) the formation of "a conspiracy among themselves or with other persons to lessen competition and restrain trade...on the production, distribution, and exhibition of motion picture films"; (2) the practice of block booking; and (3) of "acquiring or threatening to acquire theaters for the purpose of intimidating or coercing an exhibitor of films to book and exhibit films of the Famous Players-Laksy Corporation." This last point is particularly pertinent to the radio venture, although the block booking controversy received most attention at the time.[30]

Although the order stipulated that it did not "require the corporation to divest itself of any property that it has acquired in the course of the organization of the alleged conspiracy," the further acquisition of theaters would have been cut off abruptly for Paramount. At the time, Paramount owned outright a total of 128 theaters, most of which were first-run; owned a 50 percent or more share in another 141; and had a minority interest in 99 others. Paramount had just completed its greatest coup, the purchase of the Chicago-based Balaban and Katz chain from under the nose of First National, in October of 1926. The result of this policy of theater buying, according to the commission, was "a dangerous tendency to create a monopoly in the greater part of the United States."[31]

In a daring move, Paramount decided to fight the FTC's order, but interestingly chose to take issue only with report's block booking provision, ignoring the FTC's findings on theater acquisition and conspiracy to monopolize. Whether deliberately or not, Paramount's response provided the best protection possible under the circumstances for its newest program, that of theater building, by deflecting attack onto the one criticized practice on which the exhibitor forces themselves remained divided. Block booking, Paramount and other production companies argued, benefitted more often than it harmed the exhibitor by allowing profit from unexpected successes.

As a result of conflicting industry appeals, the FTC avoided litigation by instead convening a series of conferences on the trade practices of the motion picture industry. For one week, beginning on October 10, 1927, representatives from all spheres of the film business met in Washington to thrash out perceived problems and inequities. Although very little actually resulted from these conferences, aside from some half-hearted and soon-disregarded legislation against block booking, this organized confrontation of one-half of the industry with the other, as so often in the past, played an important part in the film industry's developing experimentation with radio.

The Alliance with CBS

Meanwhile, the coming storm over sound film rumbled in the distance. *The Jazz Singer* premiered October 6, 1927 in New York City, culminating the long period of experimentation with sound. In the same year Paramount had released a film, *Wings,* which tried out RCA's Photophone system as adapted and improved by Paramount technicians, but RCA, having gotten a late start, was unable to bring developments up to date in time to prevent AT&T's Electrical Research Products Inc. (ERPI) subsidiary from making a clean sweep of the industry.[32]

In his discussion of Zukor's 1929 stock transfer with CBS, Jonathan Buchsbaum constructs an elaborate rationale for Paramount's move, based on the battle between AT&T and RCA over control of the sound-film business. His theory is that in order to secure a powerful ally in the financing of theater acquisition and sound conversion, Zukor, having observed William Fox's success with the behind-the-scenes influence of AT&T, turned to RCA for similar backing. But, unable for no specified reasons to achieve this backing, Zukor instead "concluded the deal with CBS, finally gaining his safety against the looming encroachments of RCA and AT&T." The theory is hard to accept in its entirety; in 1929, CBS was still losing money and had no Morgan or Rockefeller interests behind it to help push financing through Wall Street.[33]

In addition, Buchsbaum makes no mention of Zukor's previous interest in radio networking or UIB, when the conditions he describes in his article would not have applied. In the light of Zukor's prior unconsummated interest in radio networking, his stock transfer of 1929 represents the deferral of previously existing business purposes, not the sudden access of new conditions. Buchsbaum does refer briefly to Zukor's desire for diversification, but rather than attribute this desire to the RCA-AT&T rivalry, a more pressing reason may be seen in the previously mentioned difficulties with the industry segment that radio might indeed threaten: the exhibitors.

Throughout the history of film industry participation in radio, and later television, broadcasting, it is invariably the exhibitors who have the least to gain and the most to lose by this sort of experimentation. Although one or two showmen like Rothapfel may provide the proverbial exception, most exhibitors saw radio as a threat to their business rather than an adjunct or aid. As early as 1925, *Moving Picture World* reported on the latest box-office troubles in Milwaukee under the headline, "Radio and Snow Blamed for Slump." According to Fred Seegert, president of the Motion Picture Theater Owners Association of Wisconsin, "Radio is becoming a greater menace each day and even those who scoffed at it at first and characterized it as a passing fad are beginning to realize its danger." Milwaukee theater owners feared that with a season of heavy snow, former movie viewers would forego the frigid outing to the movie theaters in favor of remaining in a warm home to listen to the radio.[34]

The producer, on the other hand, may have been able to compensate for any revenues lost from theaters by finding new avenues of profit for his products. To take one step further Huettig's analogy of the producer/distribution and exhibition arms of the industry as a "chronically quarrelsome but firmly married couple," it can be said that the marriage remains firm as long as neither party seeks new opportunities outside the relationship. And it is the production-distribution forces that, historically, have had the more roving eye, being less firmly wedded to theaters as their only outlet than the exhibitors who depend on film as their sole source of profits. So in the context of the producer-distributor-exhibitor relationship, Paramount's reasons for first broaching, then abandoning, plans for participation in radio networking— along with the actions of other studios, which will be discussed later— take on new substance.

First, Paramount had recently completed the Balaban and Katz purchase totaling sixty-nine theaters, a huge investment coming on top of numerous smaller ones in the course of an eight-year acquisition campaign. Although profits were good, Paramount's indebtedness climbed to a new high in 1926 and showed signs of mounting higher as the sound era dawned. Heavy investment in radio networking, a fledgling industry with uncertain profits as well as indefinite future financial requirements, may well have required a larger commitment than Paramount could reasonably make, at least without thirty days' option.

A second possible reason behind Paramount's postponement of radio investment plans centers on the growing turmoil over sound-film technology. By mid-1927, it had become obvious that the entire film industry would have to proceed quickly with conversion, using either the RCA or the AT&T system: no other alternatives then existed except Fox's Movietone, which still possessed some serious flaws. To choose Fox would have been to elevate that studio to permanent dominance over the entire industry, breaking one of the film business's most basic laws: thou shalt not willingly enrich a competitor. So the prospect remained of a future dependency on one or the other of the broadcasting giants, both of whom profited from the as yet unchallenged supremacy of the NBC chain: RCA through direct profits and access to wires, AT&T through the exclusive line rental arrangement.

To alienate either company by encroaching on the broadcasting business may have looked less and less like a good idea as 1927 drew to a close and the "standstill" agreement neared the end of its terms. On the other hand, a little muscle-flexing by bringing in names such as Senator Watson of the Interstate Commerce Committee or Clarence McKay of Postal Telegraph may have been intended to provide the industry with a bargaining tool in its future negotiations with the broadcasting powers. Third, the FRC had been instituted as a regulatory body in February 1927, and during most of that year would-be broadcasters rushed to submit applications for frequency allocations, in a "now or never" atmosphere. But the opportunity to get into radio broadcasting as an innovator, before the economic and regulatory system had settled irrevocably (as was to happen within the next two years), coincided with the Federal Trade Commission investigation and order discussed previously.

Although the FTC order by implication extended to the entire industry, it was only Paramount-Famous Players-Lasky that the July 10 report specifically indicted. Proceeding with a further expansion into the government-protected business of radio broadcasting would have done little for Zukor's assertions of nonmonopolistic intent. At any rate, Keystone Chain plans were dropped, not to be resurrected until the 1929 stock trade with the fledgling CBS.

More Experimentation: The MGM Chain, "Telemovies"

Although Warners and Paramount attempted the largest and noisiest forays into broadcasting territory, others in the film industry experimented with radio in various ways as well. For example, Carl Laemmle at Universal Studios inaugurated the "Carl Laemmle Hour" over WOR in 1927, presenting vaudeville and feature stars and giving previews of upcoming pictures. Across the country, theater owners collaborated with local radio stations in shows such as WARS Brighton Beach's "Theater Hour," used to publicize pictures playing or soon to play at local houses. First National used WJZ for publicity. In California, Washington, and Oregon, a theater chain, West Coast Theaters, joined resources with a small NBC-affiliated string of stations to form the Pacific Broadcasting Corporation. Warners continued broadcasting from KFWB, as other studios built broadcasting facilities and went on the air. Loew's operated WHN out of the Loew's State Theater at 1540 Broadway. MGM had also been providing programs for other stations with favorable results, as *Variety* reported on August 17: "MGM for some time has been utilizing radio through 22 individual stations. Public reaction was excellent. It proved its value for good will and went beyond that in actual box-office reaction."[35]

Perhaps as an outgrowth of this activity, the startling announcement that MGM and Loew's would enter chain broadcasting appeared on September 27, 1927. Envisioning a network of sixty stations in more than forty cities, the venture would broadcast from WHN and from WPAP at the Palisades Amusement Park in Fort Lee, New Jersey. Unlike the May headlines proclaiming Paramount plans, which were based on indirect reports and never directly confirmed by studio spokesmen, an MGM representative openly made the announcement and provided a list of the cities that would be linked by the MGM chain. Specific stations in these cities were not mentioned, however. MGM-Loew's went on to announce that "The broadcasts of the new chain will be commercialized only to the extent of actually covering the cost of production and overhead of the system and will be commercialized only with the view of broadcasting the better elements of radio." February 1928 was named as a starting date.[36]

However, this chain was never to materalize, and indeed it is surprising that so soon after the death of Marcus Loew on September 6 such a major venture should be considered at all. A report in *Moving Picture World* may provide one clue to the potential network's disappearance from the scene. It reports, "contracts for land wires for a nation-wide hook-up involving from $1 million to $3 million annually are being negotiated with AT&T." Faced with the three-year delay in obtaining wires originally accorded CBS, and without the necessary "connections" in Washington, MGM may simply have allowed the idea to lapse. Or again, a desire to throw a scare into exhibitors two weeks before the scheduled trade conferences in Washington could have precipitated an announcement designed more for its immediate effect than for eventual action.[37]

But MGM had other plans for radio as well. Since the summer of 1927, MGM had been experimenting with a novel kind of radio program which the studio dubbed "teleshorts." Every week, using MGM newsreels currently playing in the Loew's State Theater downstairs, WHN would broadcast an "aural" version of the newsreeled events, using an announcer who described each shot and "narrated" the news story, with a musical accompaniment and sound effects. These proved so successful and popular that in December 1927 MGM expanded its efforts to embrace its biggest first-run film of the season: an adaptation of *Anna Karenina* succinctly entitled *Love*, starring no lesser names than Greta Garbo and John Gilbert as Anna and Vronsky. Advertised as the world's first "telemovie," a blow-by-blow account of the film, along with music and sound effects, would be transmitted from the Embassy Theater in New York by wire to WPAP across the river, and then to twenty-six radio stations across the country. Or as described by the *New York American*: "an entire motion picture will be broadcast in detail when Ted Husing will describe 'Love'...as it unreels before his eyes in a special performance at the Embassy theater...he will act as the 'eyes' for the audience in telling the screen story of 'Love'."[38]

Ted Husing, later to achieve considerable fame as a radio announcer, had until this time been known primarily for his football commentary, so *Love* may have proved a considerable challenge to his announcing skills. Much hoopla attended *Love*'s radio debut, including a nationwide stenography contest, with a grand prize trip to Hollywood to go to the stenographer whose transcription most closely matched Husing's monologue. Despite the publicity, this experiment was never repeated on such a large scale; as the following year ushered in the talkies in earnest, the idea of a movie "announcer"—going back in concept to the narrators of nickelodeon days—would no longer be necessary.

The Radio Act of 1927

At the same time as the turmoil in Hollywood, legislators and radio representatives struggled in Washington, D.C., with the final stages of the Radio Act of 1927. In 1926 the *U.S. v. Zenith Radio Corporation* case, disputing the ICC's right to enforce frequency assignments, effectively disbanded all previous legislation over radio based on the inadequate and contradictory rulings built upon the Radio Act of 1912. This breakdown of radio law speeded the passage through Congress of the bills resulting from the fourth radio conference. On February 23, 1927, the new radio control bill received the signature of the president and the first official Federal Radio Commission was born.[39]

Although one of the powers and duties specifically conferred on the commission was "to make special regulations applicable to chain broadcasting" and although the creation of monopoly powers in broadcasting was specifically censured, the next two years were to see the emergence of the advertising-based, network oligopoly structure that still dominates television broadcasting. With the quelling of movie-industry interest by the FTC investigation of 1927 and the conversion to sound, and with the operation of radio broadcasting firmly established in the private sphere with legislative safeguards against censorship, the system of advertiser-supported radio become a reality. The next chapter will trace the years 1928 to 1945, as Hollywood-based programming for radio came to dominate the industry, and as the development of television sparked renewed movie industry investment.[40]

NOTES

1. Robert Sklar, *Movie-Made America* (New York: Vintage Books, 1976); Douglas Ayer, Roy E. Bates, and Peter J. Herman, "Self Censorship in the Movie Industry: A Historical Perspective on Law and Social Change," in *The American Movie Industry,* ed. Gorham Kindem (Carbondale: Southern Illinois University Press, 1982); Jennie Irene Mix, "Good National Radio Programs Prove 'What the Public Wants'," *Radio Broadcast* May 1925, in *American Broadcasting: A Sourcebook on the History of Radio and Television,* ed. Laurence W. Lichty and Malachi C. Topping (New York: Hastings House, 1975), pp. 62–65.

2. Federal Radio Commission, "Appendix F, " *Annual Report 1928* (Washington, D.C.: Government Printing Office, 1929), pp. 166–70.

3. Federal Radio Commission, *Third Annual Report, October 1, 1928 to November 1, 1929* (Washington, D.C.: Government Printing Office, 1929), p. 34.

4. Federal Radio Commission, *Annual Report 1928,* pp. 252–55.

5. May Huettig, "This Motion Picture Industry Today," in *The American Film Industry,* ed. Tino Balio (Madison: University of Wisconsin Press, 1976), p. 233; Janet Staiger "Mass Produced Photoplays: Economic and Signifying Practices in the First Years of Hollywood," in *Movies and Methods,* vol. 2, ed. Bill Nichols (Berkeley: University of California Press, 1985), pp. 144–61; Charles Musser, "The Early Cinema of Edwin Porter," *Cinema Journal* 19 (Fall 1979): 23.

6. Musser, "The Early Cinema of Edwin Porter," p. 34.

7. Balio, *The American Film Industry,* p. 111.

8. Sklar, *Movie-Made America,* p. 148; Jeffrey Pfeffer, "Merger as a Response to Organizational Interdependence," *Administrative Science Quarterly* 17 (September 1972): 382–94.

9. Douglas Gomery, "The Coming of Sound to American Cinema," Ph.D. diss., University of Wisconsin-Madison, 1975.

10. Douglas Gomery, "Movies Become Big Business: Publix Theaters and the Chain Store Strategy," in *The American Movie Industry,* ed. Kindem, pp.

104–16; Sklar, *Movie-Made America,* p. 149; Ralph Cassady, Jr., "Monopoly in Motion Picture Production and Distribution, 1908–1915," in *The American Movie Industry,* ed. Kindem, pp. 25–68.

11. Gomery, "The Coming of Sound"; *Variety,* April 1, 1925; *New York Times,* October 13, 1927.

12. Douglas Gomery, "Toward an Economic History of the Cinema: The Coming of Sound to Hollywood," in *The Cinematic Apparatus,* ed. Stephen Heath and Teresa deLaurentis (New York: St. Martin's Press, 1982).

13. *Moving Picture World,* March 21, 1925, p. 286; Gomery, "The Coming of Sound," p. 136; Irving Settel, *A Pictorial History of Radio* (New York: Citadel Press, 1960), pp. 49, 99.

14. Samuel L. Rothafel and Raymond F. Yates, *Broadcasting: Its New Day* (New York: Century, 1925), p. 156.

15. Rothafel and Yates, *Broadcasting,* p. 156.

16. *Motion Picture World,* April 11, 1925.

17. Gomery, "The Coming of Sound," p. 130; Federal Radio Commission, *Annual Report 1927* (Washington, D.C.: Government Printing Office, 1927).

18. *Motion Picture World,* April 5, 1925, p. 436.

19. Ibid., March 21, 1925, p. 236.

20. Ibid., January 17, 1925, p. 1.

21. *New York Times,* January 11, 1927, p. 1.

22. Ibid., October 2, 1927, p. 22.

23. NBC advertisement, reproduced in Settle, *A Pictorial History,* p. 56; Edward F. Sarno, Jr., "The National Radio Conferences," *Journal of Broadcasting* 13 (Spring 1969): 201–2.

24. Arthur Judson, "How CBS Got Its Start," *American Heritage,* August 1955; John W. Spalding, "1928: Radio Becomes a Mass Advertising Medium," and Federal Communications Commission "The Columbia Broadcasting System," both in *American Broadcasting,* ed. Lichty and Topping, pp. 219–28, pp. 178–81.

25. *New York Times,* May 24, 1927.

26. Ibid., June 6, 1927, p. 26; May 24, 1927, p. 21.

27. N. R. Danelian, *AT&T: The Story of Industrial Conquest* (New York: Vanguard, 1939).

28. *New York Times,* June 23, 1927, p. 22; Eric Barnouw, *A Tower in Babel* (New York: Oxford University Press, 1966), pp. 219–24.

29. Barnouw, *A Tower in Babel,* p. 220; Judson, "How CBS Got Its Start," p. 79.

30. *New York Times,* July 10, 1927, p. 1.

31. Ibid., July 13, 1927, p. 21.

32. Eugene Lyons, *David Sarnoff* (New York: Harper and Row, 1966), p. 237; Gomery, "The Coming of Sound."

33. Jonathan Buchsbaum, "Zukor Buys Protection: The Paramount Stock Purchase of 1929," *Cine-Tracts* no. 8 (Summer-Fall 1979).

34. *Motion Picture World,* January 17, 1925, p. 220.

35. *Variety,* April 13, 1927, p. 54; August 17, 1927, p. 11; October 12, 1927, p. 2; October 26, 1927, p. 56.

36. *New York Times,* September 17, 1927, p. 24.

37. *Motion Picture World,* September 20, 1927.

38. Ibid., September 10, 1927; *New York American,* December 17, 1927; *Film Daily Yearbook 1928* (New York: Film Daily Publications, 1928), p. 253.

39. Frank J. Kahn, ed., *Documents in American Broadcasting* (New York: Appleton-Century-Crofts, 1968), pp. 21–31.

40. L.F. Schmeckbier, *The Federal Radio Commission* (Washington, D.C.: Brookings Institution, 1932), p. 17.

3

Radio Goes Hollywood

1928-38

By the end of 1927, radio broadcasting had taken on most of the structural, economic, and regulatory features that were to characterize the radio, and later television, industry for the next fifty years. In the Radio Act of 1927 lay broadcasting's determining principles, some stated overtly, some still obscured by the circumstances and rhetoric of the day. The industry itself had begun to take shape as an advertising-based medium consisting of relatively low-power local stations strung together into networks. With the formation in 1926 of NBC, owned and operated by RCA, a period of increasing monopsony power lay in store for the broadcasting business.

Radio programming came into its own as increased advertising revenues and the backing of RCA allowed NBC to devote time and money to the improvement of old forms such as musical performances, and to the creation of new forms such as radio drama, news, and star-studded entertainment specials. The rise of the nation's second network, CBS, after 1928 provided NBC with competition and led to more rapid program development as well as increasingly overt advertising. Indeed, the twenty years between 1927 and 1947 represent radio's "Golden Age," effecting changes in the nation's social habits, business economics, and forms of art and entertainment in far-reaching ways that television, despite its far greater revenues and notoriety, did not originate but only continued.

These were also some of the film industry's greatest years, during which the "Hollywood film" became a standard and a symbol, not only in the United States but also worldwide. By the end of 1928, conversion to sound was in full swing, and suddenly Hollywood's relationship to the world of the legitimate theater took center stage as studios rushed to buy up theatrical rights to fuel the new demand for dialogue. Some in the radio business viewed the conversion to sound as a reaction to radio entertainment's growing popularity, as did William Paley in a 1930 address. "Just so has radio stimulated the legitimate theater and motion pictures. It has brought on the 'talkies,' instead of ruining the film industry by keeping the public at home to listen in, as was feared when broadcasting first began."[1]

Although the whole situation behind Hollywood's adoption of sound was, perhaps, more complex than Paley indicated, it cannot be denied that the addition of an aural component to the formerly silent medium opened new possibilities for competition and cooperation between the two industries. One other factor emerged during the early years of this period that would color the relationship: the increasing interest and advancement in television technology. In the same address, Paley also indicated something of the value of the Paramount alliance to CBS: "It is my conviction that, just as the films have utilized the resources of radio science to give the screen a voice, radio broadcasting will eventually borrow eyes from the master minds of the motion-picture laboratory. Whether we will broadcast direct performances from the studios, motion picture performances from film strips synchronized with sound, or theatrical presentations from the stage, it is still too early to say."[2]

As the decade of the Great Depression ran its course, all these possibilities would be tried out on radio, and television would disappoint many as its early promise failed to materialize. Not until after the war would television become widely available to the public, but then it would burst forth with a speed and impact made greater for the period of delay and war-time postponement that had preceded it. In a similar manner, radio and film interests coexisted fairly peaceably during the 1930s and early 1940s, each side gathering strength and making preparations for the confrontation that would finally take place in 1947 with the advent of regular commercial television broadcasting.

Selling the Public Interest:
The Rise of the Commercial Networks

As of January 1928, radio, and the shape of Hollywood's interest in it, remained relatively unformed. Structures had been set and had begun to harden, but the content of broadcasting on a day-to-day basis remained in flux. The idea of radio broadcasting as a public service provided by high-minded and highbrow corporations, encouraged and in fact mandated by the accumulating body of regulation established by the Federal Radio Commission, led to a high proportion, at first, of "sustaining" shows—originated and paid for by the network itself—financed by a small number of commercially sponsored ones. In 1928, only one-quarter of NBC's programs relied on commercial sponsorship. The rest of the broadcast day consisted of network sustaining programs, usually of a public service or cultural nature. Even so, that same year, the National Association of Broadcasters declared a new code of ethics in relation to advertising, which prohibited commercial announcements between the hours of 7:00 and 11:00 P.M.—family time, as opposed to the "business day."[3]

According to Erik Barnouw, the type of programming favored by NBC in 1928 "fostered the developing self-image of the business magnate. He was ready to become a patron of the arts; NBC gave him this chance. . . . The air of distinction which NBC managed to impart to its operation in the formative months was an extraordinary phenomenon."[4] The advent of CBS in 1928 and its rapid growth thereafter can be attributed in part to the successful exploitation of the weaknesses of the NBC policy—or rather the essential weakness of radio's regulatory situation when unsupported by the lofty ideals made much of by NBC. NBC and its affiliate stations operated under a rather complicated system by which affiliates paid the network for sustaining programs (usually at a rate of $50 to $90 per hour, which smaller stations found burdensome), while NBC paid its affiliates for carrying its sponsored programs (usually from $30 to $50 per evening hour, an amount many larger stations felt was inadequate).

The economics at NBC's only competitor, however, were quite different. With no large research department, no receiving set manufacturing division behind it whose sales could offset programming costs, CBS from the beginning presented itself as the advertisers' network. Paley himself had gotten involved in radio as an advertiser, persuading his conservative father and uncles to invest in radio advertising for the family cigar company. The strategy worked, and Paley became a radio enthusiast. The finances of the network in its early days, even with Paley's investment, made attracting sponsored shows imperative—any sustaining program originated by the network itself only lasted as such until it found a sponsor, and the quicker the better. Programs were created with the specific idea of attracting sponsors, not of providing a high-minded public service. Sponsors were free to create programming as they chose; to this day the CBS television network places fewer restrictions on comercial content than either NBC or ABC.[5]

By 1935, CBS boasted a larger number of affiliates than NBC, a testimony to the efficiency and profitability of the system. But a side effect, and one that exploited a major weakness of the regulatory structure, was that by allowing the network to take over the choicest parts of the schedule where the opportunities for revenue were greatest, the affiliate stations essentially sold their responsibility for programming to the network. Because networks fell outside the regulatory reach of the FRC, the government as early as 1929 lost most of its control over radio programming, a situation that continues to the present. By 1929, the 20 percent of all radio stations affiliated with networks received almost 80 percent of advertising revenues.[6]

Thus the existence of a second nationwide network, CBS, as a competitor to NBC's dominance of the field, while providing listeners with a well-deserved alternative source of national programming, hastened the commercialization of radio. CBS's lean and hungry operation—unsupported by income from receiver sales—could not afford the elevated and philanthropic type of sustaining programming NBC supplied; economics dictated that the lofty public-service goals put forth by the FRC and backed by RCA must give way to a more profit-oriented view. Economic pressures brought on by the depression as well as the FRC's lifting of the ban on recorded commercial announcements in 1932 (chapter 4) also contributed to the commercialization process. From a proportion of 76.4 percent sustaining hours to 23.6 percent sponsored on NBC in 1933, the percentage of sustaining shows dropped to 50.6 by 1944. During the same period "classical and semi-classical" music dropped from 26.9 to 12.2 percent of the daily schedule, while children's programming fell from 3.6 to 0.4 percent and talks and discussion declined from 7.0 to 2.4 percent. In the meantime the amount of drama of all types on the air increased from 11.2 to 26.7 percent and variety and quiz formats from 2.6 to 14.0 percent.[7]

As radio advertising became a profitable business, advertising agencies increasingly assumed control not only of aligning sponsors with shows, but also of eventually creating and producing the shows themselves. Llewellyn White, reporting for the Commission for the Freedom of the Press, links the entry of advertising agencies into broadcasting with the rise of the daytime "women's" serial, the comedy series, and the adventure and mystery drama, as well as the original impetus behind the use of Hollywood names to promote radio variety shows. Stephen Fox supports this conclusion and further emphasizes the large part played by advertising agencies in creating the so-called "soap-opera" form. Three of the earliest daytime serials, "Just Plain Bill," "Betty and Bob," and "Ma Perkins," were invented and put on the air by the Blackett-Sample-Hummert agency of Chicago as vehicles for

Kolynos toothpaste, Gold Medal flour, and Oxydol detergent, respectively. The role advertising agencies played in the development of broadcast programming will be discussed in detail in chapter 4.

Hollywood on the Air

For Hollywood, the period 1928-38 was marked by slow but steadily increasing involvement in radio programming punctuated by periods of severe intraindustry conflict. When the dust from the tumultuous year of 1927 had settled, the major studios found themselves standing on the outside of radio networking and ownership, but holding some valuable assets on the programming side of the radio game. In the scramble to convert to sound, radio took a temporary back seat, but even so Hollywood made its presence felt.

On March 29, 1928, the Dodge Brothers of Detroit sponsored the biggest star extravaganza as yet heard over the air to promote its new Dodge car. NBC, with the help of AT&T, set up a special, one-time link from Hollywood to Detroit, with a second New York to Detroit tie-up to allow WJZ and fifty-five NBC stations to switch back and forth from all three locations in the course of the broadcast. On the Hollywood end, some of the biggest names in film gathered at the home of Douglas Fairbanks, where a special transmitting facility had been set up. Not only Fairbanks but also John Barrymore, Norma Talmadge, D. W. Griffith, Charles Chaplin, and Dolores Del Rio performed over the air, interspersed with music by Paul Whiteman and his orchestra in New York City.

According to the next day's review the event was a huge success, proceeding with not a single technical slip-up. To record-size audiences across the country, each star either delivered a talk or performed a turn of his or her choosing. Fairbanks began with a short talk on "Keeping Fit," Talmadge followed with advice on "Fashions for Women," Del Rio sang the lead song from her current movie *Ramona,* and Griffith read an essay on "Love." Chaplin, according to the report, told several "characteristic stories," followed by Barrymore, who did the soliloquy from *Hamlet.*[8]

Although radio could not often duplicate the grandeur and magnificence of such an evening, as Hollywood found its voice, it turned increasingly to radio for expression. The enthusiasm for radio appearances continued for various reasons, extra publicity being the main one. For example, in 1929, *Variety* featured an article headlined "Film People Seeking Radio Dates as Mike Training for Voices." Warner Brothers continued to sponsor star "appearances" over KFWB, despite

Sam Warner's death in 1928. Paramount instituted the "Paramount Picture Hour" over KNX, located on the Paramount lot until 1932. This two-hour Sunday night broadcast featured current Paramount releases, and *Variety* reported that "studio players are eager to appear." MGM linked up with Auto-Grill, a toaster manufacturing company, to do a series of shows in 1929, broadcasting not over one of the established networks but over an ad hoc line-up of independent stations—a foreshadowing of later Hollywood strategy with television.[9]

The year 1929 also saw the merging of Paramount and CBS interests through the previously discussed stock transfer that solidified the Hollywood-radio connection, although this particular merger would prove evanescent as the depression deepened. In the meantime, the movie industry continued to experiment with new uses of radio-related technology; for example, Fox studios received its own frequency allocation in April of 1929 to transmit the sound portion of its daily rushes from location shooting in the Fiji Islands back to Hollywood via shortwave.[10]

Of course another example of radio-film interconnection is the arrival of direct radio involvement in moviemaking through RCA's establishment of RKO studios, an instant "major," in that same year, in order to develop its sound on film system in the only way left open to it since all the existing studios had opted for ERPI. On February 6, 1929, an extravagant two-page spread in *Variety* announced with typical understatement, "A TITAN IS BORN....Eclipsing in magnitude and far reaching interests any enterprise in the History of Show Business... NOW...MORE THAN EVER...MASTER SHOWMEN OF THE WORLD!" In other words, RCA was now in the business of making movies. The era of Hollywood-radio interdependence dawned in earnest. Through 1930 and 1931 the interchange continued, as the depression began to make itself felt.[11]

1932: Readjustment and Rebellion

One industry relatively unaffected by the economic downturn of the early 1930s, however, was that of radio manufacturing and broadcasting. Even in 1931, when Hollywood had finally begun to experience the box-office downturn that rapidly accelerated during the next two years, both CBS and NBC reported record income and continued to profit handsomely. *Business Week* reported that "It's like going into a different world when you leave the depression-ridden streets for the office of a big broadcasting company. Men going past are fat and cheerful. Cigars point ceilingward, heels click on tiles, the merry quip and the untroubled laugh ring high and clear."[12]

Radio broadcasting's economic health contrasted sharply to the rapidly worsening plight of the film industry, where "Thespis [was] doing an Eliza across the ice with the hounds yipping at her heels." This downturn hit the theater owners first and hardest. By the summer of 1932, *Business Week* reported that "Roxy's—'largest theater in the world,' 'Cathedral of the motion picture'—is in receivership. Other big metropolitan houses are dark... *Variety* reports that half of the 1600 Publix [Paramount] theaters have been aided [by the parent corporation] one way or another."[13]

But despite, or perhaps because of, the economic downturn, the year 1932 can be examined as the beginning of Hollywood's "readjustment" to radio. Although direct ownership of the medium on any large scale remained difficult, if not impossible, 1932 witnessed Hollywood's increasing involvement in production for radio, the growth in exchange of talent as performers trained and experienced in radio moved West to make films just as their Hollywood counterparts began to pursue radio spots, and also the sharing of dramatic properties as studios acquired ideas from radio and radio began to bring Hollywood to the airwaves. The year 1932 also produced the first serious rupture along the film industry's traditional fault line, producer-exhibitor relations, pitting the complaints of hard-pressed theater owners over radio competition against the expanding opportunities available on the production side.

The 1932 Ban

Most histories of radio and film, if they discuss industry interaction at all, make mention of the so-called Hollywood ban on radio performances of stars in 1932. As Barnouw states, "In 1932 all major studios except RKO had adopted a policy of keeping their contract talent off the air. Hollywood strategy, for the moment, was to ignore radio." This is viewed as a straightforward expression of Hollywood's feelings about radio, which in turn lead to charges of "blindness" and "ignorance" on the part of the movie industry that carried over into its later relations with television. In fact, this ban headlined in *Variety* in late December of 1932 does not represent a long-standing attitude toward radio, but the temporary appeasement of exhibitor complaints brought to crisis point by a one-time situation. The so-called radio ban of December 1932, partial at best, had by August of 1933, eight months later, virtually disintegrated. The reasons behind this short-lived ban, which has achieved an accepted historical status far out of proportion to its actual significance, indicate a quite different rationale and motivation on the part of the studios than is commonly understood.[14]

Objections such as those expressed by exhibitors at the trade conference in 1927 to the "free" performances given by film stars on radio during hours of theater operation were heard continuously throughout the 1930s. From 1925 to 1940, not a year went by without headlines in *Variety* or *Motion Picture World* proclaiming theater owners' dissatisfaction with producers' publicizing of films and stars on the air. However, the situation came to a head in 1932 with a rising crescendo of complaints by theater owners over film stars' free performances, not only on air but also, in some cities, in downtown radio recording studios where live audiences were admitted each night for free. In February 1932, *Variety* reported that an RKO broadcast had seriously angered theater interests when the announcer had gone so far as to conclude the broadcast with "Aren't you glad you stayed home this evening to listen to the 'RKO Theater of the Air'? Stay at home every Friday night for it."[15] In June 1932, a group of exhibitors complained to the press that it felt the Hays organization was "double crossing" them on a spoken agreement that film producers would be required to curb star performances on the air during theater hours. The immediate cause for this complaint was a popular star-studded charity show put on in Hollywood earlier that year.[16] The situation was exacerbated by the another source of conflict from a direction that would seem to benefit Hollywood interests, but which proved a double-edged sword. As radio became a medium increasingly dominated and controled by advertisers, and as advertising dollars expended on radio rose dramatically each year, newspapers began to feel the threat to their own economic base. As early as 1922 the Associated Press had refused to grant radio stations membership in its cooperative organization, and although many broadcasters turned to the United Press and the International News Service, the depression intensified competition between the two media. This conflict came to a head in 1932 as well, when not only the Hoover-Roosevelt presidential contest, but also the Lindberg kidnapping drama brought radio newsgathering into direct and harmful confrontation with newspaper coverage—and advertising revenue. As *Variety* stated, "Most publishers regard the $4,000,000 spent in 1931 with the two air networks as money diverted from them."[17]

The American Newspaper Publishers Association responded by cutting off all wire services from the broadcasters, and beyond that entered into an anti-radio campaign that it intended the film industry to join. Across the country, newspapers sought the cooperation of film exhibitors to fight the popularity of radio by giving increased publicity to filmed entertainment in a "campaign to weaken the radio audience." Every minute spent in the movie theater was a minute denied to the radio networks, and newspapers saw no such competition between their own product and film entertainment. Many newspapers dropped radio schedule listings from their pages altogether in an attempt to reduce support of the rival medium, and those who continued program listings at least made an effort to drop the name of the advertiser from the title of the show. But even as *Variety* gloated, "Film press agents are making the pleasant discovery that news columns these days are being thrown open to pictures as never before," those same news columns also demonstrated their willingness to publicize the complaints of exhibitors against the studios concerning radio appearances of stars.[18]

It is not hard to see the advantage in this alliance for the movie studios' publicity departments. At very little cost to themselves, since the demand for star performances on radio did not diminish, studios received free promotion of their theatrical films as a by-product of the newspapers' attempts to encourage consumers to substitute theater-going in place of radio-listening. Theater owners benefited from the free publicity, but in so doing committed themselves to an anti-radio stance that carried over into their relationship with the studios, which continued to loan out their stars for radio appearances.[19] In addition, exhibitors' feelings about radio suffered some rather severe blows in early 1932. RKO began advertising its films on the air that year and further announced a new program called "Hollywood on the Air" for which it would solicit studio participation; NBC announced that it would actively promote film-radio cooperation in the promotion of films on RKO's new show; and Irving Thalberg at MGM announced plans for participating in this scheme by broadcasting film dramatizations.

In June, just before the debut of the RKO-NBC program, a star-studded charity benefit for the unemployed was broadcast from Hollywood. Benefit performances, for charities and such things as unemployment funds during this worst year of the depression, had become so frequent that both the major networks and the studios had earlier that year placed bans on free performances by their major stars. The studios had further arranged that future requests be handled by the Hays office, so that some kind of control could be maintained without the onus of direct refusal by the individual studio.[20] The June program attracted national attention and proved popular enough with radio audiences to reawaken exhibitors' complaints. *Variety* reported that "the recent star broadcast for the unemployed from Hollywood on a national hook-up is reported to have brought the matter to a head because many of the big theaters, as well as subsequent runs, attributed a marked drop in patronage that night to the screen's personal loud speaker appearance." "Hollywood on the Air" went on in June. In August,

Columbia and Universal contributed to the program; in September, MGM made good its offer of participation by promoting several of its new releases in cooperation with RKO and NBC. On September 6, a one-time radio special produced jointly by General Motors and Warner Brothers made the news. Exhibitors' grievances increased to new heights and found an outlet in newspapers across the country.[21]

These plans, and exhibitor resentment of radio's competition for audiences, culminated in December 1932, when RKO once again attempted to recruit big names from other studios for "Hollywood on the Air." It must be remembered, at this point, that 1932 marks the definitive takeover of radio by advertising interests, as mentioned previously, and the concommittant termination of "gratis" performances by artists of all descriptions. Although free performances by actors, musicians, and other artists had, before 1932, been regarded in the light of a self-promoting public service, the changing economic conditions of radio made this attitude unrealistic, and by 1932 ASCAP, the studios, and most talent agencies demanded that their talent be paid, and paid well. Indeed, as the final barriers to the use of recorded materials on the air were removed by the FRC in 1932, radio moved firmly into the hands of the advertising agencies, intensifying the rush to Hollywood.

What networks, in the sustaining programming, had been willing to do without, sponsors now demanded: big-name Hollywood stars. RKO, by its generous offer to help publicize other studios' films, simultaneously managed to provide itself with free performances by major stars. Although MGM and other studios with those stars under contract might be willing to experiment with this concept once or twice, ultimately, in the always piquant words of *Variety,* "No Film Dough for Radio"—why should the studios give away one of their greatest assets? The recently lifted restrictions on recorded material may have contributed to the studios' new reluctance to cooperate as well: Paramount, MGM, Warners, and RKO all announced plans to distribute recorded picture promotions in October 1932.[22]

Into this complicated melange of competing interests, economic hardship, and intraindustry conflict, the RKO request for talent to appear on its program fell like a bomb. Why, as calls from advertising agencies offereing substantial sums for radio apearances began to come in rapidly, should Paramount, Warners, MGM, and 20th Century-Fox risk increasing exhibitor discontent or alienating their new allies, the newspapers, by allowing their contract talent to appear under the RKO banner, to RKO, RCA, and NBC's credit, at no remuneration to themselves? Suddenly, the complaints of the exhibitors and the self-interest of the studios began to coincide. On December 27, 1932, *Variety* announced, "Film Stars Kept Off Air...all major studios with the exception of Radio's have verbally agreed to prohibit people under contract from broadcasting under any circumstances." The article then innocently stated, "First knowledge of this airtight agreement was had when RKO asked members of the producers' association to participate in its 'Hollywood on the Air' program, with all companies refusing to cooperate. Radio and RKO will have to recruit its future programs from within its own ranks.[23]

Taking this declaration in conjunction with the other studios' previously announced plans for radio production—and those that soon followed—it is hard to arrive at any other conclusion than that of a certain duplicitousness on the part of the studio management. By agreeing—verbally—to participate in a ban on radio performances, the studios could at once appease their angry exhibitors, gain favorable newspaper publicity, and avoid contributing to a program that would not directly benefit them without overtly voicing the resentment felt against RKO and the network whose agreement with AT&T gave them virtual monopoly powers in the broadcasting field. The announcement of December 1932 seems designed to act as a temporary public relations screen behind which, after a short period of quiescence, the studios could carry on very much as before. In addition, studios had long been troubled by unauthorized star appearances—it was felt that some stars, by ill-considered or simply ill-performed stints on the air, were "using up" their box office appeal—and the ban gave studios further ammunition with which to limit and supervise contract talent appearances.

It is evident, at any rate, that the ban was short-lived. By January 17, 1933, only three weeks after the ban, Paramount was using radio dramatization to promote *Island of Lost Souls,* and Warners continued to originate radio shows over KFWB from its Los Angeles theater while admitting the public at no charge, a practice Los Angeles theater owners estimated cost them $5,000 per week in lost admissions. By January 24, independent theater owners felt compelled to issue another demand, this time that the studios ban film star performances during theater hours (noon to midnight). RKO's show went on the air regardless— with in-house talent—and by August 29, 1933, *Variety* reported that all studios except Fox had long since quietly dropped the radio boycott. (Fox had its own reasons for refusing to cooperate with radio interests; its bitter battle with AT&T and RCA over sound-film patents continued into the mid-1930s.) Also, tellingly, no agreement was ever put into writing or formally drawn up between the concerned parties; indeed,

Will Hays later advised the studios not to give in to the complaints of the exhibitors, arguing that as soon as the studios formally agreed that radio apearances in fact reduced the box-office value of screen stars, exhibitors could use this as a bargaining tool in film negotiations, driving down rental prices.[24]

In fact, throughout the period exhibitor reaction was not undivided. Although many theater owners, particularly the larger independent groups, did regard radio as a threat, others saw in radio an opportunity to promote films on the local level. This difference in reaction reflects a pattern of film industry collision of interests that goes back as far as the days of the Motion Picture Patents Trust. Janet Staiger points out that it is difficult to generalize motives for actions across large interest groups; each group may contain elements within it that, often because of local legal or business circumstances, may act in ways dissimilar with, or even contradictory to, goals of affiliated or parent organizations. Given, too, that ownership ties between the integrated studios and theater companies were often only through a fractional share of stock, interests and goals of parents and subsidiaries might differ considerably. This diversity of reaction to radio amid exhibitors is reflected in trade publication reports.[25]

In between reports on the deleterious effects of radio-listening on box-office receipts, the *Motion Picture Herald* ran several articles on radio as a medium of film publicity. On January 21, 1933, a theater owner contributed an article entitled "How to Nail Profitable Radio Tie-Ups to the Box Office." In it he recommended such promotional devices as short spots of Hollywood gossip centered on a given film or stars; locally acted and produced "trailers," dramatizing scenes from the film currently in play; organ concerts broadcast from the theater itself (a popular radio staple); broadcasting the preceding stage show; and using on-air quiz games or film-related contests.

A February 11 article discussed another use of radio: to broadcast radio shows to an audience inside the theater over the ERPI sound system now that most theaters were wired, although ERPI objected to this usage. The February 25, 1933, issue contains an article by Jack Cohn of Columbia Pictures, who urged theater owners to use radio to "get people back into the theater-going habit." One basic technique used to accomplish this benefited all aspects of the industry in a very simple manner, still employed today: "Hollywood made sure to use the names of its films as part of the titles of its theme songs, so radio—like it or not—would automatically plug its pix when announcing the song titles and recordings played."[26]

Radio Programming Takes Shape

The history of the development of the forms and structures of the radio programming wafted over the airwaves to an unsuspecting public in the early 1930s is truly remarkable; unfortunately, the medium's genuine achievements and innovations in programming, although bringing an amount and variety of entertainment to a wider audience than ever before reached by a mass medium, remain overshadowed in many accounts of that period by the rapid rise in number, and lowering in tone, of the radio advertising commercial. Yet, as the historians Robert E. Summers and Harrison B. Summers write, "beginning in 1929 and 1930, radio entered an era of program experimentation, invention, and development without parallel in any other period in the history of broadcasting."[27]

Most of this material represented borrowing and modification of existing art forms; with the exception of the talk show and the quiz or audience participation show, two possibilities novel to broadcasting, radio adapted the forms and formulas of vaudeville, theater, concert, and film to fit its burgeoning needs. Hollywood participated in the development of all these formats.[28]

A comparison of the broadcasting schedules of the networks from 1929–30, 1934–35, and 1939–40 shows three main trends. First, although between 1930 and 1934 the total number of hours in a typical week spent broadcasting music of all types rose from 59 to 74.5, it then declined from 1935–39 to 56, representing a gradual decrease in music's importance to the radio schedule. The earlier increase must be attributed at least in part to the dramatic rise in overall hours on the air; in 1929, a typical network station broadcast between the hours of noon and 11:00 P.M., or only sporadically during a longer day. By 1934, the average day began at 6:00 A.M. and proceeded with a fully packed schedule until sign-off at 1:00 A.M. or later. Most of the early-morning, late-night, and fill-in hours were occupied by music. The second noticeable trend is that the amount of on-air drama during prime-time (evening and Sunday afternoon) schedules increased from 11 percent in 1933 and 20 percent in 1939 to 26.7 percent in 1944. The third trend, the rise of afternoon serial drama, or "soap," from a negligible quantity in 1929–30 to seventy-five hours a week by 1939, later developed into another area of interplay between radio and the Hollywood "women's film."[29]

Hollywood influence played an important part in all three of these trends. The film industry's participation in radio programming occurred in two distinct stages: the period up to and including 1936, marked by sporadic involvement and the innovation of one or two variety shows, and the post-1936 period during which Hollywood-based programming proliferated and soon began to dominate over programs produced elsewhere. Once again, as with the entry of CBS into radio networking, the decisive factor in this change involved the telephone company.

AT&T and Coast-to-Coast Broadcasting

Up until 1936, although coast-to-coast long lines were in place, and had been since 1915, the telephone company maintained a policy of charging additional fees over and above normal line charges, which were themselves substantial, for broadcast hook-ups emanating elsewhere than New York City. These charges were based on a policy of figuring fees on a cost-per-circuit-mile basis, rather than actual, or air, distance. Because the major transmitting facilities of both networks were based in New York, AT&T charged the broadcasters on a per-mile basis for the Los Angeles to New York circuit in addition to charges from New York back out to stations across the country. In other words, to reach an NBC affilliate in Denver with a show originating in Hollywood, the network would have to pay first for the land lines connecting Los Angeles to the central transmitter in New York City, then for the wires connecting New York to Denver, even although direct Los Angeles to Denver wires were in place and capable of transmitting radio signals—all these charges figured per circuit mile, usually much less direct than actual distance. This practice considerably increased the relative cost of West Coast-originated shows, leading to various problems in pre-1936 Hollywood-radio cooperation.[30]

First, because the networks preferred to avoid the additional fees, film stars were encouraged to come to New York City for radio spots, a practice film producers claimed disrupted ongoing movie work. Second, the reverse borrowing of radio stars for film work (a growing trend in the early 1930s) was made difficult and prohibitively expensive. For example, when the creators of the popular "Amos 'n Andy" radio serial were invited to make *Check and Double Check* for RKO in 1931, the studio contracted to pay the comedy team's $1,000-per-day line charges so that their daily show could continue to air throughout filming. Third, the policy discouraged the building of permanent studios and transmitting stations on the West Coast; Chicago in the early 1930s remained a more thriving center of radio than Hollywood with its millions of dollars of captive talent.[31]

The situation rapidly reversed itself after 1935, but it took a federal investigation to prompt the telephone company to rethink its rate structures. On March 15, 1935, Franklin D. Roosevelt authorized

Congress to undertake a massive investigation of AT&T and other telephone company practices, both as a fact-finding study and in order to determine "the effect of monopolistic control upon the reasonableness of telephone rates and charges; and the reasons for the failure generally to reduce telephone rates and charges during the years of declining prices."

One of the particular areas of enquiry was that of interstate toll rate structure. The FCC reported that during the period of the investigation from June 1, 1935 to January 15, 1937, "as a result of negotiations between the American Telephone and Telegraph Company, long distance telephone rates were reduced on a basis equivalent to an estimated savings to the public of $12,235,000 per annum," and, more specifically, the investigation produced "revision of wire service charges to radio stations...it is estimated that these revisions will result in annual savings to broadcasters of $530,000."[32]

The removal of double rates to the coast produced a veritable deluge of Hollywood-produced programming over the next five years, with both major networks building new studios in Los Angeles. This "Trek to Hollywood" as the *Literary Digest* offically dubbed it, reflected both the public's insatiable interest in the stars, scripts, and formulas developed by the movies and the culmination of a fruitful period of borrowing and cross-interests that began in the earlier period for both industries.[33]

Hollywood's Role in Radio Programming

Hollywood contributions played a major role during the 1930s in the development of four distinct types of programming: the variety special, the dramatic series featuring big-name guest stars, the publicity-gossip show, and the radio adaptation of movie hits. Each of these made its initial appearance before 1935, but reached full stature in the later 1930s.

Variety

The variety special, based on standard vaudeville practice, combined big names, lesser stars, and regular performers in a mix of music, comedy, dialogue, and short dramatic vignettes. As described in chapter 2, Samuel Rothafel, "Roxy" to millions, pioneered this early variety forms on radio; the addition in 1928 of big-name Hollywood stars helped boost its popularity further.

Among the foremost variety shows on network radio, from its inception in 1932 throughout its lengthy life, was Maxwell House coffee's

"Show Boat." Set on a fictional paddle-wheeler that made weekly Thursday night stops at various ports, the show contained music, variety acts, and comic sketches, usually featuring one or more well-known names from Hollywood or Broadway. Making high ratings each year of its existence, "Show Boat" attracted MGM as its co-producer (with Maxwell House) in 1937, and changed its name to "Hollywood Good News" along with its format. Other popular variety shows featuring Hollywood talent included the "Rudy Vallee Show," which premiered on NBC in October 1929; the "Kraft Music Hall," debuting in 1933 on NBC; and Al Jolson's "Shell Chateau" sponsored by the Shell Oil Corporation from 1935 to the mid 1940s.

Dramatic Series

The dramatic series format, often featuring big-name stars, originated with the appearance in 1929 of the long-standing dramatic program "First Nighter," sponsored by Cambana Balm. Built around the kind of imaginary flexibility of space and time unique to radio, "First Nighter" opened with a character known as "the genial first nighter" taking a fictional stroll up Broadway to the "Little Theater Off Times Square," where he purchased a ticket and was shown to his seat by an usher just as the curtain went up. Halfway through the show "intermission" would be called to allow for a commercial break, then back to the show as the buzzer sounded and the usher cried "Curtain going up!"[34]

The plays presented ranged from adaptations of genuine Broadway shows to original creations for radio, many of them written by the well-known radio dramatist Arch Oboler, later of "Lights Out," a "Twilight Zone" predecessor. Although the show evoked Broadway and was in fact produced in Chicago, it soon became a vehicle for Hollywood talent, usually appearing on guest status among a crew of radio regulars. This basic formula would increase in popularity and presence on the radio throughout the 1930s; "First Nighter" itself lasted through 1945 in a variety of time slots and network changes. Campana Balm remained loyal; although its ratings declined from the mid-20s to a 10.8 in its last season, "First Nighter" provided a model for a score of followers, including a second shot at success launched by Campana Balm in 1933. "Grand Hotel," using a dramatic framework based on the Academy Award-winning film of the previous year, involved a series of famous "guests"—in two senses, now—in light-weight fictions by a different writer each week. It stayed on the air until 1938, then gave up in the face of a proliferation of imitators.[35]

In the 1934 season alone, four other drama programs appeared that focussed on Hollywood: "Gigantic Pictures," sponsored by Tastyeast on the NBC Blue Network; "Irene Rich Dramas" from Welch's Juice, also on NBC Blue; a sustaining NBC Blue show called "Motion Picture Dramas"; and a short-lived serial called "Sally of the Talkies" sponsored by Luxor Products on the Red Network.

The year 1935 brought to the air a show that became known as "one of the most intelligent" on the air: "The Calvacade of America," a series based on historical dramatizations and featuring top Broadway and Hollywood names on a guest basis. Beginning on CBS, then moving to NBC in 1939, it stayed on the air for eighteen years and built a reputation for thorough and accurate research as well as dramatic appeal. Sponsored by DuPont ("Better things for better living through Chemistry"), "Calvacade" drew on the expertise of a board of academic advisers headed by Frank Monaghan of Yale, and also featured special productions written by talents such as Carl Sandburg, Stephen Vincent Benet, Maxwell Anderson, and Robert Sherwood. The show's aura of seriousness and prestige attracted stage and screen actors who had formerly remained aloof; Clark Gable made his first radio appearance on "Calvacade," and serious actors such as Raymond Massey (playing Abraham Lincoln), Charles Laughton, Lionel Barrymore, Dick Powell, Tyrone Power, and Edgar G. Robinson portrayed various historical figures. Orson Welles and some of his later Mercury Theatre troupe began on "Calvacade." Although "docudrama" is a form supposedly invented by television in the 1970s, its roots, like so much of television's programming, lie in radio.

Another anthology program using film talent, "Hollywood Play-house," came on the air in 1937 on the NBC Blue Network, sponsored by Woodbury Soap and hosted by a succession of film names including Charles Boyer, Jim Ameche, Tyrone Power, and Herbert Marshall. Its run was brief, however; by 1939, having failed to gain more than an 11.8 rating, it went off the air. Another similar program, the "Silver Theater" on CBS (predictably sponsored by the International Sterling Company) met with improved success, attracting stars such as Rosalind Russell, Joan Crawford, Douglas Fairbanks, Helen Hayes, and Henry Fonda.

After 1938, the appearance of Hollywood and Broadway talent on radio, and vice versa, became so commonplace an event that it became the rule rather than the exception. However, two other program types appeared before 1938, the Hollywood gossip "column" and the movie adaptation.

Publicity and Gossip

The catalyst behind exhibitors' fears of radio was a type of program that, almost from its first days, drew on Hollywood for material: the broadcast gossip column. Louella Parsons, Hedda Hopper, Walter Winchell, and scores of lesser known gossip purveyors found an avid audience for their tales of Hollywood life. In January 1932, the Hays Office launched an investigation of "alleged slurs on film stars and studios by radio columnists," but went on to announce that despite the disreputable reporting by one or two radio columnists, the broadcasting industry and Hollywood retained a good relationship: "There is a complete understanding between radio and pictures."[36]

The movie producers' annoyance at the exploitation of their stars' names and reputations over the air remained mitigated, however, by the usefulness of the free publicity. The studios' disfavor soon shifted to a desire to avoid mismanaged star publicity; radio gossip and talk shows could be as effective a tool for movie promotion as printed ads and posters, providing that the stars themselves were protected from their own impulses.

One of the first network gossip columns appeared in the 1930-31 season on NBC Red, "Rinso Talkie Time." This program lasted only one season, but in 1932 NBC ran two new "talk" spots on its Blue Network: a show called "D.W. Griffith's Hollywood," hosted at least nominally by the director himself, and the beginning of the long-running "Walter Winchell Show," originating at first from New York and focussed primarily on Broadway. Winchell continued to broadcast from New York for most of his career, but much of his material derived from Hollywood-renowned personalities and events. He remained on the air continuously from 1932 to the years of long-form radio's bitter end, bringing listeners "lotions of love" from Jergen's lotion until 1948. In 1945 he and Louella Parsons began a cooperative venture for Jergens, featuring Winchell from New York on Sundays at 9:00 P.M., followed by Parsons from Hollywood at 9:15. A fierce rivalry between the two for Hollywood scoops kept the show's ratings high until 1951, when the advent of regular television broadcasting caused radio ratings to fall precipitously throughout the industry.

Several other lesser-known gossip purveyors appeared during radio's early years. For example, in 1933 "Madame Sylvia" went on the air, first for the Ralston Company, then for Ry-Krisp. Her twice-weekly program on NBC Red ran for only two seasons, but 1934 saw the appearance of another sucessful specialist, Jimmy Fidler "Your Hollywood Reporter," on the NBC Blue for Tangee Corporation, and later from Drene shampoo on CBS until 1941 and Carter on ABC until 1950. Another famous name joined the group in 1939: Hedda Hopper. Although never cornering the largest ratings, these shows retained a loyal audience until supplanted by television in the late 1940s. They do not necessarily represent a form of participation in radio much encouraged by the studios; however, such shows could and did quite effectively promote and publicize Hollywood films and stars. They were also to serve as a recurrent bone of contention between studios and exhibitors throughout the 1930s and 1940s. Louella Parsons herself maintained a radio presence, off and on, from 1928 through the early 1950s, in a show sponsored by Sun-Kist oranges, but "Hollywood Hotel" was her most successful effort.[37]

The Movie Adaptation

Frequently credited with having "brought radio to Hollywood," "Hollywood Hotel" first appeared in 1934 on the CBS chain. Combining the variety format with guest-star drama, the show originated with and was hosted by Louella Parsons, who used her considerable influence to persuade big-name stars to appear for free. This money-saving idea helped to offset the AT&T surcharge still in effect for West Coast transmitting. Who could risk a refusal at the cost of falling from Miss Parsons's good graces?

"Hollywood Hotel" promoted the gossip and talk format to a kind of respectability and reinforced the popularity of the star-studded variety act, but it also pioneered a new form of film-based programming that would prove the be extremely popular and mutually beneficial for both the film and radio industries. "Hollywood Hotel" featured the weekly enactment of a scene from or a condensed version of a film soon to be released by one of the studios. Often using the actual stars of the film, these twenty-minute vignettes served not only to popularize the radio show but also as excellent publicity for the films. In 1938, the radio show itself served as the basis for a movie, *Hollywood Hotel*, starring Louella Parsons in her real-life role.

The movie-adaption program best remembered by radio listeners, which represents the culmination of its type, was the "Lux Radio Theatre." "Lux" started out as a vehicle for radio versions of Broadway shows and was based in New York City; not until the AT&T line charges dropped in 1936 did "Lux" move to Hollywood, where it signed on as master of ceremonies the well-known director of screen extravaganzas, Cecil B. DeMille. From its debut on June 1, 1936— an adaptation of "The Legionnaire and the Lady" with Clark Gable and Marlene Dietrich—to its controversial loss of DeMille in 1945,

"Lux Radio Theatre" remained one of the most popular shows on the air. Gaining a 25.1 rating in its first season, the 9–10:00 P.M. Monday show hit a peak of 30.8 in the 1941–42 season. It remained one of radio's top ten shows through the 1940s and spawned a host of imitations. Its introductory words, "And now . . . Lux Presents HOLLYWOOD!" and its sign-off phrase, "This is Cecil B. DeMille, saying Goodnight to you from Hollywood," became catchphrases across the country.[38]

The show was sponsored by Lever Brothers, which seemed to be willing to spend enormous amounts of money by radio standards to make its Lux soap flakes a household word. DeMille received $1,500 per week at first, later more than $2,000, just to introduce the show each night, provide a few comments between the acts, and sign off dramatically—as well as for his enthusiastic endorsement of the product during the show. Actual direction was done by Frank Woodruff, listed as assistant director, but DeMille's name and production style proved to be well worth the cost. As one account had it, "Danker [Daniel J. Danker, Jr., head of the Hollywood office of J. Walter Thompson, Lever Brothers' advertising agency] had wanted an extravaganza, and he got it. . . . In the DeMille years more than 50 people were required for each show. Sometimes the stage couldn't hold them all."[39]

"Lux Radio Theatre" attracted nearly all the top names in Hollywood during its fifteen-year career, and many more supporting stars. DeMille claimed that more than five hundred top stars had been heard, with the sole exceptions of Chaplin and Garbo. Among the films adapted to the requirements of the hour-long aural presentation were "Dark Victory," with Bette Davis and Spencer Tracy; "To Have and Have Not," with Humphrey Bogart and Lauren Bacall; "The Thin Man," with William Powell and Myrna Loy; "Mr. Deeds Goes to Town," with Gary Cooper; and "A Farewell to Arms," with Clark Gable and Josephine Hutchinson. A few shows, such as "Dark Victory," "How Green Was My Valley," and "This Above All," were presented on "Lux" before being released to the screen. Most, however, were broadcast immediately after the film's first run and served to boost theater attendance, according to studio executives. The show was broadcast from the Music Box Theater in Hollywood before a live audience of a thousand people, in order, according to DeMille, "to give the players and director the lift that only a living audience can provide." Such a production did not come cheap; stars received a flat fee of $5,000 per performance, bringing the typical weekly production cost to more than $20,000.[40]

Although the prestige and popularity of "Lux Radio Theatre" made radio performances by top stars an acceptable and even a desireable part of movie promotion, the fact remains that the "Lux" idea originated not in Hollywood but in a New York advertising agency, and that control of the program rested in the hands of the agency and its client. Warner Brothers Studio took steps in 1938 to correct the situation. Drawing on the emerging talent in its famous "Warner's Academy of Acting," the "Warner Brothers' Academy Theatre" dramatized and promoted Warner Brothers films in production. Such budding stars as Susan Hayward, Carole Landis, and Ronald Reagan could be heard regularly; part of the show's attraction was an informal "chat" with the actors and actresses at the end of the show. Unlike "Lux," the "Academy Theater" remained under the production control of Warner Brothers, who sold advertising slots within it to the Gruen Watch Company. Also unlike "Lux," the show was not aired over a major network. Instead, Warner syndicated the series through the Trans-America Broadcasting System for sale to independents and smaller chains on an individual basis. This syndication strategy was one that Hollywood would pursue with great success later as it diversified into television production.[41]

Another tactic, producing another highly popular film adaptation show, "The Screen Guild Theater," was to compete with the high salaries of "Lux" by persuading top talent to appear free—in the name of charity. Gulf Oil sponsored the show and donated comparable amounts per star to the Motion Picture Relief Fund, which used the money—estimated at more than $800,000 by 1942—to build a retirement home for aging and impecunious actors and actresses. Some of the series' productions included "Dark Angel," with Merle Oberon, Ronald Coleman, and Donald Crisp; "Design for Scandal," with Carole Landis and Robert Young; "Altar Bound," with Bob Hope, Jack Benny, and Betty Grable; and "Bachelor Mother" with Henry Fonda and Charles Coburn. Although never achieving quite the ratings of "Lux Radio Theatre," the "Screen Guild Theater" remained solidly popular from 1938 to 1951, attracting a line-up of stars as luminous as "Lux"'s.

Other anthology dramas that evolved later and were based on this format include "Hollywood Premiere," another Louella Parsons vehicle, on NBC in 1941; the "Dreft Star Playhouse," which began on June 28, 1943 on NBC; "Hollywood Startime," an RKO production which featured interviews in the RKO commissary at lunchtime; "Hollywood Mystery Time" on ABC; "Hollywood Star Preview" running from 1945 to 1950 on NBC; the prestigious "Academy Award Theater," whose premiere production, "Jezebel" with Bette Davis, aired on March 30, 1946; the equally serious "Screen Directors' Playhouse," which opened on NBC on January 9, 1949 with a production of "Stagecoach" starring John Wayne; "Hollywood Players" on CBS; and the "Hollywood Star Playhouse" which aired first on CBS, then ABC, then NBC through the early and mid 1950s and provided Marilyn Monroe with her first broadcast date in 1952.

1938: Symbiosis

After 1938, the cross-fertilization of Hollywood and the radio industry blossomed on a multiplicity of levels, each contributing to the other in an increasingly symbiotic relationship. A score of radio programs evolving from the prototypes discussed previously emerged from 1938 through the war years, as well as a new type, the radio series based on the characters or situation of a successful film. Of this latter type, "Stella Dallas," a long-running soap-opera prototype, appeared in 1937, the same year that King Vidor's classic remake of the film (released in a silent version by Henry King in 1925) was released. The series ran for 18 1/2 years. "The Adventures of the Thin Man" came on the air in 1941, based on the 1934 film (itself based on the novel by Dashiell Hammett) that starred William Powell and Myrna Loy.[41]

Radio at the Box Office

The film industry also drew upon radio. Beginning in 1932, radio supplied the movies with a steadily increasing supply of ready-made talent and material whose established radio appeal could be used to make popular films. On January 12, 1932, *Variety* announced that Fox Pictures had just purchased the rights to a radio script for the first time: "The Trial of Vivienne Ware" by Kenneth Ellis, which had run as a serial on radio. This borrowing of story ideas and characters worked both ways; besides radio shows inspired by films, the studios soon developed the idea of basing films on radio shows or formats. One of the earliest examples is *The Big Broadcast of 1932*. Paramount produced this light-weight but successful film to capitalize on the growing popularity of such radio personalities as Bing Crosby, Kate Smith, George Burns, Gracie Allen, and Cab Calloway. Based on a thin plot about a failing radio station that is saved from bankruptcy by a star-studded revue, the idea proved so profitable that it was followed by *Big Broadcast*'s of 1936, 1937, and 1938.

By early 1933, several movies in production starred radio personalities such as Kate Smith, Rudi Vallee, Bing Crosby, Jack Pearl, George Burns and Gracie Allen, Ed Wynn, and Eddie Cantor. A few of these entertainers, well known on the vaudeville circuit, had already made films in Hollywood. For example, Eddie Cantor starred in six previous films: *Kid Boots* (1926); *Special Delivery* (1927); *Glorifying the American Girl* (1929), a Paramount musical also guest-starring Rudy Vallee, Florenz Ziegfield, Jimmy Walker, and Adolph Zukor; *Whoopee* (1930); *Palmy Days* (1931); and *The Kid from Spain* (1932). He went on to make nine more that were entertaining and fairly profitable, if not particularly distinguished. Rudi Vallee had also made one film previously, *The Vagabond Lover* in 1929, but he is remembered primarily for his work in radio, which carried him on through his extended film career.[43]

George Burns and Gracie Allen, on the other hand, as popular vaudeville and radio comedians, got their film start in the *Big Broadcast of 1932* and went on to achieve their greatest popularity in television. Bing Crosby, although starting out with a primary reputation as a radio "crooner," achieved considerable success in films. His first film, *King of Jazz* for Universal in 1930, followed by *The Big Broadcast,* established his box-office appeal; in the years between his film debut and his later success on television, Crosby starred in more than fifty films, most for Paramount, not all memorable, but at least moderately successful. Among the most popular were Crosby's "road movies" made with Bob Hope and Dorothy Lamour for Paramount in 1940, 1941, 1942, 1945, 1947, 1952, and 1962.

Many other radio stars appeared in and inspired films through the 1930s and 1940s. Other borrowing also occurred, the most famous of which is Orson Welles's switch from the acclaimed Mercury Theatre to RKO to make *Citizen Kane* in 1940. The reasons for this sudden increase and ease in borrowings between the two industries lay with the actions of a seemingly unrelated third party, the telephone company, whose belated lowering of West- to East-Coast rates sparked what came to be known in the trade as the "Swing to Hollywood" of 1936–38. With decreased transmission charges in effect, the major networks, which had originated all schedules in New York, decided to build their own studios on the West Coast—in Hollywood. NBC erected a modern structure next door to the RKO studios in 1937, "on the site of the old Famous Players-Lasky movie lot";[44] CBS purchased an existing broadcasting station and set up network transmission facilities and a new studio there. "To Hollywood! becomes a broadcaster's cry as New York agents of sponsored programs tire of chasing movie stars just off the boat from Europe, or catching flying Big Names on the wing eastward. 'A radio center as well as the movie capital' becomes the slogan for Hollywood."[45]

The Reappearance of Television

A second factor in the heightened mutual interest of film and radio centers on yet another technology: the reemergence of television as an imminent possibility. If 1931 marked the "brightest moment in television's *false* dawn,"[46] 1936 became the beginning of its true although still gradual arrival. Some commentators felt that RCA's purchase of RKO had as a hidden agenda the idea of "protect[ing] itself when television became a fact."[47] Most writers and industry personnel assumed that when television did come into its own, the film industry would play a major part in it. "Visionaries believe that the years will see radio and the screen in even closer alliance, especially with television ahead. Films are expected to be the backbone of the television art."[48] Whether these would be regular full-length Hollywood films or films made by the Hollywood studios especially for television remained a debated point, but there was no doubt about the linkage of the two industries in one way or another.

Some still scoffed, however, at the film industry's preparedness to meet the coming technological revolution. As early as 1936, the *New York Times*'s radio column leveled some familiar-sounding charges at the "film barons," stating that "here, except for a recent investigation conducted in behalf of two or three producers who wanted to check on the progress of the medium, little interest has been shown" and that, "the town [Hollywood] is unconcerned over the threat of television competition." The article was headlined, "Dodging That Big Bad Television." Its points were mitigated somewhat by the concluding statement, however: "Hollywood...feels that there are too many problems to be solved before the medium becomes a threat and...producers are confident they will be able to jump in at the proper moment and take advantage of anything the process offers." This outlook comes closer to the facts of the situation, as history shows; although much important technical and regulatory ground was laid for television in the 1930s, its presence would not be felt until after World War II.[49]

In the meantime, interest in television in Hollywood took another form: in 1936 the Academy of Motion Picture Arts and Sciences assigned its Research Council to provide a report on industry preparation for television. It concluded that "Hollywood's 'psychological preparedness' for television was in contrast to the costly 'scepticism' with which many greeted the change from silent to sound pictures."[50] Overall, the committee felt that the film industry stood well prepared, both technically and economically, for the advent of television, but that "no change is imminent."[51] Paramount's purchase in 1938 of a half interest in DuMont Laboratories—one of the innovators in television research—would appear to confirm that view. Between 1938 and 1948, other investments in television broadcasting technology on the part of the film industry would follow (chapter 5).[52]

Renewed Conflict: "Hollywood Good News"

However, one group within the industry viewed the increasing comfort and mutuality of the Hollywood-radio relationship with growing alarm. That group consisted of the never completely quiescent exhibitors, who saw in the prospect of television the fulfillment of their worst nightmares about radio. Added to this fear was the enormous popularity of the new "Lux Radio Theatre" movie-adaptation format, and plans announced in 1936 for a further film foray into broadcasting: the MGM-Maxwell House hour that began in late 1937 as a continuation of "Show Boat." Called variously "Hollywood Good News" or "Good News of 1938," the show used the same format pioneered by "Lux"—movie adaptations with the original stars, interspersed with "behind-the-scenes" interviews and previews of coming movie attractions—but this time Metro-Goldwyn-Mayer would act as producer, retaining all artistic and financial control, with Maxwell House as sole sponsor. For this MGM would receive $25,000 a week from the coffee company as well as all the increased box-office appeal it could generate. In return, it threw open its entire stable of talent ("except Garbo") to the greater glory of Hollywood, radio, and Maxwell House coffee.[53]

However, the show proved less successful that its rival. *Newsweek* wrote that radio audiences "couldn't decide whether Metro Goldwyn Mayer was trying to sell Maxwell House, or if the coffeemakers were putting out Metro Goldwyn Mayer in airtight containers." Although ratings were fairly high—a 13.2 in the first year and a 20.2 the second—MGM slowly and quietly withdrew as Fanny Brice, introduced in the show's first year, gained in popularity. By 1940, the show was known as the "Fanny Brice–Baby Snooks Hour." Most sources attribute MGM's withdrawal from the show to theater owners' protests combined with the show's excessive costs.[54]

In 1936, exhibitors' complaints to Will Hays's office had again provoked the announced intention on the producers' part of setting up a special committee within the Motion Picture Producers and Directors Association (MPPDA) to "regulate stars' radio appearances."[55] Through the late 1930s studios increasingly demanded supervision of their contract players' radio dates, including one-half of any fees or salaries earned. This response effectively answered one exhibitor complaint, that "many stars have killed their value [at the box office] by unglamorous appearances on the air,"[56] without detracting much from the growing crossover of film and radio talent. Another exhibitor complaint, that Hollywood-based radio shows aired during prime theater-going hours (defined as broadly as 12 noon to 9:00 P.M. by some exhibitors) led to the scheduling of shows at off hours, like the Paramount production on Sundays at 12:30 P.M., and "Lux"'s move to the 9–10:00 P.M. time slot.[57]

Again in 1938, after a series of small lawsuits against the distribution practices of the major studios, exhibitor complaints focussed Justice Department attention on the movie industry. In July of that year the Justice Department filed a petition in the Southern New York District, asking finally for the divorcement of exhibition from production and distribution and citing not only the five major studios (Paramount, Fox, Loew's-MGM, Warners, and RKO) but also Columbia, Universal, and United Artists. In 1940 the companies signed a consent decree, which stopped short of divestiture but did involve a modification of current practices, including any further investment in theaters. However, the timing of the suit against Paramount's purchase of its stock in DuMont laboratories may indicate the direction at least one studio was preparing to take in the event of divestiture. In 1944 the Justice Department reopened the case, leading to the decrees of 1948 that split exhibition from production-distribution and permanently changed the face of Hollywood.[58]

The movie industry was not alone in attracting the attention of federal regulators, however. Douglas Gomery suggests that the "second depression" of 1937 prompted the government to focus its criticism on large trusts and monopolies as an explanation for the economic downturn, and that the film and radio industries provided particularly large and colorful targets. The FCC initiated its investigation of chain broadcasting in November 1938, resulting ultimately in the divestiture of the NBC Blue Network, which became the American Broadcasting Company (ABC) in 1944. The creation of this third network, combined with the movie industry divestiture, would have an unforeseen effect some ten years later, when the merger of ABC with the divested United Paramount Theater Corporation finally made the last-place network into a viable operation. It also had the side effect of driving the DuMont network, partially owned by Paramount Pictures, out of business. Furthermore, while creating new and difficult business conditions for the film companies during and after divestiture, the lingering shadow of the antitrust litigation of the past two decades made the film industry's entry into the business of television much more difficult (chapters 5 and 6).[59]

NOTES

1. William S. Paley, "Radio and Entertainment," in *Radio and Its Future,* ed. Martin Codell (New York: Harper Books, 1930), pp. 61–67.

2. Paley, "Radio and Entertainment," p. 64.

3. Erik Barnouw, *A Tower in Babel* (New York: Oxford University Press, 1966), p. 203; Llewellyn White, *The American Radio* (Chicago: University of Chicago Press, 1949), pp. 45–57.

4. Erik Barnouw, *The Golden Web* (New York: Oxford University Press, 1968), p. 58.

5. White, *American Radio,* pp. 36–38; David A. Cook, "The Birth of the Networks: How Westinghouse, General Electric, AT&T, and RCA Invented the Concept of Advertiser-Supported Broadcasting," *Quarterly Review of Film Studies* 8 (Summer 1983): 3–8; *Wall Street Journal,* June 10, 1988, p. 25.

6. Robert B. Horwitz, "The Regulation/Deregulation of American Broadcasting," *Quarterly Review of Film Studies* 8 (Summer 1983): 25–33.

7. White, *American Radio,* p. 66.

8. *New York Times,* March 28, 1928; *Variety,* March 30, 1928; Paley, "Radio and Entertainment," p. 63.

9. *Variety,* March 6, 1929; April 10, 1929.

10. Ibid., April 17, 1929.

11. Ibid., February 6, 1929.

12. *Business Week,* February 10, 1932, p. 18; August 10, 1932, pp. 14–15.

13. Ibid., August 14, 1932, p. 14.

14. Barnouw, *Golden Web,* p. 103; Garth Jowett, *Film: The Democratic Art* (Boston: Little, Brown, 1976) p. 280; Christopher Sterling and John Kitross, *Stay Tuned: A Concise History of American Broadcasting* (Belmont, Calif.: Wadsworth Publishing, 1978), p. 133.

15. *Variety,* February 9, 1932.

16. Ibid., June 14, 1932; October 25, 1932, p. 2.

17. Ibid., February 16, 1932, p. 1.

18. Ibid., p. 67; March 8, 1932, p. 1.

19. Ibid., February 16, 1932.

20. Ibid., p. 67; May 17, 1932, p. 2.

21. Ibid., July 12, 1932; July 19, 1932; June 14, 1932; October 25, 1932, p. 2; September 6, 1932.

22. Ibid., February 9, 1932, p. 51; October 25, 1932, p. 3.

23. *Variety,* December 27, 1932.

24. Richard B. Jewell, "Hollywood and Radio: Competition and Partnership in the 1930s," *Historical Journal of Film, Radio and Television* 4, no. 2 (1984): 136; *Variety,* January 17, 1933; January 24, 1933; April 4, 1933; August 29, 1933.

25. Janet Staiger, "Combination and Litigation: Structures of U.S. Film Distribution, 1896–1917," *Cinema Journal* 23 (Winter 1983): 41–72.

26. *Motion Picture Herald,* January 21, 1933; February 11, 1933; February 25, 1933; February 11, 1933; February 25, 1933; Abel Green and Joe Laurie Jr., *Show Biz: From Vaude to Video* (New York: Holt, 1951), p. 358.

27. Robert E. Summers and Harrison B. Summers, *Broadcasting and the Public Interest* (Belmont, Calif.: Wadsworth, 1966), p. 54.

28. Russell Nye, *The Unembarrassed Muse* (New York: Dial Press, 1970).

29. White, *American Radio,* p. 66; Summers and Summers, *Broadcasting and the Public Interest,* p. 59.

30. Federal Communications Commission, *Report of the Federal Commnications Commission on the Investigation of the Telephone Industry in the United States,* 76th Cong., 1st sess., House Document no. 340, 1939.

31. Arthur Frank Wertheim, *Radio Comedy* (New York: Oxford University Press, 1979).

32. Federal Communications Commission, 1939, p. xvii.

33. *Literary Digest,* October 31, 1936, p. 17; Orrin E. Dunlap, Jr., "The Swing to California," *New York Times,* October 17, 1937; *Business Week,* November 6, 1937, p. 27; *New York Times,* April 12, 1936, sec. 9, p. 4; November 29, 1936, p. 24.

34. John Dunning, *Tune in Yesterday* (Englewood Cliffs, N.J.: Prentice-Hall, 1976), pp. 208–10; Frank Buxton and Bill Owen, *The Big Broadcast* (New York: Viking Press, 1972), pp. 85–86.

35. Harrison B. Summers, ed., *A Thirty Year History of Programs Carried on National Radio Networks in the United States, 1926–1956* (Columbus: Ohio State University Press, 1958, repr. New York: Arno Press, 1971).

36. *Variety,* January 5, 1932, p. 59.

37. Summers, *A Thirty Year History.*

38. Cecil B. DeMille, *The Autobiography of Cecil B. DeMille,* ed. Donald Hayne (Englewood Cliffs, N.J.: Prentice-Hall, 1959), pp. 346–48.

39. Buxton and Owen, *The Big Broadcast,* pp. 146–47; Dunning, *Tune in Yesterday,* pp. 378–81; DeMille, *Autobiography,* p. 346.

40. Bernard Lucich, "The Lux Radio Theatre," in *American Broadcasting: A Sourcebook on the History of Radio and Television,* ed. Laurence W. Lichty and Malachi C. Topping (New York: Hastings House, 1975), pp. 391–94; DeMille, *Autobiography,* p. 346; Gene Ringgold and DeWitt Bodeen, *The Films of Cecil B. DeMille* (New York: Citadel Press, 1969), pp. 370–77.

41. Dunning, *Tune in Yesterday,* p. 639.

42. Ibid., pp. 10–11, 568–69; Buxton and Owen, *The Big Broadcast,* p. 225.

43. *Variety,* January 10, 1933; *New York Times,* July 16, 1933, sec. 9, p. 7.

44. *Business Week,* November 6, 1937, p. 27.

45. *Literary Digest,* October 31, 1936, p. 17; Dunlap, "The Swing to Hollywood"; *New York Times,* November 29, 1936, p. 24.

46. Robert H. Stern, "Regulatory Influences upon Television's Development: Early Years under the Federal Radio Commission," *American Journal of Economics and Sociology* 22, no. 3 (1963): 347–62.

47. *New York Times,* October 17, 1937, sec. 10, p. 12.

48. Ibid., July 7, 1937, sec. 9, p. 11.

49. Ibid., April 12, 1936, sec. 9, p. 4.

50. Ibid., May 18, 1936, p. 14.

51. Ibid., June 14, 1936, sec. 9, p. 8.

52. Hal W. Bochin, "The Rise and Fall of the DuMont Network," in *American Broadcasting,* ed. Lichty and Topping, p. 190.

53. Dunning, *Tune in Yesterday*, pp. 240-41; "Metro's Maxwell House Air Show," *Variety*, November 10, 1937; "Radio Relying on Hollywood," *New York Morning Telegraph*, September 20, 1940.

54. *Newsweek*, November 15, 1937, p. 25; Dunning, *Tune in Yesterday*, p. 241; Summers, *A Thirty Year History; New York World Telegram*, February 13, 1939; *Billboard*, October 1, 1938, n.p.; *New York Times*, February 22, 1939, p. 19.

55. Ibid., November 29, 1926, p. 24.

56. Ibid., August 30, 1939.

57. Ibid., October 17, 1937.

58. Simon N. Whitney, "Antitrust Policies and the Motion Picture Industry," in *The American Movie Industry*, ed. Gorham Kindem (Carbondale: Southern Illinois University Press, 1982), p. 181.

59. Douglas Gomery, "Failed Opportunities: The Integration of the U. S. Motion Picture and Television Industries," *Quarterly Review of Film Studies* (Summer 1984): 219–27; Gary N. Hess, "An Historical Study of the DuMont Television Network" (Ph.D. diss., Northwestern University, 1960, repr. New York: Arno Press, 1979).

4

The "Lux Radio Theatre of the Air"

The previous three chapters have traced several key developments that led to the increased influence of Hollywood on radio programming. The reduction of AT&T land-line rates to and from the West Coast in 1936 provided, as with its bottleneck on leasing network lines in the late 1920s, a hidden but crucial factor in the ability of Hollywood interests to participate in radio production. The growing strength of commercial sponsors in program production through the intermediary of the major advertising agencies contributed to the decline of network sustaining programs; the creation of important but as yet unrecognized loopholes in the government disposition of the "radio problem" permitted both the dominance of the two major interconnected networks and their heavy dependence on the output of the agencies.

These forces, along with the regulatory and industrial strictures set in place in the 1920s (chapters 1 and 2), constitute what might be called the macroeconomics of the film-broadcasting industry interface. They are the major factors behind the subsequent development of broadcast programming, setting the basic structures and conditions of possibility for what would come later. A traditional political economy approach to the media might stop here, having delineated the necessary—but, as Stuart Hall reminds us, not necessarily the sufficient—conditions for broadcast texts to develop as they did.[1] Hall's critique of the shortcomings of the political economy model grows out of his own theoretical approach, which conceives of the communicative act as a process consisting of three "determinate moments": the process of encoding, the message form itself, and the decoding process. Although Hall's own work, and the work of the "cultural studies" school in general, has tended to focus on the decoding process—by which a message form is perceived and interpreted by a viewer—the moment of encoding occupies an equivalent and equally important position in the communication model.

> The institutional structures of broadcasting, with their practices and networks of production, their organized relations and technical infrastructures, are required to produce a programme. . . . Of course, the production process is not without its 'discursive' aspect: it, too, is framed throughout by meanings and ideas: knowledge-in-use concerning the routines of production, historically defined technical skills, professional ideologies, institutional knowledge, definitions and assumptions, assumptions about the audience and so on frame the constitution of the programme through this production structure.[2]

Thus the encoding process includes not only production techniques, but also the forces behind the development of those very techniques: the institutional structures of broadcasting, organized relations, and accepted practices, all of which contribute to the message form. And although the message itself takes on a symbolic structure, expressed through language forms or codes, which does not become complete until it is received and decoded by an audience, the moment of production plays a "predominant" role, because it is the "point of departure for the realization" of the message form itself.[3] Furthermore, as Hall develops in later works, encoding forces must be examined concretely, within the context of a specific historical period and specific circumstances, in order to arrive at an understanding of the symbolic constructions set in place by these institutions, and thus the range of decodings available to the receivers. Finally, this encoding process is a conflicted one, not expressing unity and consensus of intention on the part of the encoding institution, but instead reflecting the internal conflicts and struggle for dominance within and throughout the encoding process, as a "struggle and contestation for the space in which to construct an ideological hegemony."[4] Applying Hall's model, the question then becomes, Out of the welter of competing interests, economic pressures, regulatory restrictions and social conditions that make up the institutional structures of broadcasting, how did the unique and distinctive forms of the broadcast text arise? Out of all of the possibilities for expression and use, why did American radio evolve into its characteristic segmented, serial, disrupted discourse of primarily entertainment programs? No sweeping general rule will suffice to explain these developments; instead a close look at the specific historical circumstances surrounding the origination of individual programs, program types and categories, and the formation of the broadcast schedule, is needed within the institutional structures that support and, to a certain extent, determine them.

This institutional approach to the encoding process has been most fully developed in the study of the early days of the film industry. A number of works have been published that examine the emergence of the characteristic narrative and signifying aspects of the Hollywood film. Among these are Janet Staiger's study of the effect of early production and marketing strategies on the evolution of signifying practices, Douglas Gomerey's analysis of the development of sound film and its effects, and Charles Musser's study of Edwin S. Porter and the shift in creative control from the exhibitor to the cameraman-director.[5] The early days of the broadcast medium are just beginning to benefit from similar institutional analysis. For example, in his examination of economic and institutional pressures on the rise of the soap opera, Robert C. Allen concludes that "There is little doubt... that the primary generative mechanisms responsible for the origination of the soap opera form and for its perpetuation over nearly fifty years can be located in the institutional requirements of American commercial broadcasting."[6]

This is equally true for other types of broadcast texts. Yet Allen's work remains the exception rather than the rule. Even with the recent increase in attention to the broadcast discourse from a number of critical directions, it is troubling that, first, television's very direct roots in radio broadcasting are so often overlooked, and second, that even in the existing literature on radio and radio programming so little attention is given to the role played by advertisers and their creative agents, the large advertising agencies. Popular anthologies of radio programs, sparse though they may be, share the common characteristic of foregrounding stars, storylines, and occasionally network involvement but very rarely mentioning the agencies that created and produced the shows. Also ignored are the clients, whose interests at all times needed to be considered in planning and execution of programs, hiring of talent, and placing the show in a time slot. These accounts thus exclude key factors that entered into the creative process behind much of the innovation in radio broadcasting.

The major radio networks, influential though they may have been in determining the basic structure of the broadcasting industry and providing the framework within which innovation could occur, served increasingly during the 1930s and 1940s as simple conduits for those sponsors and agencies that could afford to buy time on the air. Under these circumstances the networks themselves had very little input into the creative process, particularly of those shows aired during the most popular times, until the development of spot advertising strategy in the late 1950s. This lack of network control can be seen in the fact that successful shows on radio often network-hopped in mid-run, switching networks according to time slot available or more favorable rates.

Contemporary historians and analysts of television, projecting the decisive role played by today's network programming departments backward onto radio, neglect the true originators of most of the broadcast forms still with us: the major advertising agencies. This version, or vision, of responsibility for programming better fits the concepts and regulatory structure enforced over the years by the FCC, which regulates broadcasters, not advertisers. A closer look at the creative process behind radio programming may also reinforce the arguments of some critics and analysts of the television text that the television (or radio) program cannot be considered outside of its commercial context, that the commercials, rather than providing brief and irrelevant "interruptions" to the text, are in fact a vital component of the "supertext," including both creative and structural forces as well as the reading process. Indeed it seems clear from an analysis of the origins of radio program forms that Raymond Williams's view of television as "commercials interrupted by programs" is not merely a theoretical construct but has firm roots in actual historical conditions.[7]

However, researching the contributions of advertising agencies and their clients to the development of radio programming is not an easy task. Very few historical accounts discuss the agencies' role in any systematic way. A thorough history is needed of the role of the advertising agency in the development of broadcasting in this country. Although most agencies retain archives, information on broadcasting activity appears to be scattered, and most institutions that preserve material on the history of broadcasting and other media tend to ignore the "intrusion" of the commercial side into field of "art."[8]

But as Nick Browne observes, the role of the advertising agency is that of the "central mediating discursive institution" linking the economic interests of the producers of media with the cultural use and signification of the texts produced.[9] This chapter will examine more closely the role of the advertising agency in the production of radio, and by extension, television, texts. I have selected an episode of the "Lux Radio Theatre of the Air" to use as the location for this study for several reasons. First, since the overall concern of this work is the interrelationship of the film and broadcasting industries, the position of "Lux," specifically occupying the interface between the two as a radio adaptation of a film format, highlights most of the economic, regulatory, and aesthetic issues relevant to this history. Second, the show's continuing popularity as one of the long-term highest rated on radio recommends it for study, because success itself says much about the particular context of a given text. Third, it is a key text in the history of radio programming forms, giving rise to many similar shows patterned after its success, and in its rise and fall it followed closely the major historical trends and forces more than, perhaps, a less popular, less successful, more eccentric or marginal show might. In addition, its success has ensured that more materials are available, including tapes of the shows themselves, than would exist for a lesser program, somewhat easing the problems of the historical study of radio.

Advertising Chatter

By the end of the 1930s, programs produced by advertising agencies dominated the airwaves, particularly during evening hours. According to Llewellyn White, the percentage of commercial as opposed to sustaining programs for the entire broadcast day grew from 23.6 percent in 1933 to 49.4 percent in 1944 on NBC, and on CBS from 22.9 to 47.8 percent in the same period. By 1944, evening hours consisted almost entirely of sponsored programs. In terms of concentration of advertising and programming power within the agencies themselves, by 1944 three of the nation's largest advertising agencies (J. Walter Thompson; Dancer, Fitzgerald; and Young and Rubicam) between them controlled about one-fourth of total commercial time on the three major networks. In 1945, almost half of CBS's total billings of $65,724,362 came from only six advertising agencies representing seven sponsors.

Although Stephen Fox quotes the radio writer Carroll Carroll as saying, "You can't imagine . . . with what crushing surprise radio made its guerrilla attack on all advertising agencies. It caught few ready for it but all prepared to fake it," the speed and enthusiasm with which the agencies adjusted to the age of radio is attested to by James Playstead Wood: "For the first time advertising had a medium which it controlled." Unlike magazines, heretofore the dominant advertising medium, a separation between the editorial content and the advertising adjacent to it was no longer necessary; with radio, the advertiser created the "content" as well as the commercial message.[10]

Although individual advertisers moved to include radio in their advertising strategies quite early—WEAF's list of clients in 1923 included Macy's, Colgate, and Metropolitan Life—some resistance to the medium existed in the more established agencies during the 1920s.

One reason for this had to do with opposition from within the existing media market. Worried by potential competition for the advertising dollar, the newspaper and magazine industries opposed radio in its early years, influencing some agencies to take a cautious stance toward radio advertising in order to protect their good relations with established media outlets. Also, the practice of "indirect advertising," although attracting many companies through shows such as the "Lucky Strike Dance Orchestra," the "A&P Gypsies," the "Cliquot Club Eskimos," and "The Palmolive Show," limited the amount and type of advertising that could be done over the air. Before the establishment of the large networks, programs had to be placed on a station-to-station basis. Because no ratings system yet existed, many advertisers preferred not to trust the audience estimates of local stations and to stick instead with the measurable circulation figures of the print media. But with the formation of NBC in 1926, a far larger audience became possible, and both NBC and CBS took active steps to promote the concept of radio advertising. In 1930, the Cooperative Analysis of Broadcasting (Crossley) rating system was established as a joint venture of the American Association of Advertising Agencies and the Association of National Advertisers. According to Ralph M. Hower in his history of the N. W. Ayer advertising agency:

> Until 1930, all agencies tended to look for attractive programs and then to seek advertisers who would take a fling at broadcasting. After 1930, much of the original glamor and mystery of radio had vanished, and men had to take a more realistic approach. The Ayer firm rapidly developed the view that an agency must start with the client's sales problems, determine whether radio can help, and then devise a program which will achieve specific ends in terms of sales. The complete reversal of the method is significant.[11]

This process, of examining the client's sales problems and, if necessary, devising a radio program to fit, was often a lengthy and complex one. According to the N. W. Ayer history, the Radio Department of the agency became a separate entity in 1928. "Its duties were to assemble information about all phases of broadcast advertising, build up programs, hire talent, direct production, and handle the leasing of station time and all other details connected with broadcast programs. . . ." The very largest sponsors, such as Procter and Gamble, created and maintained through their advertising agencies—in this case, Blackett Sample Hummert—an ongoing radio production department. Because Procter and Gamble was one of the first companies to see the immense potential in radio for advertisement of their household products, Blackett

Sample Hummert must be regarded as one of the most important sites for radio serial development, employing a stable of writers, most of whom were women, under the direction of Anne Hummert. These writers turned out an amazing number and variety of radio programs, including such long-running shows as "Ma Perkins," "Just Plain Bill," "Betty and Bob," "Jack Armstrong," "The Romance of Helen Trent," "Pepper Young's Family," and many more. Other smaller sponsors might put together a one-time show, which if successful could be continued. The process of bringing client, network, talent, and concept together fell to the agency radio director.[12]

A useful glimpse into the process of radio origination is provided by an article published by the *Saturday Evening Post* in 1938, "One Minute to Go: Backstage with an Advertising Agency's Radio Director" by Kenneth L. Watt, a radio director in real life. Watt traced the process by which a radio show got from initial impetus to the air. After consultations with the company president, its treasurer, sales and advertising directors, and other higher executives, the basic concept for the show was agreed upon, in this case a star-studded Hollywood variety show complete with dramatic segment, orchestra, comedian, singers, and announcer. The next step was negotiating with agents over the Hollywood contribution, and finally two current, but affordable, stars were selected. Next came the hiring of writers who would provide the script for the dramatic segment to be enacted by the stars, followed by the selection of the emcee, in this case a comedian "like Cantor or Jack Benny," who would not only provide his own comic material but would also tie the show together through introductions and transitions. Another announcer was chosen to deliver the commercial messages. At this stage, or as early as possible, negotiations with the network began, to secure an option on a favorable, and available, time slot. After choosing the emcee and negotiating with his agent, the orchestra and singer were hired; throughout each of these steps the radio director, although nominally in charge, deferred constantly to the wishes of the company president, advertising manager, and other company employees who all wished to have a hand in the process.[13]

Next came the writing of the script, which was supervised by the agency man as well as the client's advertising director. The script went through several revisions; before it was finalized, the commercial announcements had to be written and approved, and the decision made about whether to integrate the message with the show or to handle them as discrete "breaks." The commercial announcements were created by the advertising agency copy department but approved by a committee the client formed for that purpose. With this approval, the rehearsals began. Not until the final rehearsal before broadcast did the show move to the network studios, where sound levels were taken and the whole sequence run through before going out live over the network hook-ups. During the stage before the run-through, the radio director's talents were fully engaged. As Watt put it:

> Preparing the schedule, or formula, for a radio program is much like having eggs, flour, sugar and shortening for a cake. Too much of this or too little of that can make an unholy mess and result in a waste of good material simply because the ingredients are not assembled properly. My ingredients consist of: One movie star, male; one movie star, female; one master of ceremonies; one stooge—maybe more; one singer, male or female; one orchestra with leader; one announcer; sundry actors, actresses, script writers, sound effects men, production men.[14]

Next came another important step—submitting the completed script to the network censor for approval, so any material in controversial or questionable taste could supposedly be eliminated. Once this was accomplished, the final rehearsal was scheduled, with actors and actresses for the bit parts in the script hired at the last minute. At this point the agency radio director assumed the role of production director, coaching players, smoothing transitions, and determining the order of the show.

Watt's account makes clear the large role played by the advertising agency radio director in the radio program origination and production process. The radio director resembled a film producer and director combined, supervising every step of a show's production and providing important creative input, always in consultation with a sponsor whose wishes were, after all, the motivating factor behind all this activity. *Fortune* magazine provided another glimpse of the production process, this time through the eyes of the company president whose decision it was to advertise on radio. Although the process remained the same, focus from *Fortune*'s perspective tended to center on costs of such a production, and each successive decision—stars, singers, script writers, etc.—was discussed from the point of view of its price tag. *Fortune* listed some of the most popular shows on the air in terms of their production and time costs:[15]

Table 1. *Fortune*'s Cost Analysis of Top Radio Shows of 1938

Program	Production	Time	Total
Chase & Sanborn Hour (McCarthy)	$20,000	$15,900	$35,900
Jack Benny (Jello)	15,000	11,500	26,500
Kraft Music Hall (Bing Crosby)	13,500	17,100	30,600

Program	Production	Time	Total
Lux Radio Theatre (guest movie stars)	15,000	17,300	32,300
Eddie Cantor (Texaco)	15,000	11,900	26,900
Al Jolson (Lever Bros)	12,000	10,400	22,400
Major Bowes' Amateur Hour (Chrysler)	25,000	20,100	45,100
Burns and Allen (General Foods, for Grape Nuts)	10,000	10,600	20,600
Town Hall Tonight (Fred Allen, sponsored by Bristol-Myers Co.)	10,000	15,800	25,800

Source. *Fortune,* May 1938, p. 54.

The programs are listed in order of their ratings according to the Cooperative Analysis of Broadcasting, or Crossley Report. In addition, as *Fortune* noted, "All but four of the ten 'big' shows listed...are produced in Hollywood, and so, for that matter, are most of the other important evening network programs."

As programming strategies developed, so too did the art of the radio commercial. One important feature of original radio advertising, now virtually a thing of the past, was the integrated commercial message: an advertising plug arising so smoothly out of the program action, or actually written into the narrative, that it was indistinguishable from the dramatic structure. Ma Perkins endorsed Oxydol detergent and frequently found cause to use it in the course of her domestic activities on radio. Fibber McGee and Molly likewise found frequent reasons for using Johnson's wax on their show. Allen cites a proposal for a soap opera from Irna Phillips for Kleenex in which the show opens with the main character sitting at her dressing table removing her makeup with—surprise—Kleenex.[16]

Jack Benny and his troupe made Jello commercials famous by working references to the product into their comic routines—although this kind of "gag" announcement could backfire, making the radio director of the *Saturday Evening Post* article advise his hypothetical client to avoid such a format. More common was the straight commercial plug read or enacted by members of the program cast. As Roland Marchand wrote, "The Maxwell House program, a pioneer in the interwoven commercial, scrupulously maintained the continuity of mood. Program characters delivered the commercials as they gathered around the table with the program host, the Old Colonel, to share coffee and reminisce about olden days at the Maxwell House Hotel (the program's setting), when Teddy Roosevelt had characterized the coffee as 'Good to the last drop.'"[17] When the program cast member was a Hollywood star, the integrated ad took on the properties of a celebrity testimonial, lending a ready-made aura of glamour to the product. The celebrity testimonial remains one of the major advertising strategies today, and the agency known for its innovations in this area is J. Walter Thompson, not surprisingly also the creators of the "Lux Radio Theatre."

The Creative Site: J. Walter Thompson

The J. Walter Thompson firm has a long history in the development of advertising. Its founder, James Walter Thompson, got his start in 1870 in New York and contributed to the rise of magazines as an advertising medium and as a part of American culture. One of the first to see the immense advertising potential in the weekly and monthly publications, Thompson's list of magazines under exclusive contract by the turn of the century included the *Atlantic, Century* (successor to *Scribner's*), *Harper's, Lippincott's, Godey's, Peterson's,* and the *North American Review.* The firm went on to become one of the prototypes of the complete advertising agency. It tended to specialize in products appealing to women as consumers, from soaps and cosmetics to food products. In 1916, Thompson sold out to a group of employees headed by Stanley Resor, who in 1917 married another top JWT employee, Helen Lansdowne. Lansdowne was one of the first women to rise to the top of the advertising profession; her influence helped to make JWT successful with the female market it pursued. Her successful campaign for Woodbury soap was influential in Procter and Gamble's 1911 decision to employ JWT to advertise its Crisco cooking oil, the first time the large consumer products company had employed an outside advertising firm. Together Helen Lansdowne and Stanley Resor managed the J. Walter Thompson firm for the next thirty years and were influential in its innovative move into radio.[18]

Helen Lansdowne Resor must also be credited with a JWT trademark which led directly to the "Lux Radio Theatre" strategy: the celebrity testimonial. Although the testimonial is one of the oldest advertising strategies, Resor's contribution lay in attaching the product testimonial to a famous name. Her first coup, in 1924, involved persuading Mrs. O. H. P. Belmont, a New York socialite, to endorse Pond's cold cream in exchange for a hefty donation to a charity of her choice. Other "great lady" endorsements followed, including Queen Marie of Rumania, Mrs. Reginald Vanderbilt, and the Duchess de Richelieu. From the crowned heads of Europe, it was a short step to Hollywood.[19]

JWT's involvement in radio began in the 1920s. One of its earliest successes was the bringing together of Rudy Vallee with Fleischmann's yeast in 1928, one of the most successful shows on the air at the time. That same year JWT sent a representative to Hollywood, one of the first of the major New York agencies to do so. This representative, later head of the Hollywood branch office established in 1934, was Daniel J. Danker, Jr., a Harvard-educated promoter who became something of a celebrity in his own right during his influential career in Hollywood. By 1930, JWT had put together radio programs for eighteen of its clients, accounting for more than twenty-three hours per week of network time.

One of JWT's more important accounts was the manufacturing giant Lever Brothers. The Cambridge, Massachusetts, company was a wholly owned subsidiary of "gigantic" Lever Brothers and Unilever Company, nominally under Dutch ownership but managed from London—in fact, according to *Fortune,* "among the three largest British investments in the U.S." Lever Brothers' U.S. product line included Rinso soap flakes, Lifebuoy health soap, Lux flakes, Lux toilet soap, Spry vegetable shortening, and a few lesser brands. In terms of sales volume in the soap and vegetable fat trade, Lever Brothers ranked second only to Procter and Gamble in the U.S. market, with earnings of more than $90 million in 1940. For products such as these, aimed at a consumer market primarily consisting of housewives and requiring a large volume of sales to a widespread and relatively undifferentiated consumer pool, radio represented the perfect advertising medium. Both companies maintained large radio presences from the early 1930s until the switch to television. Indeed, it is possible that in terms of radio program innovation, an examination of the rivalry between the soap giants, Lever Brothers and Procter and Gamble, may reward the serious scholar far more than a study of the rivalry between the two major networks.[20]

Large advertisers such as the two soap companies often split their accounts between several agencies. In the 1930s, JWT, Lever's first agency in the United States, handled the prestigious Lux flakes and Lux toilet soap accounts. Rinso and Spry were handled by the Ruthrauff and Ryan Agency, who also had Lifebuoy until it was given to the William Esty Agency in the mid-thirties. Another Lever product, Lipton tea, was managed by Young and Rubicam, which as of 1940 stood to gain a few more Lever accounts. Thus, although the actual creative work was accomplished within the agencies and differed in approach according to agency style and specialization, the client company made the decisions about which campaigns to select and in which medium to place them. The link and corporate identity behind advertising campaigns can be seen in the fact that in 1940 Lever Brothers maintained a total of six radio shows on the air, two during the day and four evening shows, produced by different agencies for different products. Such data demonstrate two points: first, that the advertising agencies of the network radio era resembled today's television production companies (largely branches of Hollywood studios), which actually create and produce the shows, whereas the manufacturers and advertisers on radio resemble today's network programming departments, making the overall conceptual and scheduling decisions; and second, that the soap companies and their agencies influenced far more than the "soaps." Lever Brothers in particular was known for its sponsorship and innovation in evening prime-time shows.[21]

The Evolution of "Lux"

Conceptually, the beginnings of the "Lux Radio Theatre" radio show can be traced to the celebrity advertising campaign developed by the J. Walter Thompson Agency for Lux toilet soap. As noted, JWT frequently relied upon the celebrity testimonial, and in the case of Lux soap had become known by 1928 for its use of Hollywood star endorsements. Magazine copy demonstrates a progression from the generically chic society ladies of 1925 to specific celebrities. For example, in a 1928 advertisement, E. Mason Hopper, a "director for Pathé DeMille" states, "Beauty may be 'only skin deep' but nothing is more essential than the loveliness of a girl's skin. A star's adoring public and exacting director demand that beauty first of all." This opinion is accompanied by a picture of Phyllis Haver, who confirms the issue by stating, "No star can hope to look lovely unless she has really velvety smooth skin—studio skin. Lux Toilet Soap leaves my skin so gently smooth that I have no fear of the high powered lights of the close-up." A 1929 advertisement features the "Wampas Baby Stars," who "all use Lux Toilet Soap for smooth skin" and the famous line, "Nine out of ten screen stars use Lux Toilet Soap." Although a few of Lever's other products use the occasional star endorsements, the campaigns for Lux soap flakes and Lifebuoy, for example, remain distinctly different, the one emphasizing the "gentleness" of the flakes on hands and clothing, the other developing the famous "B.O." theme and emphasizing health aspects. Lux soap's focus on Hollywood celebrities led directly to the strategy behind its radio show.

One person who must be given credit for the success of Lux's appeal is Danker, the JWT Hollywood bureau head, who handled negotiations with screen stars and other personnel so successfully that, according to *Fortune,* most stars were not even paid for their endorsements. "Making the right friends and doing favors for them with the flair of an Irish politician, Danker succeeded partly by sheer personality, and later on by pointing out to picture players that Lux testimonials meant free national advertising. Finally it became fashionable for actresses to sign exclusive releases for Lux." Whether or not this is strictly true, the fact does remain that Lux, via Danker, was singularly adept at obtaining these endorsements. However, some of this luck may also be linked to the hefty fees paid to stars on the "Lux Radio Theatre," who frequently doubled in the other advertisements. Danker remains a key figure behind the radio show; his good relations with the studios and their executives and personalities helped in obtaining studio cooperation along with a perception of the radio show as a boost for film publicity rather than competition. Although once he had gotten the show off the ground Danker's day-to-day participation seems not to have been critical, he functioned as chief negotiator for film properties and stars, a process in which his flamboyant personal lifestyle apparently served him well.[22]

The "Lux Radio Theatre" was created by JWT for Lever Brothers in 1934 as a vehicle for radio versions of Broadway plays; it was to be similar to the popular "First Nighter" program, also broadcast from New York City. Starting on the NBC network on Sunday afternoons, it switched to CBS in 1935 and to the more favorable 9:00 P.M. Monday time slot, where it stayed for the rest of its radio existence. When ratings began to slump in the second year, attributed by one source to a "severe shortage of adaptable Broadway material," J. Walter Thompson assigned the young account executive Danny Danker to the task of pulling up the show's ratings. Mindful of the success of "Hollywood Hotel" and of the increasing practice of using Hollywood talent in variety shows, Danker made the recommendation that the show move in its entirety to Hollywood. With AT&T service to the West Coast finally improved and affordable, JWT approved the change and "Lux" broadcast "live from Hollywood" for the first time on June 1, 1936. Danker is also credited with the decision to hire Cecil B. DeMille as emcee.[23]

The decision to hire DeMille was critical in setting the tone that led to the program's success. The factors that led to the decision, however, are clearly presaged in JWT's previous radio experience and practice, particularly with its most successful show of the time, the "Fleischmann's Yeast Hour," a variety show hosted by Rudy Vallee. Put on the air in 1929, this show pioneered many of the elements of the variety series, creating spin-offs in situation comedy, drama, and even documentary form that later became staples of radio broadcasting. Vallee himself served as emcee-announcer, bringing a different group of guests together each week in the setting of a fictional nightclub created, like the theater of "First Nighter," from the endless flexibility of time and space available to radio. Vallee's role as the nightclub host allowed him to provide the same kind of framework and interconnections later supplied by DeMille for "Lux": introducing the show, performing numbers himself, then bringing out the different guests, even working the commercial announcements into the fabric of the show:

> During a simulated intermission the host, crooner Rudy Vallee, sauntered among the tables introducing his guest to fans until they happened to overhear a conversation at one table. Vallee said, "Let's listen," to his friend (and to the radio audience). A change in tone quality signaled a change in microphone; then the radio listener found himself joining Vallee in eavesdropping on a young couple who were marveling at the man's great success in business since he had been taking Fleischmann's Yeast.[24]

To further the fictional device, Vallee's guest introductions often took the form of a personal reminiscence, as he recounted how he had met the guests and realized how perfect they would be for his show.

By setting Vallee up not only as on-air host, but also as producer, writer, director, and talent scout for the program, Vallee tied tighter together the dramatic illusion desired by the program's true producers, JWT and Fleischmann's, by obscuring the functions of the advertising agency and sponsor personnel in creating the program. Vallee acted as a kind of screen behind which the commercial interests of the variety hour could hide. His presence emphasized the program's entertainment function over its economic purpose—a goal constantly pursued by the broadcasting industry. In fact, as Marchand quotes a J. Walter Thompson internal memo, "The facts are that Vallee doesn't know now what is going to be rehearsed this afternoon. He doesn't write one word of the script. All of the things about how he first met these people, etc., we make up for him." The strategy had proved so successful, according to the JWT memo, that "all the theatrical publications are now hailing Vallee as the greatest showman in radio."[25]

JWT employed an identical strategy with the "Lux Radio Theatre." In many ways the decision to hire DeMille as the emcee-host, then, contributed more than any one other element to the character of the show; the entire structure would be created around the personality, or persona, of the host. Thus DeMille was similarly perceived by his audience as the main creative force behind the program, personally selecting film properties, inviting stars to recreate or reinterpret the roles in the film, bringing them out during "intermission" or at the end of the show for an informal chat during which the sponsor's product often just happened to figure in the conversation. Certainly, DeMille evolved into the focal point around which popular discussion of the show took place. Introduced each evening as "Ladies and gentlemen... your producer...Mr. Cecil B. DeMille!," the famous director received credit for almost every aspect of the show, as demonstrated in a 1944 article in the *Christian Science Monitor* magazine: "No one could have been better prepared to take the show over its early hurdles than DeMille. To the opinion of the experts, who said no one would listen to a solid hour of drama over the air, he replied, 'Let's try it, anyway.'" Actually these decisions were made long before DeMille came on the scene. But the public character of "Cecil B. DeMille" as created by the director himself over the years also played an important role in the show's overall success. Known as a director of "screen extravaganzas," DeMille lent an aura of glamour and importance to the ephemeral nature of the radio experience. His presence imparted an immediate perception of the show as "top of the line," far more effectively than could the name of a lesser-known although perhaps equally successful director.

The true creative work of the "Lux Radio Theatre," however, was accomplished by a group of radio and advertising professionals rarely acknowledged in the popular press. The adaptation of the screenplay from its film to a much-reduced radio version was accomplished for many years by George Wells, who later became a scriptwriter for MGM, where his credits included the Academy Award-winning *Designing Woman*. He was replaced by Sanford Barnett, formerly the show's director. The "frame," or introductory-connecting-commercial announcement structure, was written by J. Walter Thompson copywriters, among them Carroll Carroll, who also worked on the Rudy Vallee show and continued with Thompson well into the 1960s. Sanford Barnett was replaced as director by Fred MacKaye, a former bit actor on the show. The sound man, an important position in a radio production, was Charles Forsyth. This team had been assembled by the program's true "producer," Daniel Danker, and actually put on the show. Their contributions will be discussed in depth in the analysis of the program selected. In fact, DeMille's presence was required only for the final dress rehearsal and the live performance itself; the previous stages of the process took place in his absence, and creative decisions were handled solely through Danker's office and JWT.

The basic concept behind the "Lux Radio Theatre" was the adaptation of Hollywood films to radio. This description is slightly misleading, however, in that other materials were sometimes presented as well, notably classics or Broadway materials, the film rights to which had been purchased but not yet (or perhaps never would be) made into films. This is particularly true during the first seasons of the show; once its popularity had been established, studios became much more eager to allow their recent releases to be adapted for "Lux." Although, as noted, a few films were actually previewed on "Lux" or aired simultaneously with box-office release, of the ninety-five shows aired from October 1938 through November 1940, only thirteen were aired close to the time of their first release with original stars performing the radio roles. Most of the other "Lux" features aired from one to four years after the film's box-office run. Also, roughly half of the lead performers in the radio adaptations had starred in the theatrical film, although the percentage increased as the show went on and gained higher ratings; a few actors and acresses became "Lux" "regulars," for example, Don Ameche, Brian Aherne, Barbara Stanwyck, Claudette Colbert, and Fred MacMurray, playing roles for which the original stars were unavailable or unwilling to appear.

In terms of studio participation, all the major and minor studios allowed "Lux" to use their film properties at one point or another, as well as independents such as Goldwyn, Selznick, and Korda. Goldwyn in particular participated heavily in "Lux," using the radio show to preview many of his films or to air them simultaneously with theatrical release, far more frequently than other producers and studios. Lacking the huge promotion departments of the major studios, Goldwyn as an independent may have found "Lux" an extremely affordable means of box-office publicity. Though no other one independent used the show's promotions possibilities as often as Goldwyn, independent producers were much more likely to use this prerelease or simultaneous-release strategy than the established studios. They were also far more likely to use the original film stars in these presentations.

The use of "Lux" for publicity points to an inherent conflict not only in this particular show, but also in most of the radio endeavors in which Hollywood studios or talent were involved. These programs served two different purposes: for Hollywood, as a means of promoting, either for first- or subsequent-run, current or fairly current films, and for boosting the fame and familiarity of their stars; for the advertisers and their agencies, as a source of ready-made "glamour" and attraction to draw people unwittingly into the commercial message. The conjuncture of these two interests had many favorable aspects for both: glamorous settings for Lux soap messages on the one hand, and inexpensive publicity for films on the other.

But if either factor were allowed to dominate over the other, or if one aspect were perceived as detrimental to the other, the delicate

balance between the interests of the studios and the interests of the
advertiser would collapse. For example, should the advertiser demand
that the adaptation of *Casablanca* be rewritten to show Ingrid Bergman
using Lux soap before she goes out to the climactic meeting with
Bogart, the studio, in this case Warner, would be rightfully indignant
about misuse of its commercial property, and benefit would cease to
accrue to the studio in terms of favorable publicity for its own product.
On the other hand, should the film property and personas of the stars
be allowed to dominate the commercial message completely, or should
the commercials come to be seen as an annoying and unnecessary
interruptions, benefit to the advertiser for such an expensive show would
be reduced greatly. Hence the utility of the "frame," or staging of the
show, in "Lux"'s case accomplished so ably by DeMille—and by the
team of agency copywriters headed by Carroll Carroll, whose task it
was to compose the frame and to integrate it within the fabric of the
evening.

This frame underwent changes as the radio show progressed and
gained in popularity and prestige. The earliest shows, such as "Lux"'s
initial Hollywood broadcast of "The Legionnaire and the Lady" (based
on the 1930 Paramount film *Morocco*), featured far more direct hype
for both Lux products and for current and forthcoming studio projects,
with more direct involvement in actual commercial endorsements by
DeMille and studio personnel. During the broadcast, DeMille used
one "intermission" segment to bring forward Fred Datig, casting
director of Paramount Studios, who endorsed Lux Toilet Soap in these
terms: "I look for players who screen well—who have lovely figures,
good features, and fine complexions. This means a lot to both stars
and extras—Lux Toilet Soap is the official soap over on the Paramount
lot and every other great studio in Hollywood."[26]

To even out the balance of publicity power during the evening, at
the end of the broadcast DeMille introduced Jesse Lasky, who spoke
for a few minutes of Paramount stars and productions, mentioning
Adolph Zukor and Samuel Goldwyn in the course of his talk, and
ending with a final glowing recommendation for Lux soap. During the
following interviews with Marlene Dietrich and Clark Gable, stars of
the evening's broadcast, each managed to insert a plug for his or her
upcoming film. Dietrich further reinforced the Hollywood glamour of
the production by singing "Falling in Love Again" from *The Blue Angel*.
DeMille closed with a further short endorsement of several productions
about to be released by Paramount and other leading studios.

This, however, was a somewhat atypical broadcast, because it represented the program's Hollywood premiere and included a larger than

usual studio audience composed of leading Hollywood figures. Later, as production became more routine, the show became a vehicle for Lux soap flakes advertising, rather than the toilet soap. A separate, less prestigious announcer was used to narrate the commercials, which were inserted at two different "intermissions" occurring at roughly twenty-minute intervals. And although lesser-known stars sometimes directly mentioned Lux soap in their post-program talks, Hollywood's hotter properties confined their enthusiasm to studio, rather than Lever Brothers, products.

A more typical structure of the "Lux Radio Theatre" went something like the following: After a transition announcement about "Lux"'s imminent broadcast by the network announcer, a blare of trumpets and a musical fanfare preceded the famous "And now...Lux Presents HOLLYWOOD!" [more fanfare] "Ladies and Gentlemen...your producer...MR. CECIL B. DEMILLE," over applause from the studio audience. DeMille then took over the microphone, gave his greetings and a bit of chit-chat, and announced the upcoming attraction and stars, working in at least one relatively low-key plug for the Lux product. Then, as a different musical score appropriate to the film about to be heard played in the background, DeMille in effect exited from the commercial frame of the show and entered the fictional construction, playing the role of the dramatic narrator essential to setting up the scene for the action to follow. In the analysis of the adaptation of "Dark Victory" that follows, it is evident how important the role of the narrator was in making this transition, not only from commercial to dramatic setting, but also from visual to purely aural presentation of the narrative. The actors then took over, in a version of the film property in which most details of action, character, and setting had been compressed into dialogue and in which sound effects played an important part.

Then, between acts of the three-part presentation, intermission was called. The transition from dramatic material to outright commercial was accomplished by a musical cue and applause, followed by the voice of the program's commercial announcer, who narrated the commercial announcement itself. After the advertisement for Lux soap flakes—which could run on for two minutes or more—DeMille came back on the air in his "bridging" function, leading back into the narrative. A similar testimonial was enacted at the end of the hour after the close of DeMille's narrative and a commercial announcement; DeMille then brought out one or more stars or technical personnel such as make-up experts or costume designers, often leading the conversation to the utility of Lux soap in the normal Hollywood work day. After this, with further musical bridging and thanks and congratulations all around, the show closed.[27]

"Dark Victory"

The Academy Award-nominated film *Dark Victory* starred Bette Davis, Humphrey Bogart, and George Brent in its theatrical version. I choose to examine this film's adaptation to a "Lux" episode for pragmatic as well as theoretical reasons. First, this particular program happens to be one for which an audio recording is available; not all of the "Lux" episodes were recorded for posterity, and of those that were, not many are available outside archives or museum settings. Second, the success of *Dark Victory* both as a film and as a "Lux" episode makes it worthy of consideration; audiences found it to be a particularly satisfying film, and the ratings for the broadcast version testify to the accuracy of spokesmen's reports that "the most popular plays...are those which are supposed to appeal more directly to women: plays such as 'Dark Victory', 'The Constant Nymph', or 'Wuthering Heights'."[28]

Third, this particular property has a more interesting history than most: beginning as a moderately successful Broadway play by George Brewer and Bertram Bloch, it enjoyed a fifty-one-performance run at the Plymouth Theatre in New York, opening on November 7, 1934, and starred Tallulah Bankhead as Judith Traherne.[29] Purchased by Warner shortly thereafter, it was next performed on "Lux" in a lesser-known version starring Barbara Stanwyck and Melvyn Douglas that aired on April 4, 1938. It is unclear whether this release occurred before or after the decision to film the story had been made. In 1939, *Dark Victory* appeared in its best-known reincarnation as a theatrical film, starring Bette Davis, George Brent, Humphrey Bogart, Ronald Reagan, and Geraldine Fitzgerald, among others. The adaptation was written by Casey Robinson, the director was Edmund Goulding. In general, the film was received as a standard tearjerker, "emotional flim-flam," a "gooey collection of cliches," and "a glutinous star vehicle,"[30] but audiences flocked to see it. Next came the second, more prestigious "Lux" version, starring Davis and Spencer Tracy, that aired on January 8, 1940, presumably leading up to or reinforcing the film's Academy Award nomination for best picture. In 1963, the property was remade as *Stolen Hours* starring Susan Hayward; the made-for-television version followed in 1975 as "Dark Victory," starring Elizabeth Montgomery. Gooey and glutinous the story may be, but obviously possessed of staying power.[31]

Framing the Narrative

Analysis of the "Lux Radio Theatre" version of the film *Dark Victory* is complicated, however, by the multiple frames, or contexts, involved in the presentation of the material, all of which contribute to the overall meaning of the program. It is important to establish, first, the pertinent material of this analysis, an issue often made difficult in the analysis of broadcast forms. Rather than an uninterrupted presentation of a clearly discrete, coherent, and autonomous work (as in the case of a theatrical film), the broadcast presentation intersperses the primary dramatic material with commercial announcements, commentary, and promotional material having to do with upcoming programs, the network or station itself, etc: what Raymond Williams refers to as the "flow" of the television discourse.[32]

The same is true for radio; indeed, because network radio originated this "flow," it is especially pertinent to study its utility within the overall institution of broadcasting, as well as its function in the show itself. This notion is particularly relevant to radio program analysis in that, unlike television's spot advertising structure, where relatively unrelated materials are joined by the networks or stations in a relatively unpremeditated manner, network radio operated by signing over the entire time slot to one sponsor, thus putting the entire range of material broadcast in the hands of one unifying creative department. To concentrate merely on the ostensible "subject" of a broadcast program, then, as many studies have done, is to create an artificial and unrepresentative construct having little relation to the real broadcast event as it was both produced and experienced.

Thus three dominant institutions are concerned in the production of "Lux": the network or broadcasting institution, the commercial purpose of the sponsor as mediated by its advertising agency, and the "Hollywood" institution, which provides the dramatic heart of the program. These dominant interests can be seen in the structures of the text, in what I will refer to as *frames*. By the term *frame* I refer to recognizable units of textual structure and organization that reflect, and result from, the interests and goals of the different groups concerned in its production. I use the term *frame* first to represent the limiting and determining function of each level of radio discourse, by which the "textualized" needs and interests of each successive institution to a certain extent "contain" and control the next; and second, because it often occurs in discussions of discursive structures. For instance, in his "Encoding and Decoding" article, Stuart Hall refers to the "meanings and ideas" that "frame" the constitution of the program within the communication structure. A definition of the term *frame* in Hall's work, and as I will use it, might be "a discrete, identifiable structure of codes or signifying practices used by an institution." This adds to Erving Goffman's use of the term as the "organization of experience" or "definitions of a situation...built up in accordance with principles of organization which govern events" by postulating an element of intent, of organized interest that *produces* meaning, as opposed to Goffman's more passive, empiricist definition (e.g., organization is simply "there," we perceive it).[33]

Each frame represents the site of intersection and "textualization" of the intentions and participation of one identifiable group or institution involved in its production; each frame, in turn, employs its own structure of codes and signifying practices to produce "meanings and ideas." The outside frame, Frame 1, mediates through various types of narrative or forms of address the conventions, needs, and economics of "a program on radio." Frame 1 reflects primarily the interests of the network, consisting of scheduling, time constraints, and the general economic structure and function of network broadcasting, which sells time on the air for money, promising exposure to an audience through linkage with a number of local broadcasting stations. Frame 1 also functions to reconcile the commercial purposes of broadcast radio with the regulatory structures of the federal government. It is made apparent in the text, not only through largely "invisible" limiting and structuring factors—such as time limitations, acceptance and scheduling of programs, and technical and content restrictions—but also through the voice of the network announcer, which leads into and out of the program, or may intervene for station identification (and a reminder that the network is there) during the show. This frame is the largest context for radio analysis and would affect almost any program on radio similarly. Frame 2 articulates the commercial function of the program: the interests of the sponsor as mediated by its chosen advertising agency. In terms of program material, then, Frame 2 includes the sponsor's introduction of the program, the narrator's presentation of the content of a specific show, the commercial messages themselves, and other materials belonging to the program but not to the film adaptation itself. In the case of "Lux," this frame is divided between the outright commercial interests—the voice of the sponsor's spokesman and other characters featured in the actual commercials for Lux soap flakes— and the "Hollywood" component of the program, personified by "producer" Cecil B. DeMille.

The Hollywood referent is an important component of Frame 2. Because Lever Brothers and JWT chose this particular kind of program precisely because of the glamour, prestige, and "pre-marketed" interest a Hollywood-based advertising strategy could add to a marketing campaign, the choice of DeMille as narrator was critical to the program's success. DeMille's invocation of the Hollywood mystique, introduction of stars, background information on the film properties, references to studios and backstage personnel, conversations with celebrities, and so on are used, implicitly and explicitly, to tie the appeal of Hollywood to the Lux soap product. Without this mediating frame, within which Hollywood interests (promoting films, stars, and general atmosphere for future box-office impact) could be brought forward, little would exist to either attract studio support of the effort or to distinguish these film adaptation programs from the general run of serials and original radio dramas that made up the bulk of radio dramatic programming. Almost all film adaptation programs employed this second frame in some way, although "Lux," through judicious use of the DeMille persona, was able to give the Hollywood frame far more weight and glamour than some of its competitors, perhaps one of the reasons for its leading position in program popularity.

The third and inner frame consists of what could (and later, with television, would) be called "the program itself": the adaptation of the film of the evening. This is the dramatic material used as "bait" for the other frames, the central core of entertainment or interest used to draw listeners to the radio set. However, unlike the dramatic structure of the traditional theatrical film, whose economics dictate a form quite different from the radio program, the "inner frame" of the broadcast program is permeable, segmented, not marked by forms and discursive practices designed to tie the entire work together in a seamless whole, but rather designed to be interrupted, to lend itself to segmentation and disruption, to provide opportunities for the audience not only to enter the diegesis but to *exit* it as well (but only as far as the surrounding frame). Because this disruption, this permeability, is a dominant characteristic of the commercial broadcast discourse, both in radio and television—and a necessary one to broadcast economics as they developed in this country—the transitions from one frame to another become particularly important.

Transitions play a crucial role in the broadcast text because they provide the integrating force that unites the work and the various (and in some ways competing) aesthetic and economic needs of and for which the program is constructed. Music is the device most commonly used to effect and to mark transitions, but it is frequently reinforced by narrative explanations. In the following discussion of the show, the transitions will be given particular consideration, for it is here that the seams in the continuous and smoothly flowing broadcast narrative are revealed, along with the "sutures" required to lead the listener into the text. In textual transitions some of broadcast's codes are revealed as they attempt to obscure some of the forces at work behind the scenes.

Roland Barthes, discussing the codes at work in the novel, states "our society takes the greatest pains to conjure away the coding of the narrative situation...the reluctance to declare its codes characterizes bourgeois society and the mass culture issuing from it: both demand signs which do not look like signs." The radio program's framing structure, by which the listener is led from the narrational situation into the artificial construct of the narrative, corresponds to the examples Barthes uses of "narrational devices which seek to naturalize the subsequent narrative by feigning to make it the outcome of some natural circumstance and thus, as it were, 'disinaugurating' it"—such as epistolary novels, manuscripts supposedly discovered by the author, stories told to the author by some participant, films that begin before the credits, without the "marker" that states "this is a film," and so on. (One thinks of the elaborate narrational framing of semiotician Umberto Eco's popular novel, *The Name of the Rose*).[34]

And, although all forms of creative expression act to obscure some of their generative forces and techniques, the broadcast medium is particularly adept. The reasons for this again can be traced back to the fundamental economic structures of broadcasting, by which entertainment is used as bait for commercial messages. Because time is held captive by both the broadcast and the film—both must take place in a set pattern, during a set time, unlike reading a printed text—the ability of the audience to skip over or screen out commercial material is greatly reduced. In order to hold the audience's attention, overtly commercial material—which in itself may have limited entertainment value, or which the audience may resist, or, more important in the broadcast institution, which may not necessarily be construed as serving the public interest, convenience, or necessity—must be surrounded and enclosed by more appealing material in an attempt to obscure the hook behind the worm, the purpose behind the text. Hence the elaborate framing mechanism of the broadcast discourse.

Frame 1

The "Lux Radio Theatre"'s presentation of "Dark Victory" opened with the first, important transition from Frame 1, the broadcasting frame, to Frame 2, the program-as-program, the radio program aware of itself as such and not embarrassed to reveal its commercial purpose. As with most transitions in radio, music plays an important part in "cuing" the listener, as does the applause of the "live studio audience," drawing on conventions already well established and understood by 1936. With the well-known declaration, "Lux Presents Hollywood!" made by the show's announcer, followed by a rising musical overture of the show's theme, the program effects an exit from what was, at this time, the rather "vacant" world of the network into the sponsored program; CBS, as the network most receptive to the programming needs of its commercial sponsors, tended during prime time to fade from the foreground almost completely. Thus the transition from Frame 1 to Frame 2 is rather suppressed, existing more in significant absence than in presence, especially on CBS, the advertisers' network. NBC during this period remained somewhat more obtrusive, in keeping with its organization and economics.[35]

Frame 2

The transition from Frame 1 to Frame 2 would be followed by the announcer's introduction: "The Lux Radio Theatre brings you Bette Davis and Spencer Tracy in 'Dark Victory'. Ladies and gentlemen, your producer, Mr. Cecil B. DeMille!" [music rises to climax, applause]. The announcer's role in the case of this program took on overtones of the theatrical variety show or vaudeville, providing the "Lux Radio Theatre" with a plausible means of exiting from the previously broadcast material and entering the world of the Hollywood spectacle presided over by DeMille. After the applause died down, DeMille would confirm the unique "Hollywood" element of the second frame with the equally well-known line "Greetings from Hollywood, ladies and gentlemen." He would then launch into the introductory "frame" material so carefully prepared by J. Walter Thompson scriptwriters, combining Hollywood lore and glamour—in the case of this broadcast, the recent Oscar awards won by Davis and Tracy—with an initial plug for the sponsor's product, given an equal dramatic weight by DeMille's charged delivery. "Tonight even the unemotional lights in front of the Lux Radio Theatre have a special glow of pride in our players and our play, 'Dark Victory'. Our stage is set for a prize-winning achievement— and so is the stage in your home, when Lux Flakes is starred. Many domestic producers have discovered that casting Lux Flakes in a leading role is good business at the household box office."[36]

This rather forced analogy is a typical feature of the "Lux" interior frame. To use another example, after an adaptation of the W. C. Fields movie *Poppy*, Fields and co-star Anne Shirley spoke with DeMille as follows: after a short humorous monologue in which Fields recounted his experiences as a "valet de chambre" to a circus elephant and refers to his face turning red as a result of a small boy mistaking his nose for that of an elephant, Anne Shirley giggled and stated, "But Mr. Fields, don't you know that anything washed in Lux never changes color? Might I recommend that you dip your trunk—I mean, nose, excuse me!—into a noggin of those beautiful Lux suds?" Fields then replied, "Madame, do you too wish to impugn my honor? I shall be heckled no more! Mr. DeMille, I bid you good night!"[37]

For "Dark Victory," however, the Oscar nominees were not subject to such crass commercialization—so as not to tarnish this particularly highly burnished Hollywood gloss, no taint of hucksterism was allowed too close to Davis or Tracey. Instead, atypically, the two stars were never required to talk about anything other than the Hollywood component, including their recent and forthcoming films and small plugs for other studio-related material. During this particular "Lux" performance, the actual commercials were all read by the show's announcer (not DeMille, but a faceless voice later given credit by DeMille as Mel Ruick). For the first "intermission," the transition occurred immediately following the show's first major climax: after the operation on Davis's brain tumor, the doctor closed the first act with the line, "She'll die within a year" [rising tragic music, crash of gong, applause]. The announcer's voice then came on the air saying, "You have just heard Act 1 of 'Dark Victory' starring Spencer Tracy and Bette Davis. Mr. DeMille brings you Act 2 in just a minute. But first, I have some important news for you. Listen a moment, and you'll hear how it sounds on the wires [sound of telegraph key]. The telegraph key is saying just three words. Here's what they are: New Quick Lux. Yes, that's our big news for millions of housewives."[38]

A dialogue then ensued between the announcer and another commercial character, introduced as "Sally," who interjected, "You know, I thought Lux flakes just couldn't be improved. They're so swell!" After a minute-long promotion of Lux flakes, the announcer closed the commercial and effected the transition back to the second frame with the words, "Now our producer, Mr. DeMille." DeMille came back on the air—with a shift of microphones to produce a slightly more "distanced" effect than the close-up mike techniques used in the commercial announcement, creating an impression of theatrical space—to announce: "Act 2 of 'Dark Victory', starring Spencer Tracy as Dr. Frederick Steele and Bette Davis in the role of Judith Traherne, with Earline Tuttle as Ann" [theme music up, then falling under DeMille's voice]. DeMille then shifted into the other important aspect of his role as emcee, that of narrator.

A similar transition occurred during the second intermission. After rising music and the familiar gong crash, the announcer said, "In just a moment, Mr. DeMille brings you Act 3 of 'Dark Victory'" and then proceeded with annother conversation with "Sally" extolling the virtues of Lux flakes, during the course of which a testimonial letter from a Lux user was read. At the end of this commercial the hour's sole overt manifestation of Frame 1, the "network" frame, occurred, as a voice said, "This is the Columbia Broadcasting System." Frame 2 quickly reasserted itself with rising music and DeMille's introduction to the third act. The routine varied slightly with the final commercial break after the conclusion of the play. This transition exited not only to the commercial framework but also introduced the main part of the Hollywood component, usually occuring in the form of a dialogue between DeMille and the stars of the performance after its conclusion. This time the announcer would state, "In just a moment Mr. DeMille returns with our stars" and close with "Now Mr. DeMille is bring our stars to the microphone."

Thus Frame 2 is dominated by the persona of DeMille, who served as an important bridge between the commercial purposes of the program and the Hollywood component, not only in his persona, but also in his function as he introduced the inner frame and provided the first and last commercial plugs. Rather than disrupt the flow of the fictional narrative with an abrupt transition to the commercial voice, DeMille's function as the narrator and master of ceremonies allowed the "closed" and fictional world of the film adaptation to give way gradually to the alien voice of the Lux salesman, smoothing over what otherwise would be an abrupt "break" between closed fictional narrative and the direct address of the commercial announcement and mediating between the conflicting needs of the show's commercial sponsors, on the one hand, and the demands of the Hollywood fictional film on the other. Although as the broadcast medium developed, and its forms became conventionalized and accepted, this buffering function became abbreviated, it can still be seen on broadcast television in the form of program "markers": logos or still frames, often with a voice-over, marking the transition from program to advertisement.

As previously noted, the Hollywood elements involved in the production of the "Lux Radio Theatre" played an important role in its overall popularity and in the "mise-en-oreille" of the program as a whole. DeMille played the role of the Hollywood impresario, bringing stars and screenplays together for an appreciative audience, constantly involved in the creative process of bringing the glamour of Hollywood to the air. The following excerpt from his opening introduction on the "Dark Victory" broadcast is a good example.

If there's a little more grey in my hair this week, believe me it came from the task of finding the right dramatic material for such splendid artists as Bette Davis and Spencer Tracy. In fact we considered and rejected dozens of plays before selecting the one we think is perfect, "Dark Victory." As a producer, I've always disliked the type of play known as a "vehicle," one that's designed for the actor instead of the audience. And when there are two noted players in a cast, there's a double danger that the play will turn out to be a double vehicle. But "Dark Victory" has grip and power and human appeal. And when our curtain falls on the third act, I believe you'll agree with me that this play is really a great emotional experience. Each woman in our audience will unconsciously put herself in the place of Judith Traherne; each man will wonder what he would have done as Dr. Frederick Steele."[39]

At the end of the program, DeMille traditionally interviewed the stars of that night's performance and perhaps included a commercial message within the interview. For "Dark Victory," DeMille led Davis and Tracy into a conversation that focussed firmly on Hollywood, with the stars discussing their mutual regard for and past appearances with each other. However, at the end, Davis was allowed to inquire, "What are you planning for the 'Lux Radio Theatre' next week, Mr. DeMille?" and after DeMille's announcement that the next week's broadcast would be "Sing You Sinners" with Bing Crosby and a few further credits, she closed the show with "I know we're all going to enjoy that, Mr. DeMille"—a fairly standard exchange for the better-known performers. In general, the closing interviews provided an opportunity for the unseen radio audience to "listen in" on an informal, out-of-character chat among the famous director and the stars of the performance just heard, and perhaps recently viewed in the theater. The intimacy of the radio experience gave audiences the chance to participate in a casual moment with the stars, often involving a small joke or piece of monkey business, in their off-screen personas—an opportunity rarely accorded film viewers before the days of television. This listening in, intimate atmosphere also enhanced the efficacy of the commercial message—if Anne Shirley or Evelyn Keys happened to endorse Lux soap casually, how much more compelling than a regular commercial. The air of intimacy cultivated by the stars and host of the show could also be used in their absence to sell the product: before beginning the narration of the 1946 performance of "To Have and Have Not," host William Keighly implicated the "Bogart family" (Lauren Bacall and Humphrey

Bogart, that night's stars) in a Lux endorsement, although they never spoke for themselves in the matter:

> To bring the Bogart family to rehearsals, we had to lure them from their brand new mountain home . . . if you should drop in on a friendly visit of inspection, as I did, you'd find Lux flakes doing their part in washing curtains, bedspreads, blankets, etc. etc. etc. When I commented on this fact, Bogie assured me that on his fifty-four-foot yawl in Newport Harbor, which is the Bogart's home away from home, Lux flakes are a standard part of the equipment, making this family loyal to Lux flakes on land and sea."[40]

These endorsements, whether actual or imputed, provided the necessary smooth transition, or suture, between the commercial function of the program and one of its entertainment functions, the glimpse into Hollywood and its processes. But the other function of the host of the show, whether DeMille or one of his successors, tied this secondary commercial-entertainment function to the inner frame, or primary dramatic material of the evening. The narration, together with sound effects and music, made it possible to condense and take away the visual aspects of a film, yet still present a recognizable narrative.

The Inner Frame

One of the first tasks facing the sciptwriters of the "Lux Radio Theatre" consisted of attempting to squeeze an hour and one-half to two hours of visually dramatic material into a fifty-minute, audio-only narrative. Although some films made the translation better than others, the basic Hollywood precept of narrative always received primary consideration— the narrative had to make sense as a story, possessing a beginning, middle, and end—no matter what kind of thematic and symbolic reduction had to take place to achieve this. This is certainly the case with "Dark Victory," in which most elements not directly related to the relationship of Judith with Dr. Steele were jettisoned immediately. In addition, economics of production mandated that as few actors and actresses be used as possible: because of DeMille's salary, substantial fees paid to the studios for the use of their stars, plus the Hollywood-style production values of the program, the cost of producing the show was heavy. In order to afford the top stars who provided the show's main appeal, cuts had to be made in other places. Where it proved impossible to eliminate peripheral or minor characters from the radio version, the show's regular staff of relatively unknown talent came into play.

The basic plot of "Dark Victory," in stage, screen, and broadcast version, involves the character of Judith Traherne (Bette Davis), a young, wealthy Long Island socialite, who is diagnosed by Dr. Steele (George Brent, Spencer Tracy) a brain specialist, as having a brain tumor. Although an operation performed by Dr. Steele temporarily relieves her symptoms, her "prognosis negative" means that she has only a few months to live. Despite the efforts of her secretary-companion, Ann (Geraldine Fitzgerald, Earline Tuttle) and those of Dr. Steele, with whom a love interest develops, to keep her imminent demise a secret from Judith, the truth slips out and a period of wild living and denial of her feelings for Steele follows. During this period brief dalliances with a playboy figure (played by Ronald Reagan in the film version) and her stable manager (Humphrey Bogart) occur, but only lead her to realize that to die "decently, beautifully, finely" she must stop denying her fear and admit her love for Steele. They marry and move to Vermont, where Steele has set up a laboratory to conduct serious research. Soon thereafter, the fatal symptom of darkening vision occurs, and Judith dies after first having selflessly sent her husband away to receive an award for his work.

In the radio version of the story the playboy character played in the film by Ronald Reagan is eliminated entirely; the stable manager's role played by an oddly miscast Humphrey Bogart is not only reduced, but also changed significantly. The relationships between Ann and Judith, and between Ann and Steele, through simplification become much more schematized and sparse in connotation. In addition, the lack of time and background information reduces the complexity of characterization overall. Characters become in many cases little more than stereotypes, thus limiting the realistic and affecting properties of the text. To substitute for lack of depth in the radio diegesis, the role of the narrator, performed once again by "our producer, Mr. Cecil B. DeMille," becomes crucial.

DeMille must accomplish two primary functions in the structure of the "Lux Radio Theatre." First, to compensate for the reduced amount of dramatic material necessitated by the time constraints of the broadcast version, he provides bridges that summarize and provide background material for the story; second, this narration must lead the listeners smoothly into and out of the inner frame of fictional diegesis, back to the commercial frame. As an example of the former function, as DeMille returns the listener to the inner frame after the second commercial break, he states (over a musical transition): "With only a few months of life before her, Judith Traherne lives desperately, cramming her days and nights with excitement, striving vainly to forget."

Here the words "desperately," "cramming," and "excitement," although unable fully to translate the twenty minutes of screen time devoted to this plot development, still manage to convey important information regarding Judith's activities and frame of mind. DeMille follows this line with, "At a horse show in New York, her reckless jumping has won her first prize, and now she stands at the bar, receiving the [slight pause] congratulations of her friends." Thus the scene is set, and although it takes an attentive listener to pick up on DeMille's slightly ironic use of the word "congratulations" (following the term "reckless"), which indicates the damage done by Judith to her reputation and standing with her friends during the preceeding period, enough information is given to smooth the transition back into the narrative as it proceeds.

To accomplish the second task of the narrator, the "Lux Radio Theatre" quite deliberately and specifically leads the interpretation back to the "Hollywood" frame by playing up the stars of each evening's performance in monologue and interview, clearly establishing the actor or actress's presence in the production, often of a more intimate level than possible in the filmic production. Thus, although we cannot see Bette Davis as Judith Traherne in the radio version, we are made well aware of her real-life presence in the broadcast studio and of her star qualities by DeMille's beginning monologue. Throughout the show, although the character created on radio may not be as convincing or as affecting as the one created in the film, we are aware of the presence of Davis as that character—perhaps more so, because the relative permeability of the radio text disrupts our process of identifying the actress as fully with the character she plays—and because the much shorter time period allotted to the drama forces a simplification and reduction of its dramatic material.

The transformation of "Dark Victory" into a broadcast production, then, involves a process of simplification and segmentation that encloses the narrative within a series of intentional frames and provides frequent transitions from one to another. This strategy may also begin to account for one of the characteristics of the broadcast message, its seemingly shallow diegesis, constantly subject to interruptions and self-referential elements that contrast with the intense identification demanded by the film: DeMille's function in "Lux" is in effect to lead the viewer repeatedly out of the fictional frame, back to an awareness of those concerned in its production, who then in turn endorse a product. In other words, the audience is led, not deeper into the fictional world created by the drama, into the thoughts of its characters and deeper consideration of its themes, but instead is constantly pulled back, interrupted, made aware of the presence of stars and producer—of Bette Davis, not Judith Traherne, of Spencer Tracy, not Dr. Steele, of DeMille the showman—and thence led to the product being advertised.

Structures of the Commercial Broadcast Text

The Hollywood film has traditionally been regarded as a "closed" representational system using a predominantly linear method of plot development and strict adherence to a realistic aesthetic demanding a tightly controlled diegesis.[41] No extraneous information is contained within the frame, nothing occurs that cannot be accounted for by the demands of the narrative and the conventions of the traditional style. The conventions of the "classic Hollywood film" include such techniques as point-of-view construction and self-effacing narration, which intensify the spectator's identification with the characters on the screen and heighten his or her involvement with the "realistic" enclosed world created by the film. This is certainly the case with the film version of *Dark Victory*, which changes the progression and location of the narrative to correct any "artificiality" resulting from the work's original stage setting. For instance, instead of the first scene occurring in Dr. Steele's office, as in the play, the film begins with a scene in which Judith falls from a horse as a result of tumor-induced double vision, to avoid the awkwardness of a flashback or an overdependence on dramatic dialogue to establish previous events.

The broadcast text, on the other hand, has frequently been characterized as "disjointed," with a relatively shallow diegesis that disallows the intense identification with the narrative so prevalent in film. John Ellis sees the television image as "engaging the look and the glance rather than the gaze [of the film spectator]." Television viewing's "random quality," with spectators "drifting in and out of the viewing experience over a period of time," has the effect of "greatly minimizing the possibilities for spectator engagement," producing low viewer involvement, according to Farrell Corcoran.[42] Although these writers and others attribute the source of television's unique qualities to different aspects of the broadcast medium—its multiple and varied texts, constant shifting of modes of address, continuous presence in the home, the use habits of its viewers, and its heavy reliance on the sound component of its discourse—each of these "causes" can be seen as secondary characteristics, deriving from structures, both textual and economic, originated by the early radio programs. The broadcast text as developed in the United States on the commercial networks is fundmentally a segmented, disrupted, permeable discourse because it was created by and for advertisers, for the express purpose of capturing the audience's attention only to redirect it to the product advertised.

This structure can be seen particularly clearly in an examination of early radio programs, such as "Lux," because they are the site of innovation of both the economic structure of broadcasting and its characteristic mode of discourse. The tension between the interests of the various producers of the radio program, working through a structure of frames and transitions, act specifically and primarily to lead the reader away from the dramatic narrative itself to intertextual considerations having more to do, in "Lux"'s case, with the nature of Hollywood and the carefully associated commercial product than with the presented work. Although this concept may appear almost avant-garde in its self-reflexivity, these frames are themselves products of encoding; their referents, in the case of "Lux," lie in the myth or mystique of Hollywood and similar sets of meaning that the sponsor wishes to tie to the product being advertised.

From the tightly ordered, heavily symbolic universe of the film narrative, the radio version becomes little more than a "sketch" or outline for what was the film, a permeable discourse that permits the listener to exit easily from the dramatic diegesis—but immediately "recaptures" that listener by directing his or her attention to the other sets of codes, or frames, at work. Although the audience of the broadcast version of "Dark Victory" may not become as involved with the character of Judith Traherne as does the film viewer, he or she will be led back time and again to imagine Bette Davis, the actress, playing that part, partially through specific foregrounding of the star function in the show's "Hollywood" frame, which in turn contains its references to "Lux" soap, lending associations to the product as desired by the advertiser. DeMille, whose equally encoded persona as program host presides over this process, represents the synthesizing force that mediates the tension between the program's three different frames of intent: network, advertiser, and dramatic program.

But what, then, of the structures of the contemporary dominant broadcast form, broadcast television, long after the program "host" or emcee—still present in many early TV productions—has vanished from the scene? With the emergence of the networks as the primary programming agency in the late 1950s (chapter 5), the role of the sponsor diminished to the simple purchase of thirty- or sixty-second spots adjacent to the programs selected and scheduled by the networks, and produced by the television production companies with whom the networks contract. Thus Frames 1 and 3 begin to elide, obscuring Frame

2 as the network takes onto itself the commercial interests formerly held by an independent sponsor.

To further reduce the seeming importance of the role of the sponsor in network television, the marked transitions between the various frames of TV have been played down, streamlined but not entirely eliminated. Today's transitions from the inner core of the program to the commercial break take the form of a simple fade to black, or a cut to a show's logo in still frame, perhaps with a tag of theme music. Some programs have eliminated the transition marker altogether, suspending the viewer in temporary uncertainty about the "product" status of what he or she is seeing. Perhaps this is a "psychological" marker. Today's narrator is not explicit but implied, usually invested visually in the opening sequence with which each program is introduced. The old transition, "And now, a word from our sponsor...," once so familiar, has been eliminated entirely, except on public television, the economic base of which is very different. Frame 1 becomes much more explicit, as we are bombarded by network previews and announcements ("Stay tuned for...," "Don't miss...") promoting high awareness of the network itself as a recognizable author of the television discourse—a necessary strategy in an era of proliferating channels and program services.

In effect, then, as television has evolved, the function of Frame 2, the realm of the sponsor, has been not eliminated but increasingly denied, disconnected from the content of the programs themselves, relegated to a seemingly distant source separate from the actual content and function of television. Today's commercials seem to attempt to "sneak" into the flow of programming, often taking the protective coloring of the programs themselves—or increasingly, resembling another form of programming, the music video—in order to minimize the sense of transition from one mode of narration to another, in order to obscure the source of ultimate economic power in the structure of broadcast television. Each frame identified in the preceding discussion is made up of and utilizes a complex system of codes and signifying practices that need to be examined in detail, with close attention paid to specific historical and production conditions. This analysis of the framing structures of the broadcast discourse can only point out the largest categories, but perhaps it can provide a starting point, at least, for future exploration, as the structures worked out in the early days of broadcast radio provided the starting point for the emergence of television programs and forms.

The Transition to Television

As successful as the "Lux Radio Theatre of the Air" was, we no longer experience its like today. The radio film adaptation has gone the way

of the nickoledeon and vaudeville—transformed by changing circumstances into a form barely recognizable by its former standards. "Lux"
did make the initial transition to television in the early 1950s as the
"Lux Video Theatre," but its existence was short-lived. Why was a
successful show like "Lux" forced to make that highly unsuitable
transition in the first place? The next chapter will discuss the aban-
donment of radio for television on the part of advertisers, made inevitable
by the policies and practices of the major networks. But having been
forced to be seen as well as heard, why did the video version of "Lux"
fail to live up to its predecessor? The reasons for this relate to the
economics and to the formal structures of both film and television.

The television version of "Lux" began in very much the same way
as did the radio program. From October 1950 until September 1952,
Lux broadcast one half-hour of adaptations of stage material from New
York, moving to Hollywood in September 1952 but continuing with
nonfilm, theater-based material until August 1954, when the program
moved to NBC for a full-hour broadcast slot, Thursday nights from
10:00–11:00. During that same season, 1954–55, the radio program
went off the air after several years of declining ratings. Theatrical film
adaptations became the main staple of the video program, with James
Mason as host that season, followed by Otto Kruger, Gordon MacRae,
and Ken Carpenter. As with the radio show, interviews with the stars
and studio personnel connected with the evening's performance remained de rigeur, but several factors rendered such appearances less
effective than their radio predecessors.

First, during this same season, 1954–55, Hollywood began to make
its presence felt on television using a different strategy than it had with
radio. Rather than allow others to control the production of television
programs, most major studios went into production for themselves
(chapter 5). Second, 1955 is the year in which theatrical films began
to show up on network and syndicated television. With the films
themselves available, the purpose of the Lux concept was called into
question. Why allow movie properties to be exposed to audiences in
a reduced, live, rewritten format when the films themselves could now
find a new market on TV? Technical conditions as well as economic
constraints mandated against a visual experience that could in any way
approximate the production values of a theatrical film; if inferior
productions were to be allowed to "use up" a film's appeal with a
broadcast audience, wherein lay the benefit for the film industry?

Also, with the Paramount decrees of 1947 conditions in Hollywood
itself had changed; studios no longer held stars under the kind of long-
term contracts as they had formerly, able to loan them out to radio or

other studios at will. The "Lux Video Theatre" was never able to attract the top stars and properties that the radio program drew so well, thus lessening the appeal of the commercial endorsements for Lux soap as well as the benefit to the film studios. For example, an adaptation of "Double Indemnity" (December 16, 1954), although drawing on the Billy Wilder-Raymond Chandler film scenario, lost a good part of its original appeal with such stars as Laraine Day and Frank Lovejoy in the leads. "Casablanca" (March 3, 1955), with Paul Douglas, Arlene Dahl, and Hoagy Carmichael could hardly purport to be the same property as the film. By spring 1957, more adaptations based on plays and short stories had begun to creep into the schedule, and in the fall 1958 season the show's name was changed to the "Lux Playhouse," going back to a one half-hour format and alternating on Friday nights on CBS with the "Schlitz Playhouse of the Stars." With changing circumstances surrounding both the film and broadcasting industries, the tension among the interests of the networks, the commercial sponsors and their agencies, and the studios they depended on for audience appeal shifted into a different formation. Relations between Hollywood and the broadcasting business entered a new phase.

NOTES

1. Stuart Hall, "Cultural Studies: Two Paradigms," in *Media, Culture, and Society: A Critical Reader*, ed. Richard Collins et al. (London: Sage, 1986), p. 47.

2. Stuart Hall, "Encoding/Decoding," in *Culture, Media, Language*, ed. Stuart Hall et al. (New York: Longman, 1983), p. 377.

3. Stuart Hall, "Encoding and Decoding in the Television Discourse," Occasional Papers, Centre for Cultural Studies, University of Birmingham, 1973, p. 2. David Barker applies Hall's theories to television production in "Television Production Techniques as Communication," in *Television: The Critical View*, 4th ed., ed. Horace Newcomb (New York: Oxford University Press, 1987), pp. 179–96.

4. Stuart Hall, "The Toad in the Garden: Thatcherism Among the Theorists," in *Marxism and the Interpretation of Culture*, ed. Cary Nelson and Lawrence Grossberg (Urbana: University of Illinois Press, 1988), p. 48.

5. Janet Staiger, "Mass-Produced Photoplays: Economic and Signifying Practices in the First Years of Hollywood," in *Movies and Methods,* vol. 2, ed. Bill Nichols (Berkeley: University of California Press, 1985), pp. 144–61; Douglas Gomerey, "The Coming of Sound to American Cinema," Ph.D. diss., University of Wisconsin-Madison, 1975; Charles Musser, "The Early Cinema of Edwin Porter," *Cinema Journal* 19 (Fall 1979): 23.

6. Robert C. Allen, *Speaking of Soap Operas* (Chapel Hill: University of North Carolina Press, 1986), p. 128.

7. Raymond Williams, *Television: Technology and Cultural Form* (New York: Schocken Books, 1977), pp. 90–91; Mike Budd, Steve Craig, and Clay Steinman, "Fantasy Island: Marketplace of Desire," *Journal of Communication* (Winter 1983): 67–77; Sandy Flitterman, "The *Real* Soap Operas: TV Commercials," in *Regarding Television,* ed. E. Ann Kaplan (New York: AFI Monographs, 1984), pp. 84–96.

8. Erik Barnouw does credit the agencies, notably Young and Rubicam, with providing the impetus that brought Hollywood into radio, although his attribution of specific credit can be debated; elsewhere, he mentions some of the people who played a role in writing and acting in early radio programs, but in a sporadic and anecdotal manner. The study of advertising has brought little in the way of detailed historical accounts of the actual process of program innovation; a survey of the literature of advertising gives the impression that students of that field live in the moment: for every historical account, no matter how personal or eccentric, ten studies of current techniques and strategies line the shelves. One history, Stephen Fox's *The Mirror Makers* (Random House, 1983), provides interesting and valuable detail on the history of some of the major firms; however his focus—on the development and alternation of different advertising strategies and styles—and his overall thesis, implied in the title—that advertisers merely reflect trends and forces in society rather than create them—weaken Fox's discussion of the impact agencies may have engendered on other social institutions, including radio.

9. Nick Browne, "Political Economy of the Television (Super) Text," in *Television: The Critical View,* ed. Newcomb, pp. 585–99.

10. Llewellyn White, *The American Radio* (Chicago: University of Chicago Press, 1947), pp. 54–67; Fox, *Mirror Makers,* p. 150; James Playstead Wood, *The Story of Advertising* (New York: Ronald Press, 1958), p. 413.

11. Ralph M. Hower, *The History of an Advertising Agency: N. W. Ayer & Son at Work 1869–1939* (Cambridge: Harvard University Press, 1939), p. 199.

12. Hower, *N. W. Ayer,* p. 169; Allen, *Speaking of Soap Operas,* pp. 116–17; Fox, *Mirror Makers,* pp. 159–60.

13. Kenneth L. Watt, "One Minute to Go," *The Saturday Evening Post,* April 2, 1938, pp. 8–9; April 9, 1938, pp. 22–23.

14. Watt, "One Minute to Go," April 9, p. 23.

15. *Fortune,* "Radio II: A $45,000,000 Talent Bill," May 1938, p. 54.

16. Allen, *Speaking of Soap Operas,* p. 119; Allen quotes from Phillips's proposal: "'Thus', Phillips suggested, 'the transition from commercial announcements to the story can be practically painless, and a great deal of actual selling can be done in the story itself'."

17. Roland Marchand, *Advertising the American Dream* (Berkeley: University of California Press, 1985), p. 106.

18. Fox, *Mirror Makers,* pp. 30–31, 80–82; *Fortune,* November 1947, p. 94.

19. Fox, *Mirror Makers,* pp. 88–89.

20. "Mr. Countway Takes the Job," *Fortune,* November 1940.

21. Ibid., p. 116.

22. Ibid., p. 97; "Daniel J. Danker, Jr.," *National Cyclopedia of American Biography* (Clifton, N.J.: J. T. White, 1926), 33:223.

23. John Dunning, *Tune in Yesterday* (Englewood Cliffs, N.J.: Prentice- Hall, 1976), p. 378; Bernard Lucich, "The Lux Radio Theater," in *American Broadcasting: A Sourcebook on the History of Radio and Television,* ed. Lawrence W. Lichty and Malachi C. Topping (New York: Hastings House, 1975), p. 391.

24. Marchand, *Advertising the American Dream,* p. 161.

25. Ibid., pp. 94, 106.

26. Lux Radio Theatre, "The Legionnaire and the Lady," June 1, 1936; from audio recording in the collection of the Museum of Broadcasting, New York, N.Y.

27. Several "Lux" productions were used to establish normal program structures: "Dark Victory," aired January 8, 1940 (Minneapolis: Radio Reruns, 1977); "To Have and Have Not," aired October 14, 1946 (Sandy Hook, N.J.: Radiola, 1971); "Poppy," aired March 7, 1938 (Minneapolis: Radio Reruns, 1977); "The Legionnaire and the Lady," aired June 1, 1936 (New York: Museum of Broadcasting Collection); "The Al Jolson Story," aired February 16, 1948 (Mobile, Ala.: Mobile Public Library Collection).

28. Frank Daugherty, "He Sells Soap!" *The Christian Science Monitor Weekly,* March 25, 1944, p. 8.

29. *The Best Plays of 1934–35* (New York: Dodd Mead, 1935), p. 404.

30. From reviews cited in Leslie Halliwell, *Halliwell's Film Guide,* 3d ed. (New York: Avon Books, 1984), p. 303.

31. Gene Ringgold and DeWitt Bodeen, *The Films of Cecil B. DeMille* (New York: Citadel, 1969), pp. 370, 372.

32. Williams, *Television: Technology and Cultural Form,* pp. 86–94; Michele Hilmes, "The Television Apparatus: Direct Address," *Journal of Film and Video* 37 (Fall 1985): 27–36.

33. Hall, "Encoding/Decoding," pp. 128–38; Umberto Eco, "Towards a Semiotic Inquiry into the Television Message," *Working Papers in Cultural Studies* no. 3 (Autumn 1972): 103–21; Erving Goffman, *Frame Analysis* (New York: Harper, 1974).

34. Roland Barthes, *Image Music Text* (New York: Hill and Wang, 1977), pp. 114–17.

35. Frame 1 is also remarkably hard to study historically in its textual manifestations, because it is precisely these network announcements, connectors, and transitions that subsequent recordings of radio programs deemed unnecessary and uninteresting and edited out. It is difficult to find recordings taken from radio in their entirety from the 1920s, 1930s, and even early 1940s, thus my conclusions here are highly tentative.

36. Lux Radio Theatre, "Dark Victory."

37. Lux Radio Theatre, "Poppy."

38. Lux Radio Theatre, "Dark Victory."

39. Ibid.

40. Lux Radio Theatre, "To Have and Have Not."

41. See, for example, Bill Nichols, *Ideology and the Image* (Bloomington: Indiana University Press, 1981); Daniel Dayan, "The Tutor Code of Classical Cinema," in *Movies and Methods,* ed. Nichols; Kristin Thompsom and David Bordwell, "Space and Narrative in the Films of Ozu," *Screen* 17 (Summer 1976): 42–43.

42. John Ellis, *Visible Fictions* (New York: Oxford University Press, 1982), p. 128; John Fiske and John Hartley, *Reading Television* (New York: Methuen, 1978); Farrell Corcoran, "Television as Ideological Apparatus: The Power and the Pleasure," *Critical Studies in Mass Communication* (June 1984): 141.

5

Television

FILM INDUSTRY ALTERNATIVES
TO THE NETWORKS

Incumbent in the technology of broadcasting lies a difficulty in establishing an economic base. By its very nature, broadcasting, as its name implies, involves widespread distribution of radio signals through the common airspace. Although transmitting and receiving devices can be bought and sold, and use of these devices can be monitored, it is extremely difficult to control access to a product as invisible and intangible as sound waves. Rejecting a government-financed broadcasting system along the lines of the British Broadcasting Corporation, the United States left the question of broadcasting's financial base up to the manufacturers of receiving and transmitting sets (chapter 1). In the efforts to establish a national broadcasting system, AT&T's experiment in toll-based radio was supplanted in 1926 by RCA's system based on the sale of receiving sets (chapter 2). Although NBC rather rapidly perceived that a certain amount of "indirect" advertising could help to defray programming costs, not until CBS got under way in the early 1930s did the need for a firmer economic base lead to the direct advertising system that is still prevalent.

The film industry, on the other hand, proposed an alternative form of economic support more closely related to the NBC model. An outside source of income—increased box-office revenues—could offset and justify money spent on broadcast programming, especially because talent already under contract to the studios could make such programming relatively economical. This alternative did not come to fruition for a variety of reasons, and an advertising-based system developed by which commercial sponsors served as program producers. Some of the consequences of that system, as inscribed in the broadcast text, included the tenuous balance of power between the interests of the program supplier—in this example, the Hollywood studios—and those of the sponsor and the network (chapter 4). When, with the advent of television, the addition of the visual element formerly lacking in broadcasting threatened to "use up" a vital part of Hollywood's appeal too quickly (and too cheaply), the video version of "Lux" and other similar programs lost their effectiveness as film promotion vehicles. If Hollywood were to remain involved in broadcasting, clearly a new system was required.

Beginning in the late 1940s, a few studios investigated another alternative to the commercially sponsored system of broadcasting, this time proposing to bring the direct-sale economics of film exhibition to the broadcasting business. Two methods of accomplishing this were explored. In the first, theater television, televised events could be projected on a theater screen and admission charged in the normal theatrical way. Subscription television, on the other hand, was a method of bringing the box office into the home and charging for television viewing on a per-program basis. By eliminating the "deferred consummation" of the commercially sponsored broadcasting situation, an entirely different structure of discourse could surround the broadcast event. Instead of the careful framing and balancing of interests inherent in the sponsored system, a televised program could be viewed on its merits as a program alone.

This is not to imply that the theatrical film model is free from commodification or from a balancing of commercial interests—the conflict of exhibition and production interests, to name only one, has formed an important part of this history—but the direct sale economics of the theatrical film imply a more unified formal structure that reflects the undivided nature of the product sold. And, turning this argument around, the film industry possessed thirty years of experience in producing such entertainment; no wonder, then, that it sought a new method of product distribution that could be both controlled by film interests and free from the competing structures of the commercial broadcast format.

However, some of the same problems that plagued the film industry's attempts to form radio networks were to come back to interfere with plans to put this alternative system into effect. Opposition from exhibitors and from established broadcast interests, backed by FCC protectionism and the lack of alternative distribution systems, would once again block film industry plans to move into television broadcasting in a substantial way. And again, as in the case of radio, broadcasting and film interests would establish a system of accommodations by which

Hollywood's influence over the forms and structures of broadcasting would become stronger than ever before.

Alternative Economics

The history of television begins far earlier than is generally supposed, and so does film industry involvement in the emerging medium. As early as 1927, when H. E. Alexanderson demonstrated the transmission of a few feet of film and when the initial regulatory decisions concerning television were made, through the 1930s and 1940s, the film industry was aware of, and interested in, the possibilities of television. Before 1948, the movie industry's activities in the developing medium of television had been directed at acquiring interests in equipment manufacturing firms and broadcasting stations. For example, in 1938, Paramount had purchased a 50 percent interest in the Alan B. DuMont Laboratories Company, which over the next ten years built and obtained licenses to operate two experimental television stations in New York and Washington. Through its Balaban and Katz subsidiary, Paramount applied for and August 1940 received another experimental license for W9xBK in Chicago, then applied for and was granted permission to operate commercially in October of that year. In 1947, Paramount's experimental station W6xYZ in Los Angeles received a commercial license as KTLA, Los Angeles's first television station. Thus, "with DuMont's stations in New York and Washington, Paramount had established ownership of four of the nine first TV stations in the U.S." In addition to these, as of December 1948, Paramount had applied for licenses in six other cities, usually through partly or wholly owned subsidiaries.[1]

Other applicants that lost out to Paramount for the Los Angeles television license included 20th Century-Fox's West Coast theaters subsidiary, MGM, Warner's, and Disney. Paramount's interest in DuMont may well account for its success in obtaining a license where others failed; by regulations established as far back as 1928, the FCC maintained a policy of granting experimental television priviledge only to those actively engaged in television research. However, Paramount ownership of 50 percent of DuMont was to have its negative effects as well, for both the film company and the fledgling network. Under the limitation of ownership ruling passed in 1947, no company could own more than five television stations (later expanded to include five VHF and two UHF). As of 1948, Paramount operated two stations, WBKB in Chicago and KTLA in Los Angeles, while DuMont owned and operated WABD in New York City, WTTG in Washington, D.C., and

WDTV in Pittsburgh—bringing the total owned by the two companies to the maximum five allowable. Gary Hess places at least partial blame on Paramount for the ultimate downfall of DuMont: "through the history of the DuMont network Paramount's control over the company, within the FCC's interpretation of its own regulations, affected DuMont's ability to secure a full complement of owned and operated stations. According to Dr. DuMont, the inability to secure enough stations affected the network's chances for paying its own way."[2] Hess does not explain why Paramount never affiliated its two stations with the DuMont chain, although both stations, highly successful in their markets, may have hesitated to affiliate with a less successful network.

Likewise, in a lengthy and controversial decision handed down by the FCC in December 1948, the applications of Paramount for several television station licenses were denied on grounds that Paramount already possessed, through DuMont, the full complement of permissible outlets. DuMont lobbied heavily to persuade the FCC to consider DuMont's and Paramount's holdings as separate entities, but the numerous petitions were denied conclusively in the December decision. "The fact is that Paramount can, and has exerted its authority and influence on broad questions of policy, particularly where the actions of DuMont might conflict with the interests of Paramount. . . .As long as Paramount remains the holder of all the Class B stock of the corporation and the second largest block of Class A stock. . .it does control DuMont within the contemplation of section 3.640 [of the Communications Act of 1934]."[3]

Apparently, too, relations between DuMont himself and the representatives of the Paramount Corporation were never particularly compatible, even where interests did coincide. At any rate, no permanent linkage of the two Paramount wholly owned stations with the DuMont network appears to have been contemplated, nor did Paramount attempt to provide DuMont with exclusive programming on a regular basis. This may have had to do with other plans afoot for theater and subscription television. In 1943, Paramount organized the Scophony Corporation of America, thus purchasing the U.S. rights to technology integral to the development of theater television. Among DuMont, various wholly or partially owned theater groups, and a newly formed subsidiary called Television Productions Inc., Paramount applied for a total of thirteen television licenses from 1940 to 1948, five of which became operative.[4]

But Paramount, although involved the most extensively, was not alone in its interests in television station ownership; other studios were active as well. In addition to Los Angeles, Fox applied for licenses in

New York, Boston, Kansas City, Seattle, and St. Louis. Warner Brothers tried for a Chicago license. Loew's-MGM attempted a foothold in Los Angeles, New York, Chicago, and Washington. Not all of these applications were granted, but they do indicate the active intentions of the film industry as the television age dawned. World War II brought a temporary halt to investments as government and industry devoted energies to the war effort. Although television experimentation and licensing continued, more far-reaching decisions, such as the Paramount application in 1944 for two microwave relay networks, were postponed. After 1945, applications for TV licenses increased in volume to such an extent that the FCC soon realized that existing frequency allocations were inadequate, and on September 20, 1948, declared a "freeze" on granting licenses.[5]

By 1948, the signs of television's future inroads into the theater audience had made themselves felt. In that year, television receiver manufacture quadrupled over that of 1947, and by the end of 1948, 932,318 homes in 36 cities possessed TV sets served by 52 broadcasting stations in 29 cities. Paul Raibourne, vice president in charge of television activities at Paramount, estimated that "motion picture going decreases 20% to 30% when television receivers come into the family."[6] In the movie business, the ongoing divestiture of exhibition from production created by the 1947 Paramount decrees was in the process of splitting the industry into opposing camps. On the one hand stood the producers, with film libraries and production facilities soon to be put to television use, who yet lacked their former control over all-important theater receipts and distribution assurances. On the other hand, on somewhat shakier ground, stood the theater owners, with income directly imperiled by the home screen, and bitterly opposed to any method of distribution that might bypass the box office.

Indeed, the concerted opposition of theater and broadcast interests to the idea of subscription television would effectively lead to its slow death a few years later. But in 1948, these lines had not yet been clearly drawn. Divestiture proceedings were not complete. Theater owners, noting the drop in attendance caused by major news and sports events carried by network television, grasped at the concept of large-screen, exclusive theater television. The production companies, having invested in the technology behind the process, were willing to push its development because it represented no real threat to film production.

Theater Television

Although television projection systems had been demonstrated as early as 1935, not until 1941, when RCA unveiled its new 15-by-20-foot screen, did installation in a few test theaters begin. Paramount, as part owner of Scophony, one of the originators of the large-screen process, was the first to place equipment in selected Balaban and Katz theaters. But not until April of 1948 did theater television reach Paramount's Times Square Theater, providing viewers with the first of what would prove to be theater television's greatest box-office successes—heavyweight championship fights. That year's attractions on Paramount's big screen included the Joe Louis–Jersey Joe Walcott bout, political conventions in Philadelphia, and highlights of inauguration festivities.[7]

Two methods of producing large-screen television existed throughout the five brief years of theater television's life. The direct projection method pioneered by RCA received the television transmission and by means of lenses projected it onto the screen. This is sometimes referred to as the "instantaneous projection" method because it avoids the brief delay between reception and projection necessitated by its rival system. The film intermediary method made use of fast-process film developing to receive a broadcast signal, transfer it to film in less than a minute, then project the film in the normal way. Paramount was the primary backer of the film intermediary system, which had been developed by its affiliate Scophony. In 1951, at the height of theater television success, Paramount's system used 35mm film, created a 15-by-20-foot picture, and cost $25,000 to install. Another film intermediary system produced by General Precision Laboratories (one of 20th Century-Fox's largest stockholders) used 16mm film and listed for $33,000 per theater.[8]

The RCA direct-view equipment provided a 16-by-20-foot picture, with the projector placed sixty-two feet in front of the screen, for $15,800. General Precision Laboratories slightly undersold RCA with its own direct projection system at $15,600. By far the most sophisticated version, however, promised to emerge from the Swiss "Eidophor" technology, the rights to which had been purchased in 1949 by 20th Century-Fox. This system, also direct projection, used carbon arc lights to receive and project color pictures. However, Eidophor remained at the testing stage throughout the 1951–52 height of theater television excitement; by 1953, when Eidophor was finally declared ready for commercial production, changes in the film and television industries, FCC denial of spectrum space to offset heavy telephone company charges, plus the emergence of magnetic recording technology had already rendered it obsolete.[9]

But in 1951, enthusiasm for theater television was still on the rise. Only 33 percent of American homes as yet possessed television sets. The FCC freeze on spectrum allocation had created a temporary lull in the spread of television to many markets. Television programming had not yet hit full stride, nor had sufficient advertising been drawn to the new medium to enable it to out-bid competitors for major sports and other events. The major studios still withheld their film libraries from the air for similar reasons. In the words of Barney Balaban, president of Paramount Pictures, "television can have Paramount product when it can pay for it."[10] This situation was to come about rather quickly, as history shows. However, in 1951 the movie industry retained tight control of the film product, had yet to experience major loss of audience directly attributable to television, and only sought a way to turn the television phenomenon to its own immediate benefit. Theater television proved essentially a stopgap measure despite supporters' vehement protestations to the contrary. This unwitting short-sightedness contributed heavily to the rapid closing of theaters across the country that would mark the 1950s.

By the end of 1952, more than a hundred theaters across the country had installed, or were in the process of installing, theater television. RCA dominated the market, with 75 percent of all theaters using its system. A Theater Television Network had been formed to provide major sports, public affairs, and entertainment events to participating movie houses. In 1951, it broadcast President Truman's State of the Union address as a public service, and managed to obtain exclusive rights to a series of major boxing matches as well as a number of college athletic events through the National College Athletic Association. The network lost money that year, although success was predicted as the number of affiliates grew.[11]

The year 1952 brought new heights of theater television success, with the telecast of the Jersey Joe Walcott–Rocky Marciano fight drawing a record audience to fifty participating theaters in thirty cities, producing a combined gross of more than $400,000. A live broadcast of *Carmen* from the Metropolitan Opera House made cultural news, but proved less successful financially. The first nonentertainment use of theater television, a Brooklyn clothing company's purchase of time on the network for a seventeen-city sales convention, also occurred in 1952. This particular use was to increase for awhile, then be overtaken by closed-circuit television systems.

But by the end of 1953, the tide had shifted to the point that the *Film Daily Yearbook* could report that "In contrast to the rapid growth of the TV station and syndication fields, theater television made a relatively poor showing. The high hopes held by the proponents of theater television that 1953 would be a year of wide-spread expansions failed to materialize." This change was brought about by a number of interrelated developments: in the film industry itself, in the broadcasting situation, and most important in the regulatory action—or inaction—of the FCC.[12]

Problems and Decisions

As in the days of the film companies' forays into radio broadcasting, the most immediate and pressing problem faced by theater television's proponents was transmission. In order to drive costs-per-unit down, a critical mass of theaters must be strung together as a network, able to receive a live event broadcast from a central point. In 1952, only two methods of transmission were available to exhibitors: the broadcast spectrum under FCC jurisdiction and the coaxial cables and local loops owned by AT&T. The first applications of theater television used intercity links provided by the telephone company, which were costly to lease and insufficient in many ways for video transmission. In the words of S. H. Fabian, chairman of the National Exhibitors Television Committee: "Everyone knows by now . . . that our present intercity facilities, using at best a four megacycle channel, do not serve the purpose of a quality picture on our large screens. If theater television is ever to develop its full potentialities, it must have the use of broader television frequencies."[13] Theater owners also found the costs of AT&T links prohibitive, prompting them in 1948 to request an FCC hearing on the telephone company's coaxial rates. Their petition was denied.

The answer seemed to lie in the allocation of part of the underutilized UHF spectrum to the theater networks, to be known as the "movie band." Petitions to the FCC for ten to twelve channels began in 1949. The FCC hearings on the matter began in October 1952 and continued into the spring of 1953. In June, the request for special frequencies was denied, and the theaters were directed to make use of frequencies allotted for common-carrier services. But the FCC allowed the movie companies an out: "The Commission said that if the present common carriers cannot supply the motion picture industry with 'the service they desire' the industry is free to organize its own company. If present facilities prove inadequate, it added, the theater television backers may again ask for extra frequencies." This is a rather odd decision, which would have had the effect of simply beginning the process anew had not interest in theater television declined rapidly. As of January 1954, no movie company had filed for common-carrier service.[14]

The fact was that the fast growth of home television had overtaken the need for theater exhibition. The lifting of the freeze on frequency allocation in mid-1952 boosted television growth tremendously. By the end of 1953, 334 stations were operating commercially in the United

States, with 178 more applications pending. Almost twenty-four-million homes received network television. In addition, the size of the home screen had increased dramatically since its introduction. The former nine-inch screen had given way to the seventeen-inch, then to the twenty-one-inch. Color television standards had finally been established, and it soon would appear in thousands of homes. In the meantime, the only theater television system capable of color reception, the Eidophor, remained in the laboratory. The development of magnetic tape promised to remove the necessity of live transmission permanently and to render film transfer systems obsolete.

These developments intensified changes already taking place in the motion picture industry. The B picture rapidly faded away as production for television increased and studios turned to technologies designed to emphasize those advantages clearly possessed by film over television. Industry attention focussed on CinemaScope and other wide-screen techniques, as well as three-dimensional pictures. Theater owners, many of whom had just a few months before laid out $16,000 or more for theater television, were forced to invest still more in wide-screen and 3-D equipment. Eidophor was a case in point. According to *Business Week*, "Eidophor, 20th Century-Fox's revolutionary color theater televsion system, which was believed in many quarters to be the key that would open the door to a bright new era for theater TV, remained on the shelf as 20th Fox turned all its attention an energy to the development and use of Cinemascope."[15]

The divorce of production and exhibition interests engendered by the 1947 Paramount decision was nearly complete. As the smoke cleared, production companies turned to a development designed to appeal more directly to their new circumstances: subscription television. Formerly, proponents of theater television and subscription television had pointed to a mutuality of interests, claiming that the two ideas could be best used in tandem. In 1949, Eugene MacDonald of Zenith, creator of the Phonevision subscription system, predicted that "Theater television plus Phonevision will present a compensating plus value for theater owners. The day is coming when many great national events...will be presented by Phonevision. This will mean that nobody can get a free ride for the price of a beer in the corner saloon, since these events will not be available on free television. Consequently, theaters presenting this entertainment by large-scale projection will reap a rich box-office reward."[16]

Will Baltin, of the Television Broadcasters Association, drew another kind of connection: "If a screen extravaganza is playing at the local community's Palace or Rivoli Theater and a person with a television set is not disposed to want to leave his fireside, it should be possible for him to dial the theater, 'purchase' his ticket by telephone, plug in on the 'coin box' channel and see the same movie at home." A similar plan proposed area saturation booking of a current release, with the local movie theater acting as ticket agent for the simultaneous pay broadcast of the same feature.[17]

Had the FCC in 1953 allocated the frequencies requested by the movie industry for theater networking, it is indeed possible that such a tie-in may have occurred. Certainly the existence of dedicated frequencies would have made the development of over-the-air subscription television much more feasible. Indeed, had the "movie band" been permitted to establish itself in the critical period from 1950 to 1955, it is hard to imagine that today's television-film-cable industry configuration would exist in its present form, plus perhaps providing a vital use for the still uninhabited UHF frequency range. However, the FCC, with an unerring eye for the maintenance of the status quo, rejected this vision, and the cable era slowly straggled in.

As the gulf between production and exhibition interests widened, and as enthusiasm for theater television waned, theater participation in the subscription television plan was dropped and the "free TV versus fee TV" battle moved to the fore. It is here that the movie industry made its most serious play for control over its role in television broadcasting, and here that it suffered its most resounding defeat.

Subscription Television

The main thrust of subsription television in the 1950s stemmed from the efforts of three competing systems: Paramount Picture's Telemeter, Zenith's Phonevision, and the Skiatron Corporation's Subscribervision. Throughout the history of these companies' efforts, however, a small outside voice is occasionally heard: that of the nascent cable industry. Indeed, Hollywood came closer to the cable industry in the 1950s than ever again until the 1980s. Had the movie industry only realized the full potential in the wires it proposed stringing from transmitter to home, the shape of the cable industry today might have been altered substantially.

The Telemeter system, 50 percent owned by Paramount, used a full broadcast channel to transmit its scrambled signal. To select a film, the home viewer consulted a printed guide, then dropped the appropriate coins into a box on top of his or her television set at the time of the broadcast. This caused the picture to be unscrambled, and the selection to be recorded on tape. A later version included an audio "barker" channel that could be switched on at any time, giving details of the upcoming schedule, prices, and other information. The tape and the coins were collected once a month by a Telemeter representative. In 1955, Telemeter announced a further development: the capacity to transmit two separate images on one channel. Image A, unscrambled and available to any television owner, consisted of a trailer or advertisement for Image B, the program currently available. By the time Paramount opened leasing of the Telemeter system in 1957, a full service using either wires or broadcast transmission with a three- channel capacity had been tested: in effect, a three-channel cable system.[18]

Zenith's system, Phonevision, as its name suggests, originally used telephone wires to unscramble its broadcast signal. Billing was done through the telephone company, which kept records of programs watched. Zenith filed with the FCC for permission to test its system in Chicago as early as 1949, and was granted approval in February 1950 for a ninety-day test. However, perhaps over uncertainty over cooperation of the telephone company in all localities, Zenith in 1954 adapted its system to coin box or punch card operation.[19]

Skiatron, run by Matthew Fox, an entrepreneur with a long history of involvement with the movie industry, developed with the help of IBM a system called Subscribervision based on a punch card to be inserted in the ubiquitous television-top black box. The viewer would consult a printed catalog, set a few dials or levers to the appropriate numbers on top of the box, then insert his or her card to be punched. The cards were mailed back into the Subscribervision Company for subsequent billing, in exchange for which another month's listings and card would arrive. Testing of Skiatron's system was accomplished through the close cooperation of RKO Teleradio Inc., owner of WOR-TV New York, which began experimental broadcasting of the scrambled signal in 1950. One particularly successful application was an early version of telemedicine, bringing doctors from several New York hospitals a special medical program.

Trials of these systems began in 1950 with the Zenith Chicago test, but it was Paramount's 1953 trial installation of Telemeter in seventy-five Palm Springs, California, homes that awoke the first wave of opposition across the country. Palm Springs represented an ideal market for such a test; its affluent population was cut off by a mountain range from normal television reception. A side benefit to those whose homes were wired by Telemeter was, in effect, community antenna television because Paramount erected a mountaintop relay station from which cables were laid to subscribers' homes.[20]

Amid much fanfare, Telemeter's first commercial program went out to the Palm Springs homes on the afternoon of Saturday, November

28, and consisted of the USC-Notre Dame football game at a charge of $1, followed by the Paramount film *Forever Female* for $1.35. Thereafter, subscribers would be offered the same film then playing at the local theater, along with selected sports events and an occasional "live show." Home showtime began approximately fifteen minutes after the theater's, allowing the film to be "bicycled" to the transmitting facility. Home viewers paid slightly more than the theater admission per film—as well as an installation charge ranging from $150 to $450, depending upon the home's location; a "wire charge" of $60 per year; an additional $21.75 for the Telemeter box; and a minimum of $3 per month in movie fees. The strategy of showing the film then current at the downtown theater was intended to allow Paramount to maximize potential benefit from exhibition. Results from Zenith's Chicago test had shown that 82 percent of the pictures viewed at home by subscribers were ones that they had missed on first theatrical run. Telemeter thus hoped to attract that "seven eighths of the U.S. population which never sees the average picture," while avoiding alienating theater owners through providing competing attractions.[21]

Although the owner of Palm Springs' downtown theater participated in the test in return for stock options in the new company, opposition soon arose from another quarter: the owner of the local Sun Air Drive In, who charged Paramount-Telemeter with violation of the recent antitrust divestiture decree. The prosecuting attorney argued that Paramount "is in the position of making the pictures, distributing the pictures, and is also acting as an exhibitor in the guise of Telemeter Corporation—the very thing that the Government fought for over 10 years to prevent in the distribution of motion pictures."[22]

Telemeter closed down operations soon after this, claiming that the trial had been a success, with total subscribers growing from 75 to 2,500 and revenues per household per month averaging $10 or three times the national average theater expenditure. In 1957, Paramount opened the Telemeter system for leasing, subject to FCC approval. However, when another test seemed appropriate, in 1960, it was Telemeter's Canadian subsidiary in Toronto that launched the service, just outside the reach of the antitrust controversy.[23]

In the meantime, a fourth party had entered the field rather quietly under the auspices of a southwestern theater chain, Video Independent Theaters Company (VITC), in conjunction with Southwestern Bell Telephone. That fourth party, Jerrold Electronics, had begun building and operating community antenna systems in rural areas some time earlier. The choice of the small town of Bartlesville, Oklahoma (population 19,228) for a test of pay television seemed to be a good one.

Bartlesville was the headquarters of the Phillips Petroleum Corporation, provided an isolated, fairly affluent population, and all the local theaters were owned by the Video Independent chain, thus eliminating one potential source of local opposition. Jerrold built the scrambling, transmitting, and decoding equipment for the test, which operated more like a modern pay cable system than a pay-per-view service, charging subscribers a flat monthy fee for three channels. Southwestern Bell provided and retained ownership of all wires linking stations and homes, leasing them to VITC for the substantial fee of $1,000 per month. Subscribers received regular network programs as well as a special channel of first-run movies, movie reruns, musical performances, weather, and news.[24]

By this time the "free versus fee TV" controversy raged in full force. The Bartlesville trial received vast quantities of press coverage, amid statements that "pay television has officially arrived." However, its arrival was swiftly followed by its demise in Bartlesville. Although initial results were encouraging, the novelty soon wore off. Despite a reduction in the monthly fee from $9.50 to $4.95, the total number of subscribers never exceeded nine hundred, compared to a planned three thousand by the end of the first nine months. Henry Griffing, president of VITC, attributed the failure of the Bartlesville service to three factors: first, that pole and line rental fees levied were much too high and Southwestern Bell refused to reduce them; second, that $9.50 per month represented three to three and one-half times the national average household theater expenditure, and as such was too costly; and third, that in his opinion the flat monthly fee was a mistake, forcing customers to pay for much which they did not care to watch. Griffing predicted that pay-per-view could resolve some of these difficulties. Service in Bartlesville was terminated on June 6, 1958, beginning a two-year hiatus in pay television experimentation.[25]

The Opposition

Paramount-Telemeter's 1953 Palm Springs trial marks the beginning of a tidal wave of publicity against pay television that soon swept the country, backed by a powerful coalition of private interests. The two main opposing groups consisted, on the one hand, of broadcasters whose defense of free television equated pay TV with the death of democratic choice, and on the other hand, of theater owners who feared further box-office erosion. The merger of United Paramount Theaters (the divested exhibition unit of Paramount Pictures) with the ABC television network in 1953 cemented the broadcaster-theater owner alliance against pay TV. Together they succeeded in enlisting the support of labor unions, women's groups, and religious interests throughout the country, to the extent that in 1964, a statewide referendum on whether to allow pay television to operate in California was defeated by a 2–1 margin.[26]

As one observer of this public relations battle pointed out, never has the broadcasting industry expressed so much concern for the entertainment and cultural edification of the lower-income segment of the population than in its impassioned defense of "free television." On June 6, 1955, David Sarnoff of RCA issued a statement calling for the American public to defend the current broadcasting system against the threat of pay television. He enumerated the many ways in which the quality of network programming would suffer if pay television, with its presumably greater ability to buy the top-quality products, were to siphon off the best movies, sports events, and talent. A situation would be created, fretted Sarnoff, in which those who could afford to pay for such programs would receive them at the expense of those who depended on free television for their cultural experiences.[27]

The combined forces of broadcasting and theater interests launched a well-funded and well-organized lobbying campaign that sent out pamphlets, flyers, and "fact sheets" to public interest groups across the country. One such packet, targeted specifically at women's groups, was issued by CBS in 1956. Entitled "Television in a Free World," it contained two pamphlets for distribution to group members; one pamphlet, entitled "You Be the Judge," came in the form of a blue-wrapped legal document, the other, "The World in Your Sitting Room," enumerated the benefits of free television programming. The packet also contained six "fact sheets" aimed at the woman who would address the group on this subject. Their headings indicate the broadcasters' arguments: "Free Television and Its Accomplishments," "Television Stimulates Interest in Education and Culture," "Television Provides Wide Range for Pulpit," "In Public Affairs," "The Importance of Television Advertising," and "Free Television IS Free Choice." The case for advertising—the aspect of free television most often attacked by pay television forces—was stated thus: "Television advertising, which has proven amazing effectiveness, helps make possible efficient distribution. This, in turn, results in making more goods available to more people at lower cost and keeps production and employment at high levels...that's why Free Television Advertising is an important factor in our free economy."[28]

Such an appeal succeeded in turning a fairly specialized regulatory problem into an emotionally charged national issue. Most directly, it exacerbated the initial hesitancy of the FCC to assume jurisdiction of the phenomenon of pay television and ended in embroiling Congress in the regulatory muddle. The subsequent suspicion and delay were to have strongly adverse effects on the development of pay television, particularly over-the-air pay television, in this country.

Regulation and Delay

Although technical problems and management inexperience contributed to the disappointing results of the early pay television experiment, the Federal Communications Commission must also take a large share of the responsibility. Through a tendency to protect established broadcast interests against innovative competition, indecision over asserting or denying jurisdiction, and what is surely one of the worst examples of regulatory foot-dragging in its history, the FCC managed to delay, avert, and handicap testing and operation of these systems to the point that the companies involved could no longer support their efforts.

The first petition to test pay television in this country was filed by Zenith on August 3, 1949, requesting a ninety-day period in which "to conduct an experiment regarding Phonevision." On December 8, 1949, the FCC designated the question for congressional hearing, stating that "It is not clear whether 'phonevision' should be classified as a broadcast service, a common carrier service, or other type of communication service, or what frequencies, if any, are appropriate for use in the proposed experimental operations or for use in a general commercial 'phonevision' service, in the event that such services were to be authorized on a regular basis."[29]

Zenith, wishing to avoid delay, filed a petition for reconsideration, and on February 5, 1950, was granted permission to test its system under a set of rigid restrictions without a public hearing. In his dissenting statement FCC Commissioner Edward M. Webster objected to even this limited go-ahead, stating that the Zenith test "may prove to be the first step toward the introduction of subscription television and radio into the American system of broadcasting. I do not believe that even the first step toward such a momentous change in the American system of broadcasting should be taken without the benefit of a public hearing." However, Commissioner Frieda Hennock, in a separate statement, put forth the ideas that led to the granting of permission to Zenith:

> Our duty under Section 303(g) of the Communications Act is to "encourage" new developments. I feel that we should help the proponents of any system which offers any promise of improvement in our broadcasting scheme, and the proponents of this plan suggest it as a method for the possible improvement of television programming. I believe that the holding

of hearings at this time would be an impeding rather than an encouraging move with little to be gained on behalf of the public, and therefore vote to grant the authorization.[30]

Here, the two sides of the debate that was ultimately to restrict the growth of subscription television become apparent. The first, the FCC's perception of its duty to protect the existing system of "free" broadcasting from outside innovation or competition, testifies to the success of the broadcasting industry in equating the public interest with its own. Leonard Goldenson, president of American Broadcasting/Paramount Theaters, Inc., perhaps expressed this view the best: "The FCC was created by Congress to develop and foster our American system of free radio and free television—not to authorize or encourage another system which could lead to its destruction, without first ascertaining the will of Congress." However, a close examination of the intentions and circumstances surrounding the writing of the Communications Act make this statement somewhat debatable. The opposing argument, the idea that the FCC should act as guardian of the public interest to encourage innovative use of the broadcast spectrum, would soon fall victim to intensive lobbying.[31]

In fact, the broadcasting industry found itself struggling to maintain two contradictory arguments: 1) that the American public did not want subscription television and would not pay for it, and 2) that should subscription television be allowed to get its foot in the door, it would soon dominate the field and ruin free television. The networks' success in integrating these conflicting ideas into a persuasive argument against pay television translates into a similar predicament for the FCC. As Vincent Mosco asks in his examination of the federal regulatory process, "If one assumes that there is little demand for a service...then why control it? On the other hand, if one foresees a large demand, then should not the potential value of promoting the service be given some consideration?"[32]

At any rate, Zenith succeeded in obtaining a limited permission to run a test in Hartford, Connecticut, but at the end of the ninety-day period was reprimanded by the FCC for failing to cease operations and warned that a public hearing would still be necessary. Because of the Zenith precedent, however, special temporary authorization to test the Skiatron Subscribervision system over WOR-TV was granted to RKO General Teleradio Inc. on November 22, 1950. In February, 1952, Zenith filed a petition for another test, this time nationwide, on the grounds that only such a large-scale test would allow the public to make a decision about pay television. The petition was stalled in committee, and in November 1954, Zenith brought its 1952 petition up to date. In the meantime, Paramount's Palm Springs tests whipped up public controversy, but because the trial made use of cable rather than airspace, no FCC permission was required.[33]

On February 11, 1955, the House Committee on Interstate and Foreign Commerce instituted a rule-making hearing and threw the matter open to the public. Between June and September of 1955, more than twenty-five thousand parties filed comments for and against pay television, and in April and July 1956, public hearings were held. During this period, no less than five separate bills were introduced in Congress to ban over-the-air pay television completely.[34]

On May 23, 1957, the committee, having determined that more field testing must be done before the question could be decided, requested further information from the companies involved on potential trials. Finally, on October 17, the FCC set a March 1, 1958, filing date for applications for demonstration of pay television systems under carefully controlled conditions. Trials were to be limited to major markets receiving at least four broadcast stations; no more than three markets were to be tested by any one company; and the trials were to be limited to a three-year period after which further hearings would be held. Paramount, Zenith, and Skiatron all filed applications. However, in 1958, Senate hearings on the matter were held as part of a larger inquiry into television industry practices, and as a result the FCC was asked to delay over-the-air trials until further clarification of the matter.

The FCC again authorized controlled three-year tests in 1960, and this time only Zenith, of the original three players, filed an application for a trial in Hartford, Connecticut. Opposition to Zenith's plans, led by such groups as the Connecticut Committee Against Pay Television, Stanley-Warner Management Company, Loew's Inc., Connecticut Theaters, the Manchester Drive-In Theater Corporation, and the Outdoors Theater Corporation, resulted in further delay, but in 1962 the U.S. Court of Appeals upheld the FCC's authority to permit trial operations. On June 29, 1962, after thirteen years of waiting, Zenith's Hartford trial began.[35]

RKO General (a company formed when General Tire and Rubber's broadcasting division bought RKO Studios from Howard Hughes in 1951) again demonstrated its interest in pay television by working with Zenith in Hartford. RKO purchased WHCT, a UHF station, over which it broadcast two to three hours of scrambled pay television each evening. The rest of the broadcast day was devoted to regular free daytime television. The service began with three hundred paying subscribers and ended with five thousand in 1965. Results of the test showed that middle-to-lower-income families predominated in the subscriber base, contrary to most predictions; pay television viewing comprised 5 percent of total television viewing per week. The price of the programs ranged from 25 cents to $3, with an average price of $1.25. However, by 1965, Zenith concluded that a minimum of twenty thousand subscribers was needed to achieve a profit for its pay television operation, and on March 10, 1965, it petitioned the FCC to authorize nationwide unrestricted pay television. This began the second wave of pay television controversy, leading eventually to the liberalization of cable regulation and the growth in cable-based pay television that began in the late seventies.[36]

By 1965, however, the field of players in the subscription television battle had changed, with only Zenith remaining in place. Skiatron's stock fraud scandal in 1959 occasioned its downfall. Changes in the movie industry eliminated Paramount: by 1962, most of Hollywood's library of post-1948 films had been sold to network televison, thus eliminating the program base for a movie-dominated subscription service. In the meantime, in order to compete with the allure of the home screen, Hollywood had invested substantial amounts in such new technologies as wide-screen and three-dimensional movies—all highly unsuitable for television exhibition. In addition, the 1961–62 season finally brought the turnaround in admissions for which the movie industry had waited. Lulled by profits, under the demand of production for television, and faced with unrelenting opposition from the anti-pay coalition and federal regulators, Hollywood's interest in pay television declined. Not until 1978, with the reemergence of pay television on a large scale, would the film industry again turn its attention to the scenes of its prior defeat—only to meet defeat again.

Intent and Outcome

It is indeed possible that had over-the-air pay television been allowed to experiment commercially in the 1950s it may not have succeeded, either because of technical problems, as strongly asserted by Milton Shapp of Jerrold Electronics in the 1958 hearings, or because of public indifference. But the history of its slow strangulation by federal regulation points to another scenario altogether. Two major factors seem to have worked against the early development of pay television: 1) the perceived mandate of the FCC to protect the existing broadcast system, under heavy lobbying from allied broadcasting and theater exhibition interests; and 2) attention directed by the Justice Department to the film industry, which stood to benefit from or even to control pay television, that consolidated opposition from theater owners and TV interests and created suspicion in the public's mind.

Protected Television

The first point, the FCC's perceived mission to protect and foster the "American system" of broadcasting as it had come to exist, rests in the stated purpose of that regulatory body as far back as the Radio Act of 1927, to "generally encourage the large and more effective use of radio in the public interest." Mosco has traced the evolution of this simple and vaguely defined purpose over the years into a strong perceived mandate to protect existing broadcasting interests and structures from outside interference. The arguments put forth by pay television opponents amply demonstrate this thinking. Noll, Peck, and MacGowan and LeDuc have conducted extensive analyses of the FCC's resistance to technological innovation, its protection of over-the-air broadcasting's economic base, and its tendency to suppress uses of the medium that reveal weak spots in its structure instead of using that innovation to correct the weaknesses. The stifling of cable TV growth, argues LeDuc, resulted from the actions of a federal commission that "contended that it was simply exercising its existing power to protect broadcast service from injury arising from unfair competitive use of its programming. While the FCC held no mandate to insure the economic prosperity of its stations, it did have the right to intercede . . . when the end result of destructive competition among communicators would be to 'damage service to an extent inconsistent with public interest.'"[37]

Or, in the words of *Business Week* regarding the ownership and control of television stations by the film industry, "Would movie men, if permitted to own television stations, hold back their TV operations in favor of their theaters? To the FCC, this was an important question. It doesn't care what happens to theaters, but it is directed by law to foster the development of radio and television." This chapter has demonstrated how the FCC's public interest mandate, adopted and reinterpreted by broadcast television and theater interests, became equated in the public mind with the unchallengable supremacy of the "free TV" system. Chapter 6 will trace the slow dissolution of this idea as cable and pay television technology, finally freed from its regulatory shackles, became a thriving and vital industry.[38]

Shadows from the Past

The second relevant factor in the suppression of over-the-air subscription TV, the film industry's embroilment in antitrust litigation and general poor reputation with the public, is closely related to first factor; one of the arguments made for the stifling of the pay TV "threat" was its potential for "control of television" by the movie industry. Gomery reports that in 1945, "The FCC, fresh from ending its assault on the radio industry, worried that Hollywood might try to extend its monopolistic practices into the fledgling television industry . . . FCC Chairman Paul Porter warned a meeting of executives from all the major movie companies, presided over by Will Hays, that they should not count on extensive ownership and control in the postwar television industry."[39]

This warning became reality in December of 1945, when the Justice Department moved against Paramount Pictures and its wholly owned subsidiary Television Productions Inc. along with General Precision Instrument Corporation (a large stockholder in 20th Century-Fox Film Corp.), and the Scophony Corporations of America and Great Britain, charging that the companies had conspired to halt the growth of large-screen technology through control of Scophony patents—in other words, that the movie companies were attempting to suppress a "television" technology in order to protect their own theatrical interests. Paramount was ordered to divest itself of its Scophony stock in 1949. In 1951, as a complication of the ongoing divestiture process, Balaban and Katz, now part of United Paramount Theaters, applied for a transfer of the license of WBKB Chicago to CBS. The determination of this transfer brought many other factors into question, including the issue of whether a corporation convicted of antitrust violations could hold a broadcasting license at all under sections 310(b) and 319(b) of the Communications Act of 1934.[40]

The FCC ordered on August 1 that a hearing be held to obtain more information on the past antitrust violations of Paramount and its subsidiaries, in order to determine whether or not granting a license to broadcast would serve the "public interest, convenience, and necessity" in light of the companies' "character and conduct." In an attached dissenting opinion, Commissioner Robert F. Jones asserted that this investigation was not wide enough in scope, and that the larger question to be addressed concerned, among other issues, the legality of "the concurrent operation of radio facilities and theater television in the same areas . . . the effect of owning and operating moving picture theaters and radio facilities in particular areas and on a regional and national scale . . . [and] the monopolistic effect in the entertainment field of the operation of theater television and broadcast facilities."[41]

However, outright rulings in this latter area were never made, although we have seen the effects of regulatory delay tactics on the viability of a film industry presence in television. On the more narrowly defined antitrust issue, the commission ruled in 1952 that "in general, we shall not, in passing upon applications of persons who are already licensees, consider any activities involving possible anti-trust violation which occurred more than three years before the filing of said application." Again Commissioner Jones dissented. Two weeks later, the issue was declared not resolved satisfactorily and was opened for presentation of new evidence. The process dragged on slowly until the film companies lost their place in the post-freeze rush for stations and in the developing battles over pay television.[42]

On the general public side, it is interesting to note how low public opinion of the movie industry had fallen. An article in the February 1949 issue of *Consumer Reports* expressed concern over film industry inroads into television, specifically the proposed (but never consummated) ABC-20th Century-Fox merger, the DuMont-Paramount alliance, and the Paramount-20th-Scophony suit. The article objected to movie industry involvement in television on five counts: 1) the "simple bigness" of the film companies, with fears of placing both film and television production "in single hands"; 2) the "known record" of monopolistic practices the film industry had used to "oppress independent theater owners and restrict the flow of pictures to the consumer"; 3) the possible attempt by Hollywood to "slow up the development" of television; 4) the "deterioration of public service standards" that would result if Hollywood, as opposed to radio corporations, took over television programming; and 5) the FCC's inadequacy to tackle regulation of a large industry such as motion pictures. This image of Hollywood as the big bad menace and the radio giants behind television as benificent public servants has much to do with the success of anti-pay drives across the country. It would take a further three decades of network oligopoly before public opinion, aided by the slow infiltration of cable, began to sway once again in the direction of the film industry.[43]

Another perceptive participant in the controversy provided a scenario to the Senate Committee in 1958 that sums up the results of the early pay television debacle. Solomon Sagall was president of Teleglobe Pay Television Systems Inc., a new entrant into the field whose system combined an unscrambled broadcast video channel with a separate audio line and speaker. He had founded and served as president of Scophony Ltd. of London, where he originated the technology for scrambling signals, the basis of the whole idea of pay TV. Sagall predicted that "The demand for pay television is bound to develop and grow in strength. Block pay television over the air, and within a few years the country will be covered with a vast cable network." The FCC apparently took Sagall's advice.[44]

Whether the current situation better serves the public interest is a highly debatable point. Certainly one odd result of the early pay television debate is that the networks and theater interests, in attacking an immediate threat, paved the road for cable penetration that now poses, arguably, an even greater threat and one much more likely to succeed. The growth of cable and film industry involvement in it will be the subject of chapter 7. However, the controversy over pay TV represents only one aspect of the relationship between Hollywood and broadcasting during the period. Although the efforts of the film industry to apply the direct economic exchange of the box office to the advertiser-supported business of broadcasting ended in defeat, as did its earlier efforts with radio broadcasting, a far more lasting change was occurring in the broadcasting business itself. Hollywood assumed a role in this changing configuration: from a medium controlled by the interests of its sponsors through the intermediary of the advertising agency, network television became a medium controlled and programmed by the major networks, with Hollywood as its primary supplier.

NOTES

1. Gary N. Hess, "An Historical Study of the DuMont Television Network," (Ph.D. diss., Northwestern University, 1960; repr. New York: Arno Press, 1979); Douglas Gomery, "Failed Opportunities: The Integration of the U.S. Motion Picture and Television Industries," *Quarterly Review of Film Studies* (Summer 1984), pp. 219–27; Federal Communications Commission, "In Re: Applications...," *Reports,* December 15, 1948, pp. 300–18.

2. FCC, December 15, 1948; Hess, "An Historical Study," p. 89.

3. Hess, "An Historical Study"; FCC, December 15, 1948, pp. 317–18.

4. FCC, December 15, 1948, p. 304.

5. *Business Week,* March 24, 1945; FCC, December 15, 1948; Robert Pepper, "The Pre-Freeze TV Stations," in *American Broadcasting: A Sourcebook on the History of Radio and Television,* ed. Lawrence W. Lichty and Malachi C. Topping (New York: Hastings House, 1975), pp. 139–55.

6. William L. Snyder, "Television in 1948," *Film Daily Yearbook 1949* (New York: Film Daily Publications, 1949), p. 807.

7. Snyder, "Television in 1948," p. 807; Gomery, "Failed Opportunities," p. 222.

8. Larry Goodman, "Television," *Film Daily Yearbook 1953* (New York: Film Daily Publications, 1953), pp. 139–43; John Evans McCoy and Harry P. Warner, "Theater Television: What, How, and When," *International Projectionist,* November 1949. 9. Goodman, "Television," p. 143; Gomery, "Failed Opportunities," p. 214.

10. Goodman, "Television," p. 139.

11. Ibid., pp. 141–42; *Business Week,* May 12, 1951, pp. 44–47.

12. "TV Sitting Pretty," *Film Daily Yearbook 1954* (New York: Film Daily Publications, 1954), p. 691.

13. S. H. Fabian, "Theater TV: A Year of Growth," *Film Daily Yearbook 1953* (New York: Film Daily Publications, 1953), p. 703; Gomery, "Failed Opportunities," p. 223.

14. Donald La Badie, "TV's Threshold Year," *Film Daily Yearbook 1955* (New York: Film Daily Publications, 1955), p. 680; *New York Times,* June 25, 1953, p. 26.

15. "TV Sitting Pretty," p. 691; *Business Week,* May 12, 1951, pp. 44–47.

16. E. F. McDonald, Jr., "The Movies' Role in Phonevision," *Film Daily Yearbook 1949,* p. 813.

17. Will Baltin, "The Exhibitor's Place in Television," *Film Daily Yearbook 1950* (New York: Film Daily Publications, 1950), p. 841; *Variety,* December 2, 1953, p. 7; *Business Week,* August 9, 1952, p. 48.

18. Goodman, "Television," p. 141; *Business Week,* August 9, 1952, p. 46; *New York Times,* June 10, 1955, p. 1; June 19, 1955, sec. 10, p. 11.

19. Federal Communications Commission, "In Re Petition of Zenith Radio Corporation . . . for Authority to Conduct 'Phonevision' Tests on a Limited Commercial Basis," *Reports,* February 8, 1950, pp. 459–72.

20. *Business Week,* June 21, 1952, p. 58.

21. *Variety,* December 2, 1953, p. 1; May 6, 1953, p. 25; *New York Times,* June 19, 1955, sec. 10, p. 11; September 14, 1953, p. 24.

22. *New York Times,* January 8, 1954, p. 18.

23. *New York Times,* February 12, 1955, p. 21; March 12, 1961; *Billboard,* March 30, 1957, p. 31.

24. Loudon S. Wainwright, "First Customers for Pay Television," *Life,* October 14, 1957, p. 63.

25. *New York Times,* April 9, 1960.

26. David H. Ostroff, "A History of STV, Inc. and the 1964 California Vote Against Pay Television," *Journal of Broadcasting* 27 (Winter 1983):371–86.

27. *New York Times,* June 19, 1955, sec. 2, p. 11; Wainwright, "First Customers," p. 63; *New York Times,* June 6, 1955, p. 49.

28. CBS Publicity Package, "Television in a Free World" (New York: CBS Inc., 1956).

29. Federal Communications Commission, "In the Matter of the Amendment of Part 3 of the Commission's rules and Regulations . . . to Provide for Subscription Television Service," *Reports,* December 8, 1949; Federal Communications Commission, "Comments of the Joint Committee on Toll Television, Marcus Cohn, Cohn and Marks," *Reports,* June 6, 1955; FCC, "In Re Petition of Zenith Radio Corp. . . .," *Reports,* February 8, 1950, pp. 459–72.

30. Federal Communications Commission, February 8, 1950, pp. 462, 471.

31. U.S. Senate, Committee on Interstate and Foreign Commerce, "Statement of Leonard Goldenson," *Hearings on Pay Television* (Washington, D.C.: Government Printing Office, 1958), p. 371.

32. Vincent Mosco, *Broadcasting in the United States; Innovative Challenge and Organizational Control* (New York: Ablex Publishing, 1979), p. 118.

33. *New York Times,* April 16, 1954, p. 28; April 24, p. 24. Although the FCC attempted to halt the spread of cable television where it directly threatened the interests of local broadcasters, broad authority to include cable in its jurisdiction did not come until the February 16, 1962, Carter Mountain decision (32FCC459, "In Re Carter Mountain Transmission Corp," February 14, 1962).

34. Mosco, *Broadcasting*; Committee on Interstate and Foreign Commerce, *Report on Network Broadcasting* (Washington, D.C.: Government Printing Office, 1958), pp. 35-36. Bills introduced in the House were the Celler Bill (H.R. 586); the Beamer Bill (H.R. 9629); the Madden Bill (H.R. 9690); the Powell Bill (H.R. 9706); and the Bailey Bill (H.R. 9898).

35. FCC, "In the matter of Request by RKO Phonevision Co. . . ," *Reports,* May 21, 1965, pp. 2441-445.

36. FCC, May 21, 1965; *New York Times,* March 10, 1965.

37. Mosco, *Broadcasting,* p. 225; Don R. LeDuc, *Cable Television and the FCC: A Crisis in Media Control* (Philadelphia: Temple University Press, 1973), p. 10; R. G. Noll, M. J. Peck, and J. J. MacGowan, *Economic Aspects of Television Regulation* (Washington, D.C.: Brookings Institution, 1973).

38. *Business Week,* November 22, 1952, p. 34.

39. Gomery, "Failed Opportunities," p. 225; *Broadcasting,* April 9, 1945, p. 4.

40. *Business Week,* December 22, 1945, pp. 90-93; Michael Conant, *Antitrust in the Motion Picture Industry* (Berkeley: University of California Press, 1960), pp. 84-107.

41. Federal Communications Commission, "Balaban and Katz Corp. . .for Consent to Assignment of License of WBKB-TV. . .," *Reports,* August 27, 1951, pp. 645, 646, 648.

42. Federal Communications Commission, "Memorandum Opinion and Order: In Matter of Applications of Paramount Pictures. . .," *Reports,* August 1, 1952, pp. 992-95; "Memorandum Opinion," *Reports,* August 13, 1952.

43. "TV: The Hollywood Invasion," *Consumer Reports,* February 1949, pp. 86-87.

44. U.S. Senate, *Hearings,* 1958, pp. 356-57.

6

Television

THE VAULT OF HOLLYWOOD

If there is any degradation of television service... it will come
from TV film producers and the vault of Hollywood.

—David M. Sarnoff, as quoted in
Business Week, November 24, 1956.

Beginning in the mid 1950s, a major shift took place in the economic
structure of network financing. In the early 1950s the system of program
origination developed by radio was carried over into television, and
programming power still rested with the commercial sponsors, usually
via an advertising agency. Networks sold time slots for programs, in
blocks ranging from fifteen minutes to an hour or more, to commercial
sponsors, who then originated and controlled programming according
to their own interests and desires. By 1957, a new network structure
had developed that reduced the power of the advertisers and agencies
and placed increased control of production with the networks. This
structure, known as the "magazine" format, borrowed from print
advertising the concept of a varied but unified text interspersed with
advertisements from different sources. The "Today" show on NBC
was one of the first magazine format shows; produced and controlled
by the network, time slots were sold in much the same way as magazine
advertisements. This structure ostensibly responded to the ever-increasing cost of television production by mandating joint sponsorship
of programs.

The result of the magazine format was consolidation of scheduling
decisions with the networks, leading to a new capacity to structure
television's entire flow, from programs to commercials to network an-

nouncements, free from the decisions of those whose concerns about one particular product or company might interfere with the interests of the network as a commercial institution. Rather than risk allowing one or two maverick sponsors to disrupt the most economically and psychologically useful types of programming with offbeat shows, the networks could arrange the television flow into the configurations most beneficial to the placement and effectiveness of commercial messages. The commodified medium of broadcasting extended its reach and scope from a program-to-program frame to a unified whole. As network control over the flow of broadcasting strengthened, power shifted from advertising agency radio directors to network programming executives.

The shift accounts for the difficulty many television analysts and critics have experienced in pinpointing the site of creative responsibility in television production. Although its reputation as "the producer's medium" reflects the mediating role—between network and creative talent—the producer plays in the program origination process, the success or failure of a producer's idea—and sometimes even its inception—depends on the collision of advertiser and schedule interests determined by the network programming department. However, the purpose and function of television programming remains identical to that of radio: the "deferral of consummation" of the broadcast economic exchange results in a heavily commodified aesthetic form by which the viewer is led not into a work for consideration of its thematic and ideological elements, but away from the text itself into those commercial frames that surround it.

Although the framing of American television is done at the level of the total network schedule rather than by the individual program, some of the same marking and transitional devices heard on "Lux" are still used. The narrator, however, has been replaced by a combination of visual cues—from a simple fade to black to startling computer-generated logos—and by television stars who emerge from their programs and characters to promote themselves and the network (chapter 4). Viewer sophistication and habituation to the modes of the television address have eliminated the need for explicit transitional markings and necessitated far more subtle means of persuasion and attention-getting in commercial messages than the heavy-handed "Lux" pitches. The careful integration of the commercial message within the program material more often takes the shape of repetition or reworking of program elements—stars, story lines and situations, or key visual elements—to link the programs with the more numerous and diversified commercials that interrupt them regularly.[1]

The indirect economics of television work to make communication indirect as well; the source and motivation of signification is as removed from direct view as the economic transaction that ultimately pays for "free television" is removed from the TV viewing situation. If the rhetorical—and ideological—correlation to this deferred significatory exchange of the broadcast discourse is the concept of free TV, its counterpart in the accepted aesthetics of television is the concept of the live broadcast. The concept of live or real-time simultaneous transmission of events as they happened played a large role in the development of radio broadcasting, not only in terms of the development of networks, but also as a federally defined mandate for broadcasting, which tended to operate against the film industry. As television broadcasting developed into a multimillion-dollar business, the rhetoric of "live" and the economic and regulatory structure derived from this concept increasingly obscured the slow infiltration of film-based, Hollywood-produced programming that occurred between 1955 and 1965. The networks continued to derive regulatory and public image benefit from the live aesthetic while quietly shifting to the commercial benefits of filmed programming.

The Meaning of "Live"

A point of pride for the major radio networks had always been that through their superior land lines and access to local loops, the bulk of scheduled network programming could indeed be carried live. Although transcriptions, as they were called, of live news and entertainment events were sometimes made by the receiving stations so that time-shifting could be done, the bulk of network shows were produced either in New York or Los Angeles and piped out to affiliated stations at the time of performance in the studios. Part of the reason for this has to do with the inferior quality of early transcriptions; until 1948, when tape became available, recordings were made on sixteen-inch wax discs that held ten minutes on each side, and a certain blur and scratchiness made transcriptions readily distinguishable from live broadcasts. On the other hand, technology was not the only reason. Erik Barnouw refers to the "stigma" attached to the idea of recorded programs and reports that many in the radio business viewed the broadcast of recordings as "a sort of hoax...on the listener." As late as 1942, CBS's production of "An American in England," written, produced, and directed by Edward R. Murrow and Norman Corwin, had to be performed each day at 4:00 A.M. London time because the official network taboo on recorded programs prohibited the broadcast of anything recorded, with the exception of sound effects. Why, as the necessary technology developed and radio's needs became more complex, did this self-imposed policy continue?[2]

First, it must be remembered that the one major advantage over all other would-be radio networks possessed first by NBC, then CBS and ABC, was their priority access to cross-country land lines and local wires as negotiated with AT&T in the 1920s (chapter 2). Even if other fledgling networks could afford to pay transmission costs—calculated to the advantage of heavy users, one of the factors contributing to the DuMont Network's downfall[3]—a limited amount of coaxial cable transmission space was made available by the telephone company, and established customers had priority. Without connection to either of the major networks, a local nonaffiliated station found itself having to produce all its programs locally—and they inevitably suffered by comparison to the expensive, big-name productions sent out by the networks—or attempting to buy recorded shows on a syndicated basis, very few of which existed until the late 1940s. Thus it behooved the networks to promote the superior value of live over recorded programming because the ability to transmit live belonged to the networks and to the networks alone.

Part of this emphasis, too, stems from radio broadcasting's public-service mandates: the FRC had ruled in 1928 that the broadcast of events or entertainment unavailable to the public in any other form would be considered of greater public service than those able to be received or experienced via another medium, thus the ban on phonograph records. By network reasoning, it then seems to have followed that any type of entertainment, whether manufactured specifically for the medium or not, would count as public service if it were transmitted live—a neat twist of logic most beneficial to major network market position. The FCC maintained a standing requirement that any recorded or transcribed material be identified as such before and after broadcast. In 1946, this restriction was lifted slightly to allow unidentified transcriptions of one minute or less, "Hence," according to *Newsweek*, "as every listener knows, the flood of transcribed commercials."[4]

The second factor behind the persistence of live broadcasting concerns the fact that by the late 1930s, the major networks or their parent or associated companies controlled two related areas of importance. By 1941, NBC and CBS between them had gained control over the bulk of recording technology patents and manufacturing processes, as well as ownership of the largest talent agencies, or artists' bureaus, that kept under contract much of the talent that supplied both networks and the phonograph record industry. Although, under threat of federal investigation, both CBS and RCA (NBC) sold their talent bureaus in the early 1940s, they retained interests in the music recording industry. Testimony before the Senate in 1958 claimed that the networks and their parent companies accounted for more than one-third of annual record sales. CBS's Columbia Records and RCA Victor, plus each company's many subsidiary labels, remained the two largest in the United States through the 1960s. Moreover, among them, the two networks and their affiliates owned more than 94 percent of Broadcast Music, Inc., the music rights organization formed in 1941 to rival ASCAP. Thus the major networks were in a good position to control the accessibility and use of recordings over the air. Because recorded or transcribed programs could be distributed by mail and thus bypass the wire system, they represented a strong potential threat to the supremacy of the live networks.[5]

Transcriptions

Some recorded program syndication did exist in the early days of broadcasting, however, among the first of which was one of radio's most popular shows, "Amos 'n' Andy," created by Freeman Gosden and Charles Correll out of Chicago on WMAQ in 1926.[6] At that time only ten minutes long, the show was recorded on two wax discs of five minutes' length each and distributed by the *Chicago Daily News,* which owned WMAQ. By 1928, the early syndicated network, or "chainless chain," aired on thirty stations across the country. In 1929, NBC purchased WMAQ, put "Amos 'n' Andy" on network broadcast, and the transcriptions stopped. Another station, WXYZ in Detroit, syndicated two popular shows in the 1930s, the "Green Hornet" and the "Lone Ranger." These shows aired live over the Michigan Radio Network and later over hookups to WOR in New York City and WGN in Chicago, laying the groundwork for the Mutual Broadcasting System. The transcribed program traveled by mail or other land transportation to other unconnected stations.[7]

The ice-breaking development that finally made the increased use of transcriptions on radio possible came from a combination of new technology and an extraordinarily influential entertainment figure. During the war, a German company called AMPEX had invented a method of recording on magnetic tape, a process that produced recordings superior in quality to the wax or aluminum discs used by American companies. The rights to this technology passed to American interests as part of the spoils of war. One of the first applications of the process took place within the film industry, where its use in recording film sound was quickly recognized. Radio and film star Bing Crosby, at the time working in Hollywood, recognized that this new magnetic tape was a superior means of producing his highly popular radio shows. Tape could be recorded at leisure and edited afterward, thus avoiding the split-second timing, last-minute rush, and public bloopers common to live radio production. In 1946 Crosby formed Bing Crosby Enterprises, Inc. to improve and market the technology. Crosby's popularity was such that, according to *Newsweek,* "the American public will take him any way it can get him. . . . And this time he also proved to radio executives that the listening public would take transcriptions." Crosby's show aired as a transcription over the ABC network, setting a continuing precedent there.[8]

By 1948, both ABC and Mutual regularly employed transcriptions over the air, and a network devoted entirely to transcribed programming had sprung up; the Keystone Broadcasting System served approximately 325 small stations "beyond Metropolitan America" with recorded shows. Because transcriptions were sold according to the stations' market size, they could be relatively inexpensive for advertisers in smaller markets. An advertiser could buy a fifteen-minute show, made "open-ended" so that the sponsor's commercial announcements could be inserted, and place it on one or more local radio stations for a transcription rental of as little as $3.75. The same program might cost a New York City advertiser $500 or more. One of transcription recording's pioneers also figures highly in the later field of independent television production: Frederick W. Ziv. One of the largest transcription producers, Ziv grossed $10 million in 1947 on 24 shows that aired on 850 stations across the country.[9]

Most of these programs were considered of inferior quality, however—lowbrow shows compared to those broadcast live via the major networks. With a few exceptions like Crosby, both NBC and CBS continued to broadcast live, an emphasis that carried over to the early years of television. It should be remembered that in the absence of videotape, the only alternative to live production would have been theatrical film. Filmed programs for television did not begin to appear until 1949; since broadcasters would have had to purchase such material from film producers, it is no wonder that the earliest television shows remained exclusively live. A look at the network TV schedule for the 1945-49 period shows a heavy emphasis on the transmission of real-life events that had entertainment or information value in themselves, such as sports, political, and cultural events, with live sports coverage dominating prime-time hours: "Gillette Calvacade of Sports" on NBC;

"Wrestling from Jamaica Arena" on DuMont; "Sports from Madison Square Garden" on CBS; and "Wrestling from Washington" on ABC.

Simulcasting

Television's yawning schedule soon required more programming than real life could provide. One way to capitalize on radio program investment while bringing out material new to TV was to borrow from radio; to accomplish this yet disrupt radio schedules as little as possible (since television remained in the experimental stage with radio bringing in the profits), the networks turned to simulcasting.

Simulcasting involved broadcasting a show performed live before TV cameras while simultaneously sending radio affiliates its audio portion. Two of the earliest successful simulcast shows were "Arthur Godfrey's Talent Scouts" over CBS, first airing December 6, 1948, and NBC's "The Voice of Firestone," which went to simulcast in September 1949. Both belonged to the musical variety format, a type of program, like game shows, far easier to adapt to simultaneous audio presentation than were dramatic shows. By 1947, a few variety, game, and dramatic shows begin to appear on television, often drawn directly from network radio. In January 1948, DuMont carried over Ted Mack's "The Original Amateur Hour," itself the continuation of the "Major Bowes' Amateur Hour," which had descended from one of the first shows on radio— "Roxy and His Gang." In May, NBC transferred its "Texaco Star Theater" to television, and shortly thereafter used it to create television's first real star, "Mr. Television," Milton Berle.[10]

Simulcasting continued to be common until 1951–52 because until that time television reception remained limited to only a small proportion of the country. The FCC's freeze on station construction in 1948 left some communities with no broadcasting facilities available until its lifting in 1952; AT&T completed its first coaxial cable to the West Coast in 1951, allowing network operations to begin. And until both of these conditions were resolved, television could not afford original programming of radio quality because advertisers perferred radio's larger reach and spread.[11]

The practice of simulcasting, although understandable enough from the perspective of networks eager to draw upon their radio expertise to fill in the yawning schedule gaps of early television, hastened the demise of radio as a vital public medium. The popular scenario presents the decline of radio as inevitable because the arrival of a new and superior medium automatically seduced the public from their radio sets and rendered them indifferent to the "obsolete" technology overnight.

In fact, as with the silent film, many people, public as well as critics, felt that there should be room for both radio and television entertainment. Families without access to television, or that preferred the imaginative experience of radio-listening, kept ratings for radio high until 1952, when the FCC lifted its freeze on television expansion. Suddenly, almost everyone could receive at least one TV signal.

Those still outside TV's reach or loyal to radio soon noticed a strange phenomenon: instead of shows developed specifically for radio, they were now listening to the simulcast soundtracks of shows produced for television, complete with inexplicable silences as some purely visual business occurred, or a sudden burst of laughter at something invisible to the radio audience. As the attention of the radio industry turned to television set production, with its superiority over the saturated radio set market, radio became expendable. Instead of nurturing two distinct forms of entertainment, the radio program on the one hand and forms unique to television on the other, the networks and advertisers followed a conscious policy of sacrificing radio in favor of television.

One reason for this was economic: in order to finance the technological development of television, manufacturers drew on radio profits to feed TV. According to Peter Fornatale and Joshua Mills, "In June, 1946, the NBC research department prepared a memo that predicted an $8 million loss from television in the next four years. It suggested that radio should be made to finance that loss and estimated that $3.5 million in federal taxes could be saved by applying radio profits to television development costs. In effect, the radio networks would be made to finance their own burial."[12]

With the radio set market saturated, and with the development of television resting in the hands of the same companies that controlled radio programming, development of the television receiver market logically took precedence over maintaining network radio's popularity. If that immense success could be transferred, whole or in part, to television schedules, so much the better for receiver sales. Simulcasting the audio portion of a live television show, or kinescoping the show and playing back the recorded audio portion on radio at a later time, allowed the transition to television to occur with a minimum of new investment—and ensured the decline of the radio audience.

Thus early television schedules were dominated by live sports and variety and quiz shows, often carried over from radio, with a few anthology and serial dramatic programs beginning to emerge in 1949. In the case of the serials, simulcasting of the sound tracks over radio continued in many cases into the mid-1950s, but the dramatic anthology programs proved to be less suitable for simultaneous broadcast, and serious writers and directors began to address themselves to the unique demands of visual drama. Among the first and best of these were "Studio One," "The Philco Television Playhouse," and the "Masterpiece Playhouse."

The years from 1950 to 1955 are often referred to as the golden age of television, based largely on the rise of live dramatic anthologies. Writers such as Rod Serling, Paddy Chayefsky, Mac Hyman, and Reginald Rose contributed to the development of this new dramatic form, the first—and some would say the only—original contribution of the television medium to dramatic art. The live anthology drama brought something new to viewers across the country, as writers and directors struggled to impart a unique aesthetic to the unexplored medium. Written especially for television, performed live, addressing a variety of subjects and bringing new talent before the public, these shows have been eulogized by historians, and many mourn the passing of the golden age. However, many of the programs proved controversial at the time, and ratings for most were never as high as for other contemporaneous, less highbrow offerings such as "I Love Lucy," "Dragnet," and "Cheyenne."

So the period 1949 to 1955, while remembered primarily as the golden age of live dramatic production, also marked the appearance of the first independent producers of filmed programming who pioneered a form of entertainment soon to become standard TV fare. However, the gradual establishment of filmed programming as the backbone of television generated considerable debate in the early 1950s. The reasons for this have to do with the economics of the networks versus those of independent stations. In the structural tension between the stations and the networks, a disjuncture was created that Hollywood forces, denied major entry into television on the level of ownership and networks, moved to fill. Once again the economics, technology, and discursive structures of the film industry would slowly filter into the medium of television, first in opposition to, and later in cooperation with, the major television networks, creating the hybrid form of the commercial television program.[13]

If live TV necessitated access to a complex and expensive wired transmission route, television films, or "telefilms" (filmed series or serials) could be distributed alone or in packages to the hundreds of stations across the country not tied by a web of telephone lines to the major networks. These nonaffiliated stations, dependent entirely on local production and local advertising revenues, grasped eagerly at a source of polished, big-name programming of a quality outside the scope of local production. But even network affiliates began to see advantages in syndicated filmed programming; advertising revenues generated by sale of spots on these shows reverted 100 percent to the station, as opposed to the 30–70 split common to network practice. Some stations went so far as to preempt network feed to air their own purchased programming, especially where advertising spots on a syndicated filmed show proved easier to sell to local merchants than on less popular network shows.

Thus filmed programming represented a very real alternative to network dependence. Once again, Hollywood's potential for supplying an alternative type of programming threatened the networks' domination of television economics. This would become particularly true in the case of theatrical films on TV. But the networks themselves took steps to control this threat.[14]

The Kines

The networks' own use of kinescopes from 1948 to 1952 finally broke through the stigma attached to non-live programming and made possible the eventual domination of network schedules by prerecorded shows. Kinescopes, or *tele-transcriptions* as the DuMont Network called them, played a brief but important role in the history of television. A kinescope consisted of a live television show filmed as it came over the receiver. Thus, even although film was employed, these kinescoped programs were essentially live shows, conceived and produced from a "live" aesthetic, with film serving merely as an intermediary transmission device providing a source of programming not dependent on wires.

Freedom from the restriction of wire hookups proved especially useful to the networks before 1952, when coast-to-coast cables were still being built. In order to "reserve" affiliates in unwired sections of the country, the networks needed a way to provide programming to these stations until live hookups could be established. Filmed programs, or live shows kinescoped by the networks, could then be sent to unconnected affiliates by mail, or even by plane for those events, such as the 1948 inauguration of Harry S. Truman, that had an urgent appeal. Most shows appeared "within a week or two" of their live broadcast. In 1949, networks distributed more than two thousand hours of kinescoped programs to outlying affiliate stations, even though kinescope equipment was expensive and the quality of the image fairly poor. But unwired stations needed TV programming, advertisers wanted additional markets, and the networks needed to supply unique and high quality programming in order to win over future wired affiliates before a rival program producer could entice them away. DuMont began to bill itself as a "teletranscription network" because its small number of wired affiliates made outlying penetration even more important. Thus, by breaking down their own restrictions against the use of recorded programs, the major networks paved the way for the gradual disappearance of unwieldy and unpredictable live programming and the rapid rise in the use of film, as Hollywood wedged a toe in the door by means of syndicated film series.[15]

Vault 1: Production for Television

Among the first syndicated shows to be marketed to TV stations was a serial originally made for theatrical release: "Hopalong Cassidy," distributed by its star and producer William Boyd in 1949. The television version of another popular film serial, "The Lone Ranger" (based on a radio series) appeared in the same year. The popularity of these shows among younger audiences sparked a host of Western imitations, including in 1950 "The Gene Autry Show." Autry later produced a string of popular horse operas, including the "Range Rider" series, "Death Valley Days," "Annie Oakley," and "Rocky Jordan." Roy Rogers went on the air over NBC in 1951. Bing Crosby Enterprises carried its transcription activity into filmed series, producing "Fireside Theatre" for Procter and Gamble in 1950; "Fireside Theater"'s originator, Gordon Levoy of Republic Pictures, continued to collect syndication revenues as production shifted to Hal Roach Studios in 1951.[16]

Much of the impetus behind the switch to filmed programming seems to have come from advertising agencies and their clients. Seeking more control over production and distribution of a sponsored show than the demands of live network television would permit, advertising executives began to look to sponsorship of syndicated series to showcase client products. Filmed programming worked especially well for medium-to-smaller size companies that could not afford the costs of sponsoring an entire show over a major network. But soon the "anti-fluff insurance" offered by film began to attract major advertisers for prime-time shows. As early as 1951, the success of filmed programs was such that "there were many who even deprecated the need for a coast to coast coaxial cable on which to transmit live programs. Except for such special events as news and sports, the film industry, said its exponents, could—and would—fill in the broadcast day."[17]

It must be remembered that until around 1955, sponsors still controlled the programming process. Typically, a filmed television program would be produced by an independent production house, usually in consultation with an agency that might have one or two specific sponsors in mind, but sometimes the program was made purely on speculation. The series could then be sold—either as an idea, a pilot and one or two episodes, or as a full season's worth of shows—to an advertiser, usually via an agency that would then place the show according to the advertiser's needs. A large firm with a need to advertise nationally would usually negotiate with a major network for national network distribution. A smaller advertiser, or one whose products were only distributed in certain regions of the country, might instead opt for syndicated sale, negotiating with individual stations in the desired areas for air time.[18]

An alternative route, which began to grow in popularity on the network level after 1953 when the networks introduced the "magazine," or spot advertisement concept, commonly occurred in the case of independent stations from 1950 on: the station itself would buy the show from the syndicator-producer and find local sponsors to pay for adjacent advertising spots. Series that had already aired on the major networks often did quite well on second-run syndication—as is still very much the case for independent stations.

By 1953, *Business Week* reported that even on national networks the proportion of total programming originating on film was 22 percent; 78 percent of the shows continued live.[19] On nonaffiliated stations the proportion of filmed programming was far higher; in April 1955, KTTV, an independent Los Angeles station, reported that 62 percent of its programming originated on film. Although nearly all of this filmed programming was produced in Hollywood, most of it came from small independent producers, who often leased studio space from the major studios. Not until 1953 would the major studios venture into production for TV, for reasons that had more to do with the development of competing technologies than with short-sightedness, as the events related in chapter 5 demonstrate. In the meantime, some of the independent producers rose to such heights of success with filmed TV series that they later acquired major status themselves.[20]

The Rise of the "Indie" Producers

In addition to Boyd, whose sixty-six episodes of "Hopalong Cassidy" not only started a deluge of Westerns on TV but also boosted the popularity of his films in theatrical rerun, two other former Hollywood theatrical film producers struck it rich in the telefilm business. Hal Roach, Sr., shifted production from feature film to filmed TV series in 1949, placing his son Hal Roach, Jr., in charge of the company. Some of their early successes included "Fireside Theatre," "Public

Defender," "Duffy's Tavern," "Code 3," "Racket Squad," "Passport to Danger," "My Little Margie," and several "Magnavox Theater" episodes.[21]

Jerry Fairbanks, a former Hollywood theatrical-short producer, went into "telepix" production in 1947, when NBC hired him to produce films for its newscasts. Although in 1948 the network switched to Fox Movietone, Fairbanks had already developed his innovative "multicam" system, employing several cameras to shoot simultaneously from different angles rather than using the cumbersome Hollywood multiple-take system. He went on to bring episodes of "Silver Theater," the "Bigelow Theatre," and "Front Page Detective" to the air, as well as numerous specials. Desilu, with its first-place show "I Love Lucy," soon expanded into other productions and later purchased the RKO studios.[22]

One of the most successful and prolific of the "indie telepix" producers, Frederick Ziv, had already made a name for himself in the radio transcription business. "The Man Called X," "I Led Three Lives," "Cisco Kid," "Boston Blackie," and "The Falcon" were all popular Ziv productions, in many cases growing out of his transcribed radio shows and all distributed by syndication. The Ziv Company was later purchased by Universal, which had itself begun producing for TV as early as 1950. Its fifteen-minute weekly "Hollywood Flashes" and its "Moviestar Album" (1952) were both used to promote Universal films; Universal also turned out numerous filmed commercials for Lux, Chevrolet, and Pepperell, among others.

1953: Entry of the Majors

Although 1953 marks the turning point in production for television of the major Hollywood studios, most had ventured into television production in one way or another even before this date. As early as 1945, RKO produced a series of filmed commercials for the Bulova Watch Company. In 1946, in conjunction with its Pathé news subdivision, RKO announced the availability of two prospective series for TV broadcast: a quiz show called "Do You Know?" employed clips from the RKO film library, and "Ten Years Ago Today" was a clever way to make use of old RKO-Pathé newsreels. These shows were syndicated to independent stations, although "Do You Know?" did appear on CBS daytime in the 1963–64 season.[23]

Paramount used its wholly owned independent television station KTLA to produce a package of telefilms in what Paramount called a "film network," using theater television film intermediary equipment as a kinescope device. Paramount Video Transcription distributed the programs, among them "Time for Beany," "Frosty Frolics," "Yer Ole Buddy," "The Spade Cooley Show," and "Sandy Dreams." United Artists began distributing TV programs produced by independents in 1948. In 1950, Columbia formed a subsidiary, Screen Gems, to launch itself into television production, beginning with filmed commercials and a series of musical shorts. In 1951, Screen Gems contracted with the Ford Motor Company to produce a series of thirty-nine half-hour films for the "Ford Theatre" on NBC. Screen Gems retained syndication rights after a first and second run controlled by Ford. Ronald Reagan and Nancy Davis made their first joint appearance on one episode of this series in 1953.[24]

And it is the year 1953 that marks the decisive shift of the major film studios into television production. Although many factors contributed to their timing—the lifting of the freeze in 1952, the resultant shift of advertising money to television, the drop in theater revenues and the final throes of divestiture—one other event of that year had a large impact on the studios' actions: the merger of United Paramount Theaters with the American Broadcasting Company.

During 1952, rumors had circulated regarding several studios' interest in merging with the third-place network; both Warners and 20th Century-Fox discussed plans between 1948 and 1951, while MGM reportedly pursued Mutual. But the only plan to emerge successfully from the fray was that of United Paramount Theaters, the spun-off theater subsidiary of the Paramount Corporation. In the same decision that allowed KTLA to be transferred to Paramount Pictures—over much heated opposition in the FCC itself and in Congress—the FCC ruled that antitrust activities occurring more than three years before the proposed mergers and transfers would not invalidate the film company's bids. Permission to merge was granted on February 9, 1953. Leonard Goldensen, head of UPT, became president of American Broadcasting-Paramount Theaters, with Edward Noble, former ABC president, as chairman of the board.[25]

By the end of 1954, Disney, Warners, and MGM had all agreed to produce shows for broadcast on the ABC-PT network. Although the decision to attach the studio name to productions was a culmination of many emerging trends, it seems significant that the two ice-breaking decisions—Disney's and Warners'—came not long after the ABC-PT merger, and that both produced shows for that network. For the network's part, the signing of Disney to exclusive contract has been called by *Fortune* magazine "the turning point in ABC's fortunes."[26]

Disney's plans came to light in a June 1953 letter to stockholders announcing that the studio would begin producing television films in

"about a year."[27] Negotiations continued through 1953, and in April
of 1954 Disney and ABC-PT entered into a contract—to be called
"Disneyland"—for the 1954–55 season, in exchange for which ABC-
PT agreed to invest in Disney's fledgling amusement park in Anaheim,
California. In the 1955–56 season the "Mickey Mouse Club" appeared,
followed by "Zorro" in the 1956–57 season. Not only did these shows
provide high-quality programming for ABC, but they also proved to
have excellent publicity value for both Disney theatrical films and the
Disneyland park.[28]

Disney's shows did not come cheap, however. Disney licensed the
"Disneyland" show to ABC exclusively, at $2 million for twenty-six
one-hour shows. Each show cost $65,000 to produce, and line charges
added an additional $70,000 per broadcast. Thus the total cost per
episode of the Disney show amounted to $135,000—far too high for
one sponsor to assume. Finally, ABC split sponsorship between American Motors, the American Dairy Association, and Derby Foods.
Although skeptics doubted that such an expensive show could last, by
1957 *Fortune* reported that "It . . . was an immediate and smashing
success. In many one and two station markets where ABC programs
had seldom been seen, CBS and NBC primary affiliates found ways
to schedule *Disneyland* in excellent viewing periods. It quickly moved
up among the ten top-rated television programs, a heady experience
for a network whose own affiliates had been doubtful of its ability to
come up with really popular programs."[29] Efforts to find sponsors for
the similarly expensive five-times weekly "Mickey Mouse Club" proved
more difficult, but the show remained on the air, becoming a central
childhood memory for millions of Americans.

Although rumors about Warners' eventual involvement with television had circulated since 1951, no formal announcement appeared
until April 1955, when Warners declared that, under its own name, it
would produce three rotating TV series based on three popular Warner
Brothers films: "Casablanca," "King's Row," and "Cheyenne." These
would appear as alternating segments of a larger show, "Warner
Brothers Presents," which would also feature Hollywood news and clips
and other promotion of upcoming Warner Brothers attractions. Although only "Cheyenne" continued to thrive after the first season,
becoming a long-running series in its own right, "Warner Brothers
Presents," along with "Disneyland," represents a formal attempt by
the film industry to assume production control over the previously
pervasive but scattered use of Hollywood film stars and general glamour
on television.[30]

As with radio, the aura of Hollywood served to dress up even the humblest quiz show productions. Guest appearances of known or less-known Hollywood names on panels, quiz, and discussion shows were constantly being sought by networks and TV producers, usually paying no fee to the star in question but allowing generous opportunity for publicity of any upcoming film. This practice became so widespread that in 1955 the Screen Actors Guild stepped up enforcement of its prohibition on such free appearances. Movie studios also used variety shows for film publicity; one of the most popular of the shows, Ed Sullivan's "Toast of the Town," often aired clips from new Hollywood films to enhance a guest-star turn. The annual Academy Awards presentation went on the air in 1953, at the networks' request, with a $100,000 payment going to the Academy—proof of Hollywood's established popular draw. Studios continued to contribute stars and properties to such shows as the new "Lux Video Theatre," "Calvacade of America," "Hollywood Opening Night," "Four Star Playhouse," and "Ford Theatre."[31]

In addition, as early as 1948 the film industry had begun advertising its films on television; Sam Goldwyn pioneered in the production of video "trailers" similar to those shown in movie houses but for distribution to local television by theatrical exhibitors. Many exhibitors objected to supporting the broadcast medium in this way, but others saw it as good for business. By the end of 1953, all the major studios either had on the air, or had announced plans for, their own television production, which would organize the exploitation of Hollywood properties and stars over TV. In addition to Disney and Warners, Paramount contributed its film properties and original casts to "Lux Video Theatre," and in 1954 began producing "The Colgate Comedy Hour" on NBC opposite "Toast of the Town." Featuring Dean Martin and Jerry Lewis as hosts, it provided a showcase for Paramount's "star roster, upcoming young players, properties, musical scores, and clips of pictures both in release and in the preview stage."[32] 20th Century-Fox premiered its "20th Century-Fox Hour" sponsored by General Electric, again as a film-based show, and in June of 1955, MGM announced that it had agreed to produce "The MGM Parade" over ABC, having also been wooed by both NBC and CBS for the broadcast rights.[33]

However, these self-promotion vehicles, although indicative of Hollywood's continuing interest in and recognition of the importance of television, proved to have far less effect in the long run on the television broadcasting industry—and on the film industry—than did production of the less glamourous but more profitable filmed television series with which Hollywood slowly came to dominate broadcast schedules. The studio most actively involved in this field—and the only one not to produce a self-promotion vehicle—was Columbia through its Screen Gems subsidiary. By the end of the 1955–56 season, Screen Gems was producing and distributing ten shows: "Ford Theatre," "Father Knows Best," "Rin Tin Tin," "Captain Midnight," "Damon Runyon Theatre," "Jungle Jim," "Celebrity Theater," "You Can't Take It with You," "Big Playback," and "Jet Jackson." Of these, more than half were syndicated, off-network originals.

While the big self-promotion vehicles of the other studios soon collapsed under inflated production costs (the "20th Century-Fox Hour" reportedly cost upward of $200,000 per episode), the half-hour serials made money in both first-run and syndication sales, as did 20th Century-Fox's other TV entry, "My Friend Flicka." In 1956, Columbia decided that it could afford to move into a more prestigious line of programming to promote itself and signed on with CBS to produce a few filmed plays for the prestigious "Playhouse 90" series in the 1956–57 season.[34] By the end of 1956, the proportion of network programming, mostly filmed, originating in Hollywood stood at 71 percent; "the long-postponed marriage between television and Hollywood was nearly complete."[35] However, the "marriage" was shortly to run into a particularly rocky spot over the next phase of Hollywood integration: the release of theatrical films to TV.

Vault 2: Theatrical Films on TV

Good film programming will kill the competitive and best live programming in most instances.[36]

One lesson that the ABC-PT network learned in 1954–56 was that high-quality, high-cost filmed programming promoted dependency on network structure and economics as effectively as did live TV. Instead of capitalizing on local affiliates' dependence on a network's web of wires for live shows, local stations' inability to afford big-name, Hollywood-style productions could also be used to tighten the apron strings, as "Disneyland" proved, if the producers were tied to network contracts rather than allowed to peddle their shows independently. It is no coincidence that during these same years the magazine concept appeared. Although credited to Sylvester (Pat) Weaver at NBC, who did indeed endorse the philosophy most publicly, it was ABC, writes Barnouw, that "pioneered with shared sponsorship in which each sponsor dominated a segment of a program."[37]

This practice at once opened the door to bigger, slicker production budgets, and to smaller-size companies wishing to advertise on TV. A two-tier TV production and distribution strategy began to influence Hollywood's economics: big-budget, big-name productions went to the major networks; low-budget, half-hour series were distributed to independents. This plan bears striking resemblance to the A and B movie system, with the networks playing the large first-run features and the independents receiving the low-budget and rerun productions. But with the distribution of theatrical films, several film companies took steps to see that the order was reversed.

In 1951, *Variety* estimated the value of the films in Hollywood's vaults—features, shorts, and cartoons—at nearly $250 million, counting 4,057 features and in excess of 6,000 shorts from 1935 to 1946 alone. The first films to appear, however, made many viewers doubt that assertion. Three main reasons have been given for the failure of major studio films to appear on the air before 1955: 1) the studios' desire to protect their relationship with exhibitors, who objected strongly to TV competition; 2) interest in alternative means of exhibition such as theater and subscription television; and 3) the inability or unwillingness of the networks to pay an appropriate price for quality films.[38]

Concerning the first point, some speculation existed in 1952 that one force behind the Justice Department suit against the major studios for witholding 16mm films from TV was the studios themselves in an attempt to "release their features to TV under court order to avoid a boycott by theatrical exhibitors"[39]—in other words, to protect their relations with exhibitors by allowing the Justice Department to "force" them into a practice they actually desired in the first place. The suit resulted in very little, and merely confirmed the studios' "if television wants film, let them pay for it" attitude. Until 1953, network coverage and the presence of television sets in the home were not sufficient to support high-priced programming.

The second point accounts for some studios holding back film, particularly those such as Paramount and 20th Century-Fox that were heavily involved in the competing technologies. But point three seems to have been the most salient consideration. The networks, until 1961, simply could not or would not offer the studios a very high price for films. In addition, the pre-1955 emphasis on live programming decreased network interest in paying large sums for films: if all the networks could offer was recycled Hollywood films, why should the local station buy at line-charge-inflated rates from a network when it could buy direct from a distributor? So reasoned the networks, and so also reasoned the local stations, both affiliated and independent.[40]

One of the first packages of films to air over American television came not from the networks but from independent station WPIX New

York, which in 1948 bought twenty-four major films from British film producer Alexander Korda; the productions starred such heretofore unseen-on-television actors as Vivien Leigh, Lawrence Olivier, and Charles Laughton. While the networks continued to resist the use of feature film—"All three networks, with varying degrees of firmness, have taken stands against showing features, particularly in 'prime time,'" *Business Week* reported—WPIX and other independent stations found that advertising revenues from feature film spots did very well.[41] Even network owned and operated stations bought off-network films (WCBS-NY purchased MGM's big film package in December 1956). However, between 1948 and 1955, available films tended to be British, Western, or B-quality, and they were generally minimally profitable for the distributor. Monogram, Republic, and Eagle-Lion began to release their products in 1948. Universal's United World Films subsidiary distributed more British features from J. Arthur Rank—seventy features in 1949, bringing in only $300,000 for the television rights.[42]

Monogram immediately encountered difficulties with the complicated question of residual royalty payments for materials in redistribution. When in 1950 it attempted to release 144 features made before 1946 to television, the American Federation of Musicians (AFM) objected to uncompensated use of its members' copyrighted performances and called a strike, refusing to work for Monogram until all 144 films could be rescored using the same number of musicians employed for the original, plus a payment of 5 percent of the fee for the films. Monogram also negotiated an agreement with the Screen Actors Guild whereby an actor would receive 12.5 percent of his or her original salary for films sold for less than $20,000, and 15 percent of those grossing more than $20,000. The Screen Writers Guild bargained for a similar arrangement, which became known as the "Monogram formula." Monogram finally sold a block of films to CBS in 1951, which used them on its "Film Theatre of the Air" program, an 8:00–9:00 P.M. Tuesday program feature. Earlier, in 1949, Universal had announced the intended television release of some of its own films, but the AFM provisions made the cost of release unmanageable. Republic also announced that it would release some of its Westerns, only to be stopped by the films' stars, Roy Rogers and Gene Autry. While this case lingered in the courts, Republic did manage to release another group by syndication to local stations.[43]

In 1951, the Screen Actors Guild drew up a new contract with the major studios, which contained a clause relinquishing rights to royalties on television distribution of films made before August 1948; in return for that concession the Guild indicated that it expected to negotiate a royalty and residual system for post-1948 products. Each producer who wished to distribute post-1948 films to televison was required to negotiate additional payments to the actors involved; failure to do so meant that the studio would run the risk of losing its contract with the Guild altogether, and with it all further use of Guild actors. The Screen Directors Guild (SDG) and the Writers Guild of America adopted the same provision later that year. However, not until the 1953–54 season did pre-1948 film from any of the major studios find its way to TV, with the bulk of pre-1948 films released between 1955 and 1957. Paramount withheld its films until 1958, as its hopes for subscription TV slowly fizzled. But theatrical films made an appearance on TV screens very early in television's history, beginning with British films in 1948 and continuing through 1952 with those from some of the smaller studios.[44]

David O. Selznick broke the A picture barrier in 1951 with the release of twelve of his films, again on a syndicated basis, for which he realized more than $2 million. Also in 1951, Quality Films, a distributor with rights to a package of twenty-six top-grade, although outdated, Hollywood features, sold them to the DuMont Network for $1.8 million. A factor in the television distribution of films that stirred up a lot of controversy at the time but accomplished very little was the Justice Department's 1952 suit against the studios for the television release of 16mm prints. Claiming that a conspiracy existed among the major studios to restrain trade, the Justice Department attempted to force the studios to release their product to broadcasters in the 16mm format that the studios used for release to the military, nonprofit groups, and schools. Theater owners were vociferous in their objections to the idea, with producers taking a more noncommittal stance. Opinion generally ran against the government, with many groups feeling that enforced sale of product, without regard to price or profit, represented a clear abuse of government controls. The studios took the case to the U.S. District Court, where in December 1955 a decision was finally reached protecting the film companies from Justice Department intervention.[45]

By 1955, the issue had become largely irrelevant; television's increasing penetration and revenues made 1955 the turning point in major theatrical film release to TV. Paramount began the trend with the sale of thirty films produced by the small independent Pine-Thomas Studios for $52,000 each, or $1.15 million for the package. ABC purchased thirty-five films from J. Arthur Rank at $45,700 each, which it used on its new prime-time "Famous Film Festival" on Sunday nights and the "Afternoon Film Festival" on weekday afternoons.

David O. Selznick sold ten more films to National Telefilm Assciates, Inc., a newly formed television distribution company, for more than $100,000 each in first-run and syndication rights.[46]

Networks versus Stations: Film Marketing Strategies

Several different methods of release to television were employed by the studios, resulting in different distribution routes and avenues of profit. Television and syndication rights to films (meaning both first and subsequent television runs) could be sold outright as a package, for one flat price resulting in that producer receiving a large outright payment taxed as capital gain and all additional revenues going to the distributor. A variation on this method gave the distributor sole rights for a set period, for example, seven years, in return for a minimum guaranteed price paid over time to the producer. Profits in excess of that set amount went to the distributor, with full rights reverting to the studio after the fixed period of time. A third method employed by the studios was to set up their own television distribution division, thus retaining all network and syndication profits, or, in a variation, to sell rights to an existing independent distributor in return for shares in that company, usually resulting in a partial cash payment, a certain number of shares, and a portion of subsequent profits. Several studios used this latter method to extend their broadcast interests substantially, using valuable film libraries as leverage.[47]

But the strategy employed by all of these television film distributors, whether independent or studio owned, was to sell not to networks but to individual stations. There are two reasons for this strategy. First, the networks took a stand against theatrical films on TV, claiming they could pay no more than $20,000 per picture at that time and instead preferred to concentrate on their own distinctive programming. Second, even should the networks change their policy, the distributors' method of "blanketing hundreds of markets around the country" with a film package, according to *Business Week*, "yields the distributors prices that the networks couldn't afford to meet, even although the price per station may be modest."[48]

The event that sparked the flow of major studio features to television was Howard Hughes's sale of the RKO film library to General Tire and Rubber Company's General Teleradio subsidiary in July 1955. General Teleradio owned and operated several radio and television stations, among them WOR-TV New York City, an independent TV station over which General Teleradio planned to broadcast RKO feature films for its "Million Dollar Movie" series.[49] However, rather than syndicate the films itself, General Teleradio in December 1955 sold the entire library of 740 features and 1,100 shorts to the C&C Television Corporation, a subsidiary of the C&C Super Corporation headed by Matthew Fox. General Teleradio reserved the right to exclusive exhibition in markets where it operated a television station, as well as first-run network rights to 150 of RKO's top films.[50]

All other rights became the property of C&C. Fox, a former film industry executive whose interest in the Skiatron subscription TV system explains part of his interest in the RKO library, devised an original plan for distribution of the RKO package. Leaving aside about 20 percent of the entire package—those films less than three years old at the time of the sale—Fox sold the remaining features on an exclusive basis to one station in each broadcast market, enabling that station to maintain its own film library—in many cases with enough films to last for six years or more under normal scheduling practices. The stations would possess these rights in perpetuity, excluding syndication rights.[51]

As of July 1, 1956, fifty-eight stations across the country had bought the C&C package, bringing Fox's profits to $25 million by 1957. Many were sold on a barter basis whereby national or local advertisers lined up by C&C would be allowed spots on each showing of the film, for a reduction of the cash purchase price for the station. C&C Super Corporation, the parent company, used some of the spots for its own products, including SuperCoola and other canned soft drinks, as well as hand power tools. Fox advertised its movie packages nationally as well around the theme "See a Movie Tonight at Home." Among the films in this package to be shown on television for the first time were *The Hunchback of Notre Dame* and *Citizen Kane*. Although many of these films had been made after the 1948 SAG cutoff point, the Guild was powerless to enforce its provisions because neither C&C nor General Teleradio was involved in film production and therefore not vulnerable to reprisals. Foreign television distribution would later prove profitable as well.[52]

Fox's actions sparked the rapid release of most other major studios' pre-1948 backlogs. Republic, likewise immune to Guild actions, released post-1948s as well. In January 1956, Columbia began releasing features through its Screen Gems subsidiary, thus relinquishing no rights to a third party. By 1957, Columbia had released 195 features in three different packages, bringing in an estimated $9,700,000 to the studio. Screen Gems later purchased the bulk of the Universal library in 1957 for a seven-year contract. In March 1956, Warners sold its library of 750 features, 100 silents, and 1,500 shorts to Associated Artists Productions, a film distributor later purchased by United Artists, for $21 million. 20th Century-Fox, in what proved to be a more astute move, announced in May 1956 that it would sell exclusive rights to 52 pictures and television rights to another 390 to National Telefilm Associates. NTA already owned the Paramount library of shorts through purchase of the UM&M company in 1955, as well as some Universal films. In return, besides a purchase agreement for $32 million, Fox retained reversion rights after seven to ten years, royalties above a fixed gross, and a 50 percent interest in NTA itself. In October 1956, NTA began operation of the NTA Film Network, providing packages of feature films to 110 affiliated stations across the country. Each station would receive one package of seventy-eight films a year for five to seven years in exchange for ninety minutes of commercial time a week which NTA then sold to advertisers. After NTA Film Network play, the films could be licensed to other independent stations with a six-month clearance.[53]

MGM shortly thereafter announced its plans for television distribution through its subsidiary MGM-TV of 750 features and 900 short subjects in June 1956. By August, another announcement followed stating that for $20 million MGM had contracted for release of 725 of the features with three CBS owned and operated stations in New York, Chicago, and Milwaukee; four stations owned by Triangle Publications in Philadelphia, New Haven, Birmingham and Altoona; two King Broadcasting stations in Seattle and Portland; and KTTV Los Angeles. Later MGM broke up the package to stimulate further sales, and by 1957 had grossed $34.5 million. *Business Week* reported that "Films in the package include such features as *Goodbye Mr. Chips, Mutiny on the Bounty, Boy's Town,* and *Mrs. Miniver,* but not *Gone With the Wind* or *The Wizard of Oz."* Not only did television distribution make a lot of money for MGM, but it also increased broadcast holdings. Of the $5 million KTTV paid to MGM, $1.6 was reinvested in the station by MGM, giving the studio a 25 percent ownership interest. In 1956, MGM worked a similar deal with KTVR-TV Denver, and in November again traded against the film package for a 25 percent interest in KMGM Minneapolis.[54]

Paramount held back its features for longer than any other film company, finally selling its library of 750 pre-1948 films to MCA in February 1958. Although Paramount received more than $50 million for the package, the sale of films outright with no residual provisions was later called "probably the most stupid mistake ever made in Hollywood" by *Forbes* magazine.[55] Paramount retained the rights to its post-1948 films, however, which would bring in profits from network, cable, and cassette sales in years to come. MCA profited enormously by the transaction, reportedly grossing $70 million by 1965 on the Paramount films. MCA accomplished this by "selling not to the networks, which then were paying only $40,000 a feature, but only to local stations." This marketing strategy allowed MCA to gross close to $70,000 per film in syndication, with the added effect, by 1965, of "encourage[ing] higher network prices by limiting supply to the networks who were increasingly desperate for movies."[56]

Networks versus Stations: Film Programming Strategy

A look at network schedules for the years from 1948 to 1961 shows an interesting pattern of film use. During the very early period, 1948–52, all networks ran some feature films in prime time, with ABC and DuMont using the largest number and NBC the least. Summer schedules show the highest frequency of regular feature film slots, reaching a peak in the summer of 1951, when no fewer than eight film series ran between the hours of 8:00 and 11:00 P.M.: four on ABC, two on DuMont, and two on CBS. On regular fall and winter schedules, feature film programming began on ABC in fall 1948, increased to five features a week in the fall of 1949 (two on CBS, three on DuMont), then fell off dramatically. From fall 1953 to fall 1955, no feature films appeared on any part of network schedules. From winter 1956 to summer 1957, use of films began again but only on ABC, with the added innovation of an afternoon film, then dropped off again to nothing from fall 1957 to fall 1961. All in all, network television made scant use of the thousands of Hollywood films released to TV exhibition from 1953 to 1958. The reasons for this rest in a combination of studio marketing strategy and independent station versus network economics, once again rooted in the film and television industries' conflict over economic base and programming form.

The increasing availability of quality Hollywood films after 1953 put the television networks in an awkward position. To compete with the prices paid by multiple sales to individual stations, networks would have had to invest heavily in theatrical films, and then promote theatrical features strongly in order to attract sufficient advertising funds to offset costs. Because of the live programming tradition on which radio network power was based, and also because of a reluctance to "give Hollywood just a new system of distribution" which, in the rhetoric of television, would "weaken TV as a medium,"[57] the networks chose to downplay theatrical film use. ABC defended its film programming strategy in 1955 by pointing out that the length of theatrical films could tie an audience to an entire evening's schedule. Thus the network aired its Sunday night films at 7:30; its tough competition, the "Colgate Variety Hour" on CBS and "Toast of the Town" on NBC, both began at 8:00.

"ABC hopes that by the time 8:00 comes around, its audience will stick with it."[58]

By the same token, however, affiliates could more easily drop an entire evening's schedule if it consisted of one film rather than of several half-hour serials, enabling the station to run its own programs—often its own independently purchased film—in place of the network offering if it chose. Using this strategy meant that all advertising revenues attracted by film adjacencies would go to the station instead of the 30 percent it would receive from the network. If ABC happened to be showing one of the little-known British films purchased from J. Arthur Rank in 1955—some never released theatrically in the United States— against a glossy and familiar MGM or 20th Century-Fox feature owned by the station, an affiliate might well decide to refuse clearance in the hopes of greater revenues.[59]

For a local, nonaffiliated station, big-name films often represented the *only* viable alternative programming to network-dominated prime-time schedules. Many stations did very well by following this particular "counterprogramming" strategy. KTTV in Los Angeles in particular, partially owned by MGM, topped all other stations in the Los Angeles market with its films. *Business Week* wrote of one film, *Thirty Seconds over Tokyo,* that "Its average rating for two and one half hours was 30.8, greater than the six other LA stations combined, and neary double the combined ratings of the three network affiliates."[60] KING-TV Seattle and KTVR Denver also did well with the MGM package. In Boston, WBZ-TV used its Warners film purchase to raise its ratings from 4.4 in August to 13.7 in September; WATU New York reported similar success with the 20th Century-Fox package. A New York City showing of *Command Decision* starring Clark Gable attracted "nearly 90% of the area's TV viewers one night in December 1956."[61] Ratings success soon intrigued advertisers, and in the fall of 1956, Colgate signed an agreement with KTTV for an entire year's worth of films at a cost of $15,000 each for sponsorship. Later Revlon and Bristol-Myers adopted similar plans. Thus Hollywood provided a viable alternative source of programming to television stations, and as such began to threaten the networks' dominance on this new front of TV programming. Chapter 7 will discuss the eventual fulfillment of this threat to the networks, based on new, nonmonopolized distribution technologies.

The networks' strategy for fighting back forms an interesting parallel with the studios' use of Cinemascope and 3-D to combat the allure of TV. Beginning in the fall of 1954, the networks heavily promoted the addition of color to the home receiver by producing a series of "spectaculars" and special programs. Because almost all of the movies being released to television were pre-1948 and hence in black and white, color provided a trump card for the networks that Hollywood films could not yet match. Although 1965 is usually regarded as the year that color TV became a reality and when the networks switched to all-color programming, a "color rate card" came out for the first time on September 12, 1954, marking the commercial debut of color TV—and color TV costs. The networks' color spectaculars drew large audiences, prompting more than eighty of the big budget ninety-minute shows to appear in the 1955–56 network season.[62]

NBC actually began financing Broadway plays, operas, and ballets in an effort to find worthy properties. Network spokesmen emphasized the contribution that color would make to the television medium as an alternative to reliance on old Hollywood properties. David Sarnoff told *Business Week* that "Too great a use of feature film on television . . . would eliminate the big spectaculars, the public service programs, and shows in color"; Sarnoff added that he "emphatically believe[d] TV's future lies in color programming."[63] The costs of color programming, in turn, contributed to the development of the magazine concept and increased network control over the entire process of television production, scheduling, and commercial sales. And although pre-1948 black and white films might eventually suffer from the advent of color, years of experience with color film would stand Hollywood in good stead as TV shows filmed in color began to appear on network schedules.[64]

In fact, throughout the 1950s and 1960s Hollywood appears to have been able to have its cake and eat it too. While feature film distribution brought in substantial profits on what—but for television—would have been obsolete, useless properties, Hollywood expertise in production soon began to dominate the television series market. Most statistics purporting to show the decline of the movie industry in the 1950s and early 1960s focus on box-office receipts. Indeed, motion picture exhibitors experienced a traumatic period of turmoil and falling profits as the number of feature films produced yearly declined drastically and television cut into theater attendance. But producers, although also entering a period of confusion and reorganization, expanded their markets in production for television, and in television sale of formerly valueless films, as well as developing the "blockbuster" phenomenon whereby enormous profits could be made one year with equally enormous losses the next. By selling most of their elderly downtown palaces and smaller neighborhood theaters, studios found themselves able to regard the plight of theaters with far less concern than before. As one director put it, "Exhibitors will have to face the situation. . . . They wanted divorcement and they have it. If TV proves a better market for producers, they [the exhibitors] can sell popcorn, not movies...and best of luck to them."[65]

Film producers' and distributors' profits, although erratic, fared fairly well during the period; 1960 was a particularly successful year for most studios. In 1961, Paramount reported a $5.7 million profit; 20th Century-Fox, $3 million; and MGM, $2.6 million. All three of these studios showed losses in 1962, but by 1963 Paramount and Fox were up again. (Great variations in accounting practices from studio to studio make these figures somewhat unreliable, however; studio stocks stayed low through the 1960s, sparking a wave of takeovers in the late 1960s and early 1970s.)[66]

As for the networks, by 1960, 40 percent of network programs were produced by the major Hollywood studios—20th Century-Fox, MGM, Paramount, Warner Brothers, MCA Universal, and Columbia Screen Gems. By 1965, major studios received one-third of network television's programming production dollars. In 1960, the Screen Actors Guild and the other guilds negotiated another contract with the studios, providing a framework for the release of post-1948 films. The year 1961 marks the first release of major films to network TV relatively soon after their first theatrical run, an innovation that brought major revenues to the studios. NBC broke the ice with its "Saturday Night at the Movies" series, premiering September 23 with *How to Marry a Millionaire*. All films aired in color, and Hollywood received top dollar for them. 20th Century-Fox received $20 million for seventeen films from ABC in 1966 just for television rights; MGM sold forty-five films to CBS the same year for $52.8 million. Warner Brothers received $1 million from CBS for two showings of the *The Music Man,* and ABC paid $2 million to Columbia for two showings of *The Bridge over the River Kwai*. Douglas Gomery traces the origins of the made-for-TV movie to the early 1960s, as scarcity of film product sent prices through the roof.[67]

By 1965 the era of live TV was virtually over. Only a few news, talk, and quiz shows remained live. Network television's dependence on film became such that, according to one story, during "an NBC meeting in early 1957 at which the following season was being charted...an executive turned to MCA VP David A. (Sonny) Werblin: 'Sonny...here are the empty spots, you fill them.'"[68] Hollywood, although similarly dependent on television as a source of income, must equally be recognized as an important contributor to the shape of network television—and not necessarily of its better aspects. But if what we see on TV is largely Hollywood, the reasons for its being there belong to the structure and economics of broadcasting.

Thus the period 1953–65 marks Hollywood's growing influence over the networks, contrary to popular impression. Although the networks' reliance on film producers for the bulk of television programming by 1965 demonstrates Hollywood's economic dependence as well, the history of the distribution of films to television shows once again the ability and desire of the film industry to provide alternatives to the networks, both in terms of programming sources (as with radio) and as a structural alternative (as with subscription and theater television). The producer-exhibitor conflict once so influential faded with divestiture into the background, but the antitrust precedents set in the course of the battle returned to haunt the studios again in the 1970s. The next period of conflict between the two industries occurred as developing technology brought an alternative to the AT&T-dominated wired network system upon which the power of the networks had rested since the 1920s, and Hollywood once again attempted to take advantage of its opportunity.

NOTES

1. See, for instance, Mike Budd, Steve Craig, and Clay Steinman, "Fantasy Island: Marketplace of Desire," *Journal of Communication* (Winter 1983): 67–77; Sandy Flitterman, "The *Real* Soap Operas: TV Commercials," in *Regarding Television,* ed. E. Ann Kaplan (New York: AFI Monographs, 1984), pp. 84–96.

2. Oliver Read and Walter L. Welch, *From Tin Foil to Stereo: The Evolution of the Phonograph* (Indianapolis: Howard Sams, 1959); Erik Barnouw, *The Golden Web* (New York: Oxford University Press, 1968), pp. 218, 163, 109; Erik Barnouw, *A Tower in Babel* (New York: Oxford University Press, 1966), p. 247.

3. Gary N. Hess, "An Historical Study of the DuMont Television Network," (Ph.D. diss., Northwestern University, 1960; repr. New York: Arno Press, 1979), p. 542.

4. Federal Radio Commission, *Annual Report, 1928* (Washington, D.C.: Government Printing Office, 1929); *Newsweek,* January 19, 1948, p. 58.

5. Barnouw, *Golden Web,* p. 171; U.S. Senate, *Hearings before the Subcommittee on Communications on the Amendment of the Communications Act of 1934... S.2834,* 85th Cong., 2d sess. (Washington, D.C.: Government Printing Office, 1958).

6. The show grew out of a vaudeville routine that Gosden and Correll originally called "Sam 'n' Henry." It aired on WMAQ under that name at first, then in 1928 changed to "Amos 'n' Andy."

7. *Broadcasting,* September 10, 1984, p. 45; Frank Buxton and Bill Owen, *The Big Broadcast* (New York: Viking Press, 1972), p. 143. For a detailed history of the Mutual Network, see James Schwoch, "The Revolution in Radio: Mutual Broadcasting System and a Reconsideration of Radio as a Model for

Television History," paper presented at the Society for Cinema Studies-University Film and Video Association joint conference, Bozeman, Montana, June 1988.

8. *Broadcasting,* September 10, 1948, p. 45.

9. *Newsweek,* January 19, 1948, p. 58.

10. Richard deCordova, "The Transition from Radio to Television," paper presented at the Society for Cinema Studies annual meeting, New York City, 1985.

11. Harry Castleman and Walter J. Podrazik, *The TV Schedule Book: Four Decades of Network Programming from Sign On to Sign Off* (New York: McGraw-Hill, 1984), pp. 3–4; Kerman Eckes, "The Kines: The Initial Period, 1948-50," paper presented at the Society for Cinema Studies annual meeting, New York City, 1985; Tim Brooks and Earle Marsh, *The Complete Directory to Prime Time Network TV Shows, 1946–Present,* 3d ed. (New York: Ballantine Books, 1985), pp. 1050–54.

12. Peter Fornatale and Joshua Mills, *Radio in the Television Age* (New York: Overlook Press, 1980), p. 3.

13. Robert Vianello, "The Power Politics of 'Live' Television," *Journal of Film and Video* 37 (Summer 1985): 26-40; William Boddy, "The Studios Move into Prime Time," *Cinema Journal* 24 (Summer 1985): 23–37.

14. Amy Schnapper, "The Distribution of Theatrical Feature Films to Television," Ph. D. diss., University of Wisconsin, Madison, 1975, p. 139; *Business Week,* August 15, 1953, pp. 108–10; April 23, 1955, p. 154; October 13, 1956, pp. 32, 34.

15. *Newsweek,* April 4, 1949, p. 54; Eckes, "The Kines"; Hess, "An Historical Study."

16. *Time,* May 1, 1950.

17. *Newsweek,* February 12, 1951, p. 78.

18. Stephen Fox, *The Mirror Makers* (New York: Random House, 1983).

19. *Business Week,* August 15, 1953, pp. 108–9.

20. *Business Week,* April 23, 1955.

21. Allen D. Larsen, "Integration and Attempted Integration Between the Motion Picture and Television Industries Through 1956," Ph.D. diss., University of Ohio, 1979, p. 146; Erik Barnouw, *The Image Empire* (New York: Oxford University Press, 1970), p. 126; *Time,* March 29, 1954, p. 78.

22. Larsen "Integration and Attempted Integration," p. 148; Barnouw, *Image Empire,* p. 41; *Newsweek,* February 12, 1951, p. 78.

23. Larsen, "Integration and Attempted Integration," p. 96; Castleman and Podrazik, *The TV Schedule Book,* pp. 138–40.

24. *Variety,* October 13, 1948, p. 5; June 4, 1952, p. 21; October 13, 1948, p. 5; June 4, 1952, p. 21; Larson, "Integration and Attempted Integration," p. 155; *New York Times,* June 15, 1952, sec. 2, p. 5; *Business Week,* August 9, 1952, p. 47; Museum of Broadcasting, *KTLA: West Coast Pioneer* (New York: Museum of Broadcasting, 1985).

25. Larsen, "Integration and Attempted Integration," pp. 123, 210; *New York Times,* May 7, 1951, p. 1; Federal Communications Commission, "In

Re: Application of Paramount Pictures for Renewal of License," *Reports,* August 1, 1952, p. 994.

26. Larsen, "Integration and Attempted Integration," p. 231; *Variety,* June 17, 1953; *Fortune,* April 1957, p. 242.

27. *Variety,* June 17, 1953, p. 3.

28. *Fortune,* April 1957, p. 248.

29. Ibid.

30. *New York Times,* April 11, 1955, p. 30; April 8, 1955, p. 16.

31. Larsen, "Integration and Attempted Integration," p. 227.

32. *Variety,* March 30, 1955, p. 1.

33. *New York Times,* July 25, 1955.

34. Ibid., p. 41.

35. Castleman and Podrazik, *The TV Schedule Book,* p. 81.

36. Broadcast Music Inc., *BMI Television Talks 1957* (New York: Channell Press, 1957), p. 184.

37. Erik Barnouw, *The Sponsor* (New York: Oxford University Press, 1978), p. 47.

38. *Variety,* February 28, 1951, pp. 3,6; Schnapper, "Distribution of Theatrical Feature Films," pp. 65–75.

39. *Colliers,* September 20, 1952, p. 78.

40. Schnapper, "Distribution of Theatrical Films," p. 93; *Business Week,* November 24, 1956, p. 134.

41. *Business Week,* November 24, 1956, p. 132.

42. Brooks and Marsh, *Complete Directory,* p. 569.

43. *Variety,* July 6, 1949, p. 2; May 4, 1949, p. 26.

44. *Variety,* Nov. 28, 1951, p. 1.

45. *Variety,* April 27, 1955, p. 5; July 27, 1955, p. 1.

46. Castleman and Podrazik, *The TV Schedule Book,* pp. 85, 86; *Business Week,* July 30, 1955, p. 54.

47. Schnapper, "Distribution of Theatrical Feature Films," p. 89.

48. *Business Week,* October 13, 1956, p. 34.

49. *Business Week,* July 23, 1955, p. 32.

50. *Business Week,* December 31, 1955, p. 46.

51. Schnapper, "Distribution of Theatrical Feature Films," pp. 84–86; *Business Week,* December 31, 1955; January 28, 1956, p. 54.

52. *Business Week,* January 28, 1956, p. 54; December 31, 1955, p. 46; Schnapper, "Distribution of Theatrical Feature Films," p. 84; Glover Delaney, "Film Programming: Advantages and Problems" in *BMI TV Talks* (New York: BMI, 1959), pp. 178–88.

53. Helen B. Shaffer, "Movie-TV Competition," *Editorial Research Reports,* January 18, 1957, p. 53; Schnapper, "Distribution of Theatrical Feature Films," p. 90; *Business Week,* November 10, 1956, p. 59.

54. *Business Week,* September 1, 1956, p. 63; *Variety,* September 12, 1956, p. 39; Larsen, "Integration and Attempted Integration," p. 250; Shaffer, "Movie-TV Competition," p. 53.

55. *Forbes,* December 15, 1967, p. 31.

56. Schnapper, "Distribution of Theatrical Feature Films," p. 93.

57. David Sarnoff, from *Business Week,* March 3, 1956, p. 115.

58. *Business Week,* July 30, 1955, p. 54.

59. Schnapper, "Distribution of Theatrical Feature Films," pp. 139–41.

60. *Business Week,* November 24, 1956, p. 134.

61. Shaffer, "Movie-TV Competition," p. 48.

62. *Business Week,* August 21, 1954, p. 41; October 31, 1956, p. 33.

63. *Business Week,* March 3, 1956, p. 115; November 24, 1956, p. 132.

64. Shaffer, "Movie-TV Competition," p. 60.

65. *Film Daily Yearbook,* 1949, p. 811, from Robert Vianello, "Rise of the Telefilm," *Quarterly Review of Film Studies* (Summer 1984): 215.

66. *New York Times,* March 12, 1961; *Forbes,* December 15, 1967, p. 23.

67. Larsen, "Integration and Attempted Integration," p. 257; Douglas Gomery, "'Brian's Song': Television, Hollywood, and the Evolution of the Movie Made for Television," in *Television: The Critical View,* 4th ed., ed. Horace Newcomb (New York: Oxford University Press, 1987), pp. 197–220.

68. Barnouw, *Image Empire,* p. 64.

7

Film/Television/Cable

SO LONG AS THEY PAY

Amid the proliferation of communications technology in the twentieth century, from telegraph to telephone to radio to television, one remarkable bottleneck or point of control, enforced and supported by government regulation, has dominated the field: the American Telephone and Telegraph Company. The preceding six chapters have traced the evolution of AT&T's wired network as it affected the broadcasting and film industries and discussed how at several key points in history the actions or inaction of AT&T contributed decisively to the final outcome of events. From the inability of the studios or other outsiders to forge radio networks in the late 1920s, to the difficulties with theater television in the early 1950s, to rate structures and national interconnection in the later 1950s, AT&T's lines form the hidden supports of the broadcasting infrastructure, a government-supported monopoly to which no substantial alternative existed until the mid-seventies. Without the active support of the telephone company and its extensive and exclusionary long lines and local loops, the business of radio and television, despite the rhetoric of scientific progress that glorified these technologies' inherent "wirelessness," could not be attempted successfully, and new entrants faced a formidable hurdle.

Not until 1975 did an acceptable alternative to the AT&T system emerge, but early efforts at circumventing the limitations of broadcast coverage to the consumer provided a partial substitute: cable, or community antenna television. It is worthwhile once again to note the contradiction that lies at the heart of broadcasting: from local station to consumer, radio and television are truly broadcast media, employing electromagnetic waves and using spectrum space; from network to local station, however, broadcasting became a wire-linked business, leasing privately owned wires from a government regulated but still private monopoly. While certain other large commercial institutions, notably the film studios, had at one point or another attempted to break into this tightly closed system with alternative distribution routes, it was ultimately the small entrepreneurs at the consumer end who were able, through loopholes in regulation, to drive in the thin end of the wedge that would eventually split the system apart.

The Rise of Cable

In 1947, in the tiny town of Mahanoy City, Pennsylvania, nestled in a deep valley in the Allegheny Mountains outside the reach of neighboring television stations, the owner of the local TV and appliance shop decided to boost his sales by providing customers with something to look at on their new television sets.[1] He erected an antenna on top of one of the mountains outside the town and ran wires from it to his store as a first step. This antenna was high enough to pick up several signals from distant stations. For a small connection charge and a monthly fee, he offered his system to those who purchased his television sets; cable television was born.

Radio's greater ability to withstand signal degradation and also its much lower operating costs had enabled even the smallest, most remote hamlets to receive radio signals, but television proved a more difficult situation. With the expense involved in television, smaller towns could not support a local station; the FCC freeze from 1948–52 exacerbated the lack of smaller local stations; and finally, some remote or geographically obstructed locations like Mahanoy City simply could not pick up even one channel clearly from its nearest TV station.[2]

Across the country, not only in Pennsylvania but also in Colorado, Utah, and other remote and rugged locations, local entrepreneurs erected large antennas on the highest available ground and strung cables to the homes of the town's residents, usually charging them not only a connection fee but also a small amount monthly. These community antennas filled a gap in television service that had been created by the actions of the FCC. The early CATV operators provided no original programming but merely relayed the signals of existing stations. Because most early CATV systems extended the range and advertising reach of the local TV licensees, no objections were at first heard. But by 1959, objections to cable's presence prompted an FCC investigation, because of two factors: existing broadcasters' complaints that in some cases importation of distant signals imperiled a local station's market base; and fear that the existence of cable TV would jeopardize the plan for local UHF band stations that the FCC in 1956 had decided to implement. However, the FCC's power to act remained limited by the fact that because cable used no part of the radio spectrum, FCC regulations were held not to apply. In 1962, the landmark *Carter Mountain Transmission Corporation* decision ruled against a microwave-linked carrier on grounds of economic injury to local broadcasters because microwave allocation clearly fell under FCC jurisdiction. Once the principle of injury to broadcasters had been established, however, it was not long before cable-based importation of signals also became subsumed under FCC authority.[3]

In 1966, the FCC issued its *Second Report and Order* on cable, calling for economic studies on cable's impact on broadcasting. By 1968, a further revision set a restrictive FCC policy on cable, calling for program-by-program consent for the importation of programming from a distant station, restriction of distant signal content for top one hundred markets, and requiring cable systems to carry all "significantly viewed" local stations. Controversy surrounding these rules in effect froze cable growth until 1971. In 1972, the FCC instituted its final *Cable Television Report and Order*, under which, with increasingly frequent revisions, the cable industry operated until 1984. The 1972 report set strict limitations on cable operations designed to minimize its ill effects on the broadcasting industry, but did provide a framework within which cable could develop under close federal and state regulation. By 1975, almost 13 percent of U.S. households subscribed to cable.[4]

During this period, subscription television continued to be tested (chapter 5), and although initial enthusiasm had been dampened considerably by public controversy and regulatory delays, some industry figures began to look to cable as a carrier of pay television services. A further technological advance in 1975 brought more regulatory furor but pointed pay TV in its future direction: with the launching of SATCOM I and the availability of satellite transmission, both the bottleneck of AT&T long lines and of FCC regulation of its broadcast spectrum could be circumvented. With the emergence in 1975 of HBO, owned by Time Inc., a cable company that owned multiple systems across the country, pay television's new era dawned. HBO's initial success with the Mohammed Ali–Joe Frazier "Thrilla from Manilla" prizefight and other events, most of which were sports, quickly spawned FCC attempts to restrict the new distribution channel, but in 1977 *Home Box Office v. FCC* confirmed a lower court decision that these rules were improper and unnecessary.[5] By 1976, HBO had a competitor, Showtime, owned by Viacom, another multiple systems operator

(MSO). The programming strategy of these pay services was fairly simple: bid more for exclusive or first rights to new theatrical films and major sporting events, show them uninterrupted by advertising, then charge the cable customer a premium for the service.

The year 1978 brought new conditions to the pay TV industry, as the FCC relaxed its restriction on the pay distribution of theatrical films. Previously, only films less than two years old or more than ten could be shown on pay cable. Most films, especially the better ones, remained in theatrical release for first, second, and third run for more than two years, thus limiting pay TV's menu to very old or second-rate material. With the new three-year limit established in 1978, pay TV finally was able to provide movie fare sufficiently interesting to cable operators. Also in 1978, HBO began to feel the effects of competition as the Teleprompter Corporation, a cable MSO heretofore one of HBO's best customers, purchased a 50 percent interest in the Showtime service. This immediately caused a drop of approximately 250,000 in HBO's subscriber rate, as Teleprompter's subscribers switched to Showtime. However, earlier the same year, HBO's parent, Time Inc., had purchased its own string of cable systems in the form of American Television and Communications Corporation (ATC), the nation's second-largest MSO with more than 675,000 subscriber homes.

Thus a situation comparable to the film industry's predivestiture arrangement began to emerge, as large companies such as Time Inc., Teleprompter, and Viacom both bought and produced programming with an assured outlet in wholly owned cable systems nationwide. The situation did not pass unnoticed by the film industry. Jack Valenti, president of the Motion Picture Association of America (MPAA), had threatened early in 1978 to file monopoly charges against HBO. The emergence of Showtime as a more formidable competitor temporarily forestalled a Justice Department investigation that year, but renewed monopoly complaints did in fact provoke investigation the following year.

By 1980, HBO still dominated the field of pay television with more than 4 million, or 60 percent, of the nation's seven million pay television subscribers. Teleprompter/Viacom's Showtime came in a distant second with 20 percent of the market, or 1.5 million subscribers. Between 1978 and 1980, several other pay television services were initiated, including Warner Communication's The Movie Channel, HBO's supplemental all-movie service Cinemax, and a few more specialized or regional services; basic cable programming proliferated at an alarming rate. But the main distinction of HBO, Showtime, and the like was that they were premium, nonadvertising-based services, sold to the subscriber at an extra charge—ranging from $8 to $10 per month—above the basic cable subscription fee. Usually the local cable system operator paid the program supplier a proportion of this charge—$3 to $5 per subscriber—plus an additional fee for every increment charged to the subscriber over a set amount. The rapid growth of the cable industry during the early 1980s was due in large part to the success of pay television services. By 1983, one-third of all cable subscribers received at least one pay service, and a growing percentage subscribed to more than one, although the trend had fallen off somewhat by late 1985.

By 1981, Time Inc.'s MSO subsidiary ATC owned 96 cable systems serving 1,625,000 basic subscribers, one million of whom also subscribed to a pay service. This put ATC in first place among the nation's MSOs, just above Teleprompter with 1,533,322 subscribers and Cox Cable with 1,109,989. With few exceptions, no ATC system failed to carry HBO, Cinemax, or both, no matter what others it carried as well; the same holds true for Showtime on its parent-owned systems. In fact, in 1981, of the 3,286 cable systems nationwide carrying only one pay service, 2,168, or 66 percent of them, offered only HBO on the premium level. Of the 713 systems offering two pay services, 192 combined HBO and Cinemax—to the benefit of Time Inc., which had a monopoly over pay services on 55 percent of U.S. cable systems.[6]

According to depositions taken in the Justice Department's 1980 inquiry into the emergence of the studio-dominated pay TV service, Premiere, HBO did not hesitate to use this market dominance as a bargaining tool to drive film prices down. The strategy worked particularly well because in 1976 HBO had acquired a distribution service, Telemation Program Services, which bought pay television and broadcast television rights to film and other properties for sale to stand-alone cable systems (systems not affiliated with a large MSO, the equivalent of independent broadcast stations). Thus HBO, by using its guaranteed revenue from ATC-owned cable systems, could easily outbid competitors for top films and thereby gain a certain amount of control over the stand-alones, giving it an even larger proportion of the market. According to Lawrence Hilford, vice president at Columbia Pictures, "Time Inc. or Viacom were in a position to be able to guarantee themselves money and guarantee themselves access to that particular program, they had leverage that we did not. Any investment we would make in pay television rights would have been speculative and would not have had such a guarantee." HBO also picked up broadcast television distribution rights for many of the films it bought for pay television. Again, leverage from its dominant position in the PTV market enabled

HBO to make favorable deals. Hilford testified that in the case of one picture, *Fastbreak*, "The producer came back to [Columbia] at the last minute and said that if HBO or Time Inc. did not get the rights to that picture the picture would never appear on HBO."[7]

Others claim that this was not an isolated incident, among them Thomas Wertheimer, vice president of MCA/Universal, one of the first companies to license films to HBO. "We had numerous meetings with HBO representatives who indicated that they only had a need for five studios' product and there were seven studios, or words to that effect. And that if I didn't get on the wagon soon, it would leave without me."[8] Other studios voiced similar complaints. When 20th Century-Fox refused to accept HBO's offer for the hit film *Breaking Away*, selling it instead for a better price to NBC, no Fox films appeared on HBO for a year. Studios also pointed to statistics showing that although pay television revenues were increasing dramatically each year, revenues to the studios actually fell from about $16 per subscriber per year to only $7.[9]

In the meantime, the Justice Department investigation of the pay cable industry begun in 1979 at the instigation of the MPAA went nowhere. The film industry began to explore other options. These discussions would ultimately result in the industry's first large-scale attempt to enter the pay TV business, much as it had attempted to break into radio networking in the 1920s and subscription TV in the early 1950s: the formation in April 1978 of the Premiere Network, a studio-controlled, movies-only pay television service to be operated as a joint venture between Columbia Pictures, 20th Century-Fox, Paramount, and Universal; the Getty Oil Corporation was to provide financing and satellite transponder space. Again, this particular venture would meet with strenuous opposition, not only from theatrical exhibitors and established pay TV interests, but also from Justice Department antitrust regulations. The defeat of Premiere, brought about by a basic imbalance in the industry and regulatory structures of cable, exacerbated by the film industry's age-old bete noir, charges of antitrust violations, reflects in microcosm the problems facing the film industry as even newer technologies, such as videocassettes and pay-per-view, promised more radical change.

The Premiere Network

Our goals are basically the same. To erode HBO's ever-increasing leverage and eliminate outside middlemen from our business. We know from the network television business what can happen to us and we don't want it

to happen again. We cannot sit idly by watching HBO gobbling up the
market with our product. The revenue potential is staggering.[10]

According to the Hilford deposition, Columbia's interest in pay television stems from 1970, when it invested in an experimental hotel
distribution system. This was not successful, and Columbia temporarily
dropped the pay TV idea to focus on the videocassette market. In
1978, interest in pay TV involvement revived, due largely to unhap-
piness over the sale of a number of picture rights to HBO. In 1979
several movie companies, including Disney and United Artists, held a
series of meetings to discuss how the movie industry could obtain a
larger share of pay TV revenues. One of the first ideas discussed was
a cooperative transponder leasing venture whereby individual companies
could schedule times at which specific films would be made available
for pick up by cable systems. The idea was dismissed as impractical
because any one film company would have only ten to twelve pictures
available at any given time, too small a number to interest a cable
operator in the attendant complicated negotiations.

Another possible arrangement discussed in 1979 involved a common
sales agent handling distribution rights for six or seven film companies.
This represented a possible improvement in negotiating power, but the
idea was rejected as one that would not change the fundamental
imbalance of the existing system. It was the opinion of the studio
representatives that, given HBO's penetration of the pay TV market,
unless a new movie-based service could be strongly differentiated from
those already being offered it could not gain a sufficient market share
to cover costs. One means of product differentiation, the one most
readily available to the film companies, was to provide recently released
movies on an exclusive basis: to institute a "window" when those films
just off theatrical release would be seen only on the movie companies'
channel, with no duplication on any other satellite-fed pay service.

In August 1979, Showtime made a proposal to at least one of the
movie companies (Columbia) to acquire long- term exclusive rights to
all that studio's product, for which Showtime would take a distribution
fee, with the remaining revenues going to the studio. Showtime was
willing to make a similar arrangement with up to three movie companies, handling each agreement separately, presumably in order to
avoid charges of collusion. Hilford summed up the studios' objections
to this scheme on three grounds: first, that each contract had to be
negotiated separately, so no film company would want to be the first
to sign up; second, that he personally would be delighted to see three
other studios sign up, thereby greatly increasing Columbia's leverage

with HBO; and third, that three film companies could not provide enough product sufficiently to differentiate the service. Hilford related Showtime's reaction:

> I remember I asked...them how they could justify it—their proposal without the window and why it made sense for them. And the answer was "We will. We are not saying there can't be a window, we are just saying we don't want to be a party to the window." I said, "You mean you don't want that to be part of the stated operating policy of the company?" The answer was "Yes." Then I said, "How in the world are your salesmen going to go out and sell?" And their answer was that it is sort of going to become obvious to everybody what you are doing. We said we didn't think that there was anything wrong with the window but that was the only way that the business could work. And in essence the conversation stopped.[11]

In November 1979, a series of discussions began with Warner-Amex over a possible arrangement by which The Movie Channel would act as a distributor for one or more movie companies. Here too the controversial exclusivity concept proved a barrier. Warner did not feel comfortable with the "window" that the studios felt to be essential, and the discussions were dropped. By this time talks with Getty had begun, and plans for Premiere got underway.

Premiere's basic plan was a very simple one, which, had it only been initiated back in 1977 like HBO, would most likely have met with considerable success. According to a network publicity package, from 8:00 P.M. to 2:00 A.M. EST, seven days a week, Premiere would show films, film shorts, and film-based programs—no sports, specials, talk shows, or commercials. These would be new films just off theatrical release and not yet available on videocassette, videodisc, or to broadcast television. For this service the customer would pay a standard pay TV fee of $8 to $10 per month; the cable operator would receive $3.75 per subscriber per month plus 50 percent of the monthly subscriber fee over $8. About 150 films per year would be shown, three on Monday through Thursday nights, four on Friday, Saturday, and Sunday. Half would come from the four partners, the rest from other producers on a nonexclusive basis.

The feature that made this plan different, and prevented its successful initiation, was the nine-month "window" for Columbia, Paramount, Universal, and 20th Century-Fox films. No other satellite-distributed pay TV service could buy rights to any of those four companies' films for nine months after the end of each film's theatrical run; until then they would appear exclusively on Premiere. This could mean that for a blockbuster film whose theatrical run might be protracted for a year or more, availability to HBO, Showtime, or any other pay TV service would not occur until almost two years after the film's initial theatrical release. For a less successful film, the period would be much shorter. Cable operators, although owned by HBO or Showtime parents, would soon begin to feel pressure from consumers to provide new feature films if existing pay services suddenly began issuing a predominance of reruns and specials. At the very least, the prices HBO and Showtime paid for films of the remaining studios would show a sharp increase.

Using such ringing phrases as "Where do the stars go after they leave the theatres? They go to work for you," and "Premiere: your Hollywood connection," Premiere planned a hard-sell publicity campaign aimed at signing up cable operators. Pointing out that "No one makes better movies than Hollywood," Premiere offered cable operators help not only in marketing Premiere to subscribers, but also in promoting the entire cable service of an operator signed to the service. To placate the operator worried about losing HBO subscribers should 80 percent of its movies suddenly be cut, Premiere claimed that its nine-month exlcusivity would eliminate the kind of duplication that currently existed on the schedules of HBO, Showtime, or The Movie Channel schedules. In other words, Premiere felt that the subscriber would want at least two services: Premiere for movies and HBO or Showtime for sports, specials, and other programming.[12]

HBO responded by recommending that the Justice Department investigate what it called "per se antitrust violations. . . it's simply illegal for companies to get together, to set up a mechanism of pricing and to boycott competitors." Showtime representatives called Premiere an "illegal conspiracy" involving "price fixing and attempted monopoly." HBO Chairman N. G. Nichols also noted that "They [movie companies] have a history of behaving in a fashion which results in their having more price leverage with customers than is normal in a buy-sell relationship."[13]

The Justice Department began its investigation of Premiere in April and filed a civil antitrust suit in New York Federal Court on August 4, 1980, charging Premiere with violation of the Sherman Antitrust Act. At that time, according to Justice Department figures, the four studios involved in the joint venture distributed 43 percent of all movies in this country that earned more than $1 million in theatrical release. If these companies were allowed to band together, they would be able to restrict availability and set prices for half the film product of the United States, thus in effect "boycotting" sale of films to other pay television networks. Sidney Sheinberg, president of MCA Inc., responded, "We may also control a number of toilets in Orange County. The relevant place to look at is the market we're trying to get into."[14]

However, by its August action the Justice Department in effect asserted that the danger inherent in the proposed venture's violation of antitrust laws outweighed any considerations of monopolistic conditions in the pay television industry as a whole. In November, thirty-one states filed amicus curiae briefs supporting the Justice Department's deision, noting two points in particular. First, as a producer-supplier, Premiere would have control over a sufficient portion of the market to enable them to raise prices to the consumer unreasonably. Second, the marketing efforts of HBO had in the past benefitted the entire cable industry. If HBO were to be weakened seriously by Premiere's corner on product, cable operators unable to receive Premiere—for reasons of channel space or lack of appropriate satellite hardware—would lose subscribers. The National Cable Television Association issued a statement against Premiere for the same reasons: the kind of competition provided by Premiere, although perhaps beneficial to the movie business, would have a weakening effect on the cable industry as a whole.[15]

Judge Gerald L. Goettel, upon issuing an injunction to halt Premiere operations on December 31, 1980, stated the case in slightly different terms. "Far more important than the interests of either the defendants or the existing industry, however, is the public's interest in enforcement of the antitrust laws and in the preservation of competition. The public interest is not easily outweighed by private interests."[16]

Developments in the financing of new films during 1981–82 complicated the issue further. As production costs went up and the number of films produced each year by the major studios declined, HBO increasingly moved into the void by investing money in independent film projects in return for exclusive pay television rights. *On Golden Pond* was one example of this kind of "pre-buy" financing, and in this case the film's success proved a windfall for HBO. HBO pre-bought exclusive pay TV rights for $3.5 million, in effect investing that much in the film's production. *On Golden Pond* went on to gross over $118 million theatrically, a figure that normally would bring in at least $14 million from pay TV sale. Other such examples include *Sophie's Choice*, *Tootsie*, and *Fort Apache, the Bronx*. The studios claimed that this fragmentation of distribution rights further increased the risks associated with producing a film because a larger and larger proportion of a film's eventual profits stems not from theatrical release, but from rights to other media.[17]

In effect, film industry spokesmen argued, the studios paid for the theatrical publicity that made a movie a success, yet were barred from a share of post-theatrical profits. So why did the studios not simply invest in pay television rights from the outset? Movie companies claimed that, again, they had no assurance of selling those rights to an existing pay TV service—which, given the numbers involved, generally meant HBO. HBO, on the other hand, had a captive market for its investment, a situation that has not changed much since 1980, despite the rise in the number of pay TV services. As of 1988, 27.4 percent of all American homes subscribed to pay cable. In addition to HBO and Cinemax, which together reach more than seventeen million subscribers, Time Inc. in 1987 added Festival, a "family" channel of primarily PG-rated movies, perhaps as a response to The Disney Channel, the Walt Disney Company's 1983 entry into the pay cable market. As of the late 1980s, however, Disney remained in control of the family movie market, with 3.2 million subscribers to Festival's .05 million. Viacom's Showtime and The Movie Channel, with more than eight million subscribers, still ranked a distant second place in the pay TV market, and a new entrant, MSO Cablevision System's American Movie Classics channel was in third place with seven million. Cablevision's Bravo, a pay service with primarily foreign films and opera, ballet, and theater and aimed at up-scale urban markets, reached half a million homes. Other entrants in the pay TV market included The Playboy Channel, The Nostalgia Channel, and SelecTV, owned by Telstar.

Despite heavy competition both from within the cable industry as the number of basic cable services offering movies and related entertainment proliferated, and from without as videocassettes ate into the cable market, pay cable managed to hold firm on its subscribers through the 1980s. One factor behind such success, particularly that of the larger players such as HBO/Cinemax and Showtime/The Movie Channel, was that in the wake of Premiere, studios put animosity behind them and signed a number of exclusive distribution deals with the pay TV networks. For example, in 1988, Paramount signed an exclusive distribution contract with its former adversary HBO for a six-year period starting in 1989; Fox, Warner, Columbia, and TriStar also agreed to similar exclusive or semiexclusive deals with HBO, as did Disney's Touchstone and Cannon with Showtime.

Since Premiere

In the meantime, another new technology—videocassette distribution—provided a challenge to the film and television industries, cutting into even the extravagant promise of pay TV. In 1985, sales of home VCRs doubled over the year before, chiefly because of declining import prices brought on by the dollar's strength; video rental chains mushroomed across the country. By mid-1984, video penetration had reached 20 percent; by late 1985, that figure had risen to 28 percent; and by 1988, just over 50 percent. Video revenues edged out pay TV and broadcasting income to take second place to box-office receipts for the movie studios. In 1986, videocassette revenues exceeded traditional box-office income for the first time in history.

Perhaps forewarned by previous attempts at vertical integration, motion picture distributions and producers have made no attempt to cut in on the retail levels of videocassette sales and rentals. In 1984 alone, more than ten thousand videocassette dealers opened up shop in the United States, and by the end of 1987 between twenty-four and twenty-seven thousand dealers opened shops nationwide. Until 1986, this end of the business remained in the hands of small, local operators competing fiercely for the rental market. Several expanded into national or regional chains—for example, National Video, Tower Video, and Video World—often under a club membership plan that helped offset high initial capitalization costs. However, as distributors lowered retail prices—from an average of $79.99 in 1983 to $39.99 in 1985—more large diversified chain stores (grocery stores, discount outlets, department stores, gas stations, convenience stores) began both selling and renting cassettes and dealing directly with film distributors as a source instead of with middlemen. Thus the era of mom and pop video may soon draw to a close.[18]

MCA/Universal was one of the first studios to see the possibilities in recorded home entertainment, attributable partially to its longstanding involvement in the recording industry. With the development of the video disc in the early 1970s, MCA formed Disco-Vision Inc. to exploit the movie-on-disc market. When the discs proved unprofitable, MCA renamed its division MCA Home Video and became a major force in videocassette distribution.

MGM, subsequent to its merger with United Artists in 1981, formed the MGM/UA Home Entertainment Group in 1982 for both pay TV and home video products. In December 1985, MGM/UA contracted with Capitol Records for distribution of its cassette library, but continued to distribute current releases through MGM/UA Home Video. In 1986, the MGM/UA film library was purchased by Ted Turner, who also owned rights to a part of the RKO and Warner collections (pp. 194–95). Warners, besides its extensive cable and broadcasting interests, also formed a Home Video division in the early 1980s. Columbia and RCA formed RCA/Columbia Home Video to distribute Columbia films. CBS and 20th Century-Fox formed CBS-Fox Video in July 1982 "to market and distribute home video products and to operate the CBS Studio Center," to which Fox brought its library of films for videocassette sale.[19]

In late 1984, HBO joined with Thorn EMI, the British entertainment giant, to form Thorn EMI/HBO Video. According to reports, "The new company will handle HBO product, Thorn EMI product, and 13 current films and 20 never-on-home-video films from Orion Pictures that are part of Time-Life Films' agreement with Orion." In addition, Thorn EMI was to handle the foreign video distribution of HBO's Silver Screen films along with other HBO productions, exchanging exclusive U.S. pay TV rights to Thorn EMI's Screen Entertainment for distribution on HBO. Disney released a small portion of its popular children's films on home video through its Walt Disney Home Video subsidiary but held back wider distribution so pay TV operations would not be hurt.[20]

Paramount Home Video moved into videocassette distribution with the biggest splash in a move based on events from the 1950s. Since Paramount—unwisely, as many felt—sold its film library outright to MCA in 1948, it possessed a far smaller library of classic films than most of its competitors; hence, as *Forbes* reported, "Paramount must make every cassette of every picture count." This strategy led Paramount in 1982 to start a trend by releasing *Star Trek II: The Wrath of Khan* for only $39.95, as opposed to the $79.95 or higher prices prevalent until then. Since 1982, Paramount has taken prices even lower, with the release of a "Christmas package" in November 1984 of twenty-five films for $24.95 apiece. These tactics have more than doubled the volume of sales possible at the higher price, culminating in the release of *Raiders of the Lost Ark* for $39.95. In 1984, Paramount Home Video accounted for 16 percent of video sales nationally, compared to only 1.5 percent in 1983; counting feature film video sales only, this figure translates to 23 percent. The release of *Beverly Hills Cop* and twenty-four other films for Christmas 1985 at the $24.95 price boosted Paramount's 1986 position even higher.[21]

Most VCR owners still prefer to rent rather than to buy. With costs for one day's rental dropping to 59 cents in some cities ($2.25 per day is the average), video rentals have increased at an astonishing rate since 1985. However, the studios net no profit from these rentals; the "first-sale" doctrine embodied in existing copyright law, hotly contested by the studios in 1982–83, prevents them from sharing in profit subsequent to the first sale of a cassette. Thus, although studios would have preferred to form a two-tier pricing structure, selling at a higher price to rental concerns and at a lower price to consumers, the first-sale rule prompted most distributors to push prices higher in an attempt to compensate for loss of rental royalties. Paramount's efforts to bypass rental stores by pricing tapes low enough to sell directly to consumers was followed by other distributors, primarily those owners of classic libraries such as Blackhawk Films and Video Classics, Inc., whose classic films often retail for as low as $9.95.[22]

Beginning in 1985, the popularity of videocassettes affected not only broadcast TV ratings, but also pay TV viewership. Cable operators reported a sudden drop of 2 to 5 percent nationwide in the number of basic cable households subscribing to at least one pay service during the May 1984–May 1985 period, although after that time subscriptions have held steady. Despite the cable industry's feeling that VCR popularity defies logic—"You have a klutzy piece of hardware, you have an upfront capital investment, and you have to run down to the store to buy the programs"[23]—some cable operators have gone so far as to begin selling VCRs and renting cassettes out of their own offices. Thus, studios like Disney, with heavy involvement in pay cable, must walk a fine line between those interests and the revenues to be gained in cassette sales.[24]

The answer to this dilemma, many feel, may lie in the much-delayed advent of workable pay-per-view (PPV) services. Although tests of this technology have proved troublesome and inconclusive since 1979, the potential for increased revenues to the film industry, in view of the first-sale restrictions on videocassettes, makes it an appealing prospect to program suppliers. PPV would essentially allow a cable-delivered service to substitute for the trip to the video store, at a cost not much above rental fees. PPV bears striking resemblance to the subscription television systems advocated by film interests in the 1940s, although it is based upon a far more sophisticated technology. PPV in the 1980s relies upon addressible converter devices, which have a two-way communication ability to allow a customer at home to select whichever film the PPV service is offering at a given time. The customer would be billed only for the cost of that film rather than at a monthly rate as with pay television.

However, the Premiere experience seems to have convinced most studios to confine their roles to program supplier agreements, and to leave the implementation of PPV systems in the hands of middlemen. The nation's largest PPV network, Request Television, is owned by Reiss Media Enterprises but owes its existence to an investment of more than $40 million since the early 1980s by several film companies: Columbia, Disney, Lorimar, MGM-UA, New World, Paramount, Fox, Universal, and Warners. By the end of the 1980s, Request served 3.7

million homes, offering two to four movies per week, along with special events such as sports and concerts. Other PPV operations include Viewer's Choice, owned by Viacom, second largest at 3.5 million addressible homes, Playboy, Home Premiere TV, Jerrold's Cable Video Store, and Graff PPV.[25]

Another field still uncertain in terms of its potential for the film industry is that of direct broadcast satellite (DBS) services. Although the thousands of back-yard dishes that sprang up across the country in the eighties motivated several program services to set up monthly membership fees, most DBS viewers remain "pirates," despite the long-delayed and still awkward switch to scrambled signals that most operators made in 1986 and 1987. With the development of KU band satellites, which transmit at higher frequencies than other satellite channels and thus allow a much smaller receiving dish, a more organized DBS program provision industry may emerge in the 1990s.

Broadcast Programming: Networks and Alternatives

Revenues from all the new technologies have not surpassed most studios' broadcast television production subsidiary profits. Both in terms of network and syndicated production, and in sale of theatrical films to networks and independents stations, the former major studios continue to dominate broadcast TV. Focusing first on network television, it comes as no surprise to see prime-time schedules filled with Hollywood-produced programs.

Network

The most significant innovation in the broadcast market in the 1980s may well have been the formation of the Fox Broadcasting Company in October of 1986. Although the Fox system ratings were less than spectacular for its first few years, several shows attracted critical and popular attention: "21 Jump Street," "America's Most Wanted" (a show based on the FBI's "wanted" list, which actually produced arrests), "Married...With Children," "The Tracey Ullman Show," and a show pulled from pay cable, "It's Garry Shandling's Show." An overall drop in network ratings in 1987—based in part on the new Nielsen peoplemeter system—led some critics to question the viability of a fourth broadcast network. Partially in response to this concern, Fox's Monday night schedule began in 1988 to feature the "Fox Movie of the Week" supplied by Fox Film Corporation.[26]

In 1987–88, Paramount Television led the pack in terms of ratings, having produced both "Cheers" and "Family Ties," shows ranked consistently in Nielsen's top ten. Paramount produced a total of seventy hours of network TV in 1987–88, but Columbia Pictures far outdistanced all the other studios with more than seven hundred hours of network programs, including "Wheel of Fortune" from subsidiary Merv Griffin Enterprises, "The Charmings," "Who's the Boss?," "Facts of Life," "Everything's Relative," "Married...With Children," "227," and more from its Embassy Communications Group. Columbia Pictures Television produced "Designing Women," "Houston Knights," "Days of Our Lives," and "The Young and the Restless," with "My Two Dads," "Buck James," and "Werewolf" from TriStar.

MCA/Universal turned out 137.5 network hours in 1987–88, including the highly popular "Miami Vice," "Simon and Simon," "Knight Rider," "A Year in the Life," "Private Eye," and "Murder, She Wrote." Warners succeeded with ninety-four hours in this season, but with two high-rated programs, "Growing Pains" and "Night Court" as well as "My Sister Sam," "Spenser for Hire," "Head of the Class," and "O'Hara." 20th Century-Fox turned out sixty-one hours, including the critical success "L.A. Law," "Hooperman," "Mr. Belvedier," and "Pursuit of Happiness." MGM/UA had a rather bad season, with only 29.5 hours on network, one of which, however, was the innovative yuppie drama "thirtysomething" (the other was "Hello Kitty's Furry Tale Theater").

The former majors are far from being the only suppliers of network programming. Several highly successful independents fill much of TV's prime hours, including Lorimar-Telepictures, Orion, MTM Enterprises, Aaron Spelling Productions, and Stephen J. Cannell Productions. In total, the studios accounted for more than 1,100 hours on the networks in the 1985–86 season, while independents supplied about 750.[27]

Syndication

Only a portion of producers' revenues comes from current, first-run network shows; the balance stems from the highly lucrative syndication market. Here, again, the regulatory system has played a role—this time to the advantage of the program producers. After its investigation of the structure of network broadcasting begun in 1958, the FCC published a series of findings through the 1960s, recommending action to remedy what it perceived to be a monopolistic situation developing out of network control of programming production and affiliate schedules. In 1970, the FCC instituted what have become known as the "prime-time access," "syndication," and "financial interest" rules which respectively freed a portion of prime time from network clearances for affiliates to program independently, prohibited the networks from themselves syndicating off-network shows, and prevented them from securing a financial interest in independently produced programs, as well as restricting the number of programs that each network could produce for itself.

However, the FCC postponed putting these rules into effect because of an appeal made by network interests, which resulted in a court order to stay execution. By 1972, although a federal court had in the meantime upheld their validity, the rules still had not been put into effect by the commission. This prompted the Justice Department in 1972 to file suit against NBC, CBS,and ABC charging each network separately with violation of antitrust statutes through monopolization of program supply and distribution.

> The government alleges that the three networks have forced outside producers to give them a financial interest in evening programs; that they have refused to show programs in which they have no financial interest, or to sell air time to advertisers and outside suppliers for the screening of independent programs; and that they are trying to control the prices of movies made for television, either by going into the business of movie production (in the case of CBS and ABC) or by contracting with a single large supplier (in the case of NBC). The overall effect, according to the government, has been to restrain competition in the production, distribution, and sale of entertainment programs, and to deprive the public of the benefits of free and open competition.[28]

The timing of this suit, however, coming in an election year after then-President Richard Nixon had openly declared his hostility to the networks, enabled the networks to argue for dismissal of the case on the grounds of "improper motivation." The courts did indeed dismiss the Justice Department charges in 1974 after two years of tortuous wrangling in the courts, but did so "without prejudice," meaning that the Justice Department could, if it wished, again file charges under presumably different motivational conditions. It did so in December 1974, with the added recommendation that the networks be completely barred from airing any programs that they themselves had produced. The suit against NBC was settled by a consent agreement signed in 1977, in which NBC in effect agreed to abide by the 1970 FCC rulings previously mentioned.

In April 1977, CBS and ABC attempted to intervene in the settlement, arguing that it set a far too restrictive precedent, but they lost this bid to review the decision in 1979. The court at the same time declined the counter-bid by "five non-network program producers" who argued for an even more restrictive settlement: Columbia Pictures, Paramount, 20th Century-Fox, MCA/Universal, and Warner Brothers. The effect of all this litiginous activity—further complicated by a 1970 suit filed by the studios to force the networks out of feature-length film production, and a further 1978 charge that networks also monopolized news and public affairs programming—was to force the FCC to implement its prime-time access, syndication, and financial interest rules which indeed, by the beginning of the 1980s, had begun to produce the desired effect of increasing the number of program suppliers.[29]

In effect, the financial interest and syndication rules enabled the studios and other program suppliers to strengthen their efforts at creation of new, often ad hoc alternative networks. One result, the much-vaunted "rise of the independent station" often attributed to the growth of cable, rests in fact on two pillars: increased freedom in program supply brought about by the financial interest and syndication rules on the one side, and enhanced distribution possibilities created by satellite-cable "superstation" delivery on the other. From the late 1970s, the major studios have loomed large in three different areas of off-network program supply: first, syndication of second-run off-network series (reruns, in other words); second, in syndication of first-run original television programming, either series, miniseries, or specials; and third, in theatrical film distribution to TV, using much the same tactics they developed in the 1950s.

Now that syndication revenues revert immediately back to the producer after an agreed-upon period on network, syndication has become highly profitable. The increase in the number of outlets for rerun programs—both VHF and UHF independent broadcast stations, cable program services, and even videocassettes—has seen the resurrection of many quite elderly, formerly valueless, series and the expanded life span even of those series whose ratings caused a suspiciously rapid network demise. A quick glance through the lavish full-page advertisements in trade magazines like *Broadcasting* during the late 1980s revealed a wealth of second-, third-, or fourth-time-around programming. For example, the following is from an advertisement for the syndicated release of an old Ziv series, circa 1950: "Originally produced on film, this all purpose classic generic Western is TV-enhanced. It looks crisp, vivid, fresh. Like it was shot last week. . . . Hitch it up to a Western block. Lead it into kids' animation shows. . . . And round yourself up some mighty big ratings, pardner, with 'The Cisco Kid.'"[30] Re-issues of such classics as "The Honeymooners" and Sid Caesar's "Your Show of Shows" attracted national attention. Often, under a standard three-to-five-year contract, reruns of a hit show were be marketed to independents or local affilliates for non-prime-time slots while the current show still ran on network.

The strong market for syndicated programming prompted a new twist in series financing: often very successful shows are marketed as "futures"—that is, syndication rights are sold as early as the first year of network run. Paramount TV announced in October 1984 that advance sales of syndication of "Cheers" and "Family Ties" had already brought in more than $1 million per episode in more than fifty markets. Producers, led by Paramount, are able to negotiate a contract with syndicated buyers even before network run, stipulating that if the network should cancel the show in its first or second year, syndicators will continue to fund productions until a full package of episodes exists—usually four to five years' worth. This minimizes producers' risks considerably. According to Paramount President Richard H. Frank: "I don't think you will see another company come out with a product after it's on the network for two or three years and not get stations to agree to take first-runs on it. That's a whole change in the marketplace that says to the networks: You're going to have to think twice now on cancelling shows because there are going to be alternatives for stations, including affiliates."[31]

Another type of syndicated programming has been dubbed "first-run syndication" by the production companies; it essentially substitutes independent stations and cable networks for the role traditionally played by ABC, CBS, and NBC as the first market for new original programming. One of the earliest organized efforts in this direction was Operation Prime Time (OPT), a loosely organized consortium of studios and distributors formed in 1977 to provide high-quality, original first-run programming for distribution to ad hoc networks. Most of OPT's productions were miniseries, often based on best-selling novels: "A Woman Called Golda," John Jakes' "The Bastard," "The Rebels," and "The Seekers," and "Blood Feud," to name a few of the most successful. All the major studios participated, with the exception of Paramount, which had attempted to put together its own first-run package based on the "Star Trek" series. Although OPT still exists, most of the majors have since moved on to permanent first-run TV production under their own names. In 1988, for example, the production houses turned out more hours of first-run syndication programs than network shows.

Paramount pioneered in this field with its show "Entertainment Tonight," as well as the cable situation comedy "Brothers," and in 1987 syndicated 285 hours of varied programming. Warner Brothers began with a ten-hour miniseries, "V," sold to fourteen markets in 1987; although it produced no new first-run programs in 1987–88, its purchase of Lorimar-Telepictures in 1988 added that company's roster of 494 syndicated hours to Warners' list in 1988. Often these first-run syndicated shows were marketed to multiple-independent station owners, mininetworks who buy for a group of stations that they own and operate.[32]

Many of these first-run shows are sold wholly or partially on a barter basis whereby the producer's package to the station includes a certain number of national advertising spots, pre-sold by the producer. This reduces costs to the stations because advertising revenues offset costs, but it also decreases the number of spots left for the station to sell. OPT began on a partial barter basis, but station operators soon requested to be allowed to sell all spots on a local basis. Some series, however, are sold on a barter basis only—as Lorimar's advertising for the "Falcon Crest" package read, "Barter only, no cash—please!" Although the revenue posiblities for local shows are sharply cut down by this practice, at the same time smaller stations can afford to run quality programming at little risk.

The financial interest and syndication rules, however, were intended to expire in 1990, and, in the late 1980s, the major broadcast networks prepared to move back into program production. CBS planned to produce about 20 percent of its own made-for-TV movies in 1988–89, along with ten to twelve series. NBC Productions, the NBC network's in-house production company, also developed series and movies for 1988–89, in addition to such programs as "Saturday Night Live" and "Late Night with David Letterman," which it already produces. ABC Circle Films, which produced "Moonlighting," planned several miniseries and made-for-TV movies for the 1988–89 season. The economics of in-house production make it attractive as financial interest rules lapse; the average made-for-TV movie costs about $2.5 million to produce, most of which is offset by advertising revenue. Add revenues of approximately $500,000 from sale of syndication rights and perhaps twice as much in foreign distribution, all of which goes directly to the network, and in-house production becomes an attractive alternative to dependence on outside producers.[33]

Films on TV

The barter method of financing distribution also extends to the third form of programming provided by the studios—theatrical films. Although increasing steadily from the mid-1960s, the exhibition of theatrical films on network TV fell off in the 1980s. Made-for-TV movies played a part in this decline; comparison of ratings of theatrical and made-for-TV films during the 1983–84 seasons shows consistently higher ratings for the made-for-TV films, with the lowest-ranked of the top five made-for-TVs ("Lace, Part 1," 28.2 rating/39 share) gaining a higher rating than the top-ranked theatrical ("Stir Crazy," 26.7 rating/41 share). Networks cite competition from pay TV and videocassettes as reason for theatrical film's falling ratings: "Now in addition to a value [ratings] reduction there is a perception reduction. It's no longer a television event. Not only have the films been seen before, they've been seen before on television" explained a network spokesman. Film producers, on the other hand, charge that networks fail to promote and schedule theatrical features properly; "Their attitude about features becomes a self-fulfilling prophecy." Made-for-TV films and miniseries also remain considerably less expensive to buy or produce, boosting network profits.[34]

But whether or not the networks are buying theatrical films, marketing films on a syndicated basis has been a profitable operation for the film companies since 1955. Syndication of packages of current films, usually on a barter basis, has begun to take precedence over the payTV market. Both MGM/UA and Universal announced the availability of pre-payTV film packages in late 1984. MGM/UA's Premiere Network came about as a response to the weakened network market for films in packages. The Premiere network plan consisted of twenty-four theatrical films never shown on commercial TV, including such titles as *The French Lieutenant's Woman*, *My Favorite Year*, *The Formula*, and *True Confessions*. The package was sold on a barter basis for a two-year period, during which the station agreed to air each film twice, once in prime time. Ten and one-half minutes on each showing would be reserved for MGM/UA, with eleven and one-half going to the local operator. After this run the films could be marketed to pay TV for a six-month exclusive run, then back to stations for purchase on a cash basis.[35]

MCA-Universal's plan, called the Debut Network, went one step further in cutting out not only network run, but also pay TV run completely, with films reverting immediately to stations on a cash basis after the initial two-year barter run. This package included films such as *Halloween II*, *Iceman*, *Sixteen Candles*, and *Cat People*, as well as three Hitchcock re-releases, *The Man Who Knew Too Much*, *Rear Window*, and *Vertigo*. Orion, Warner Brothers, and a joint venture of Viacom Entertainment and Tribune Broadcasting also announced similar packages in late 1984. However, by 1988 the success of these independent-distribution film packages had fallen off considerably, primarily because of a saturated market after the rush of the early 1980s.

Immaterial Hollywood

As the 1980s drew to a close, it became more and more difficult to separate the film, cable, and television industries from each other. The 1980s' wave of acquisitions and mergers in the communications field accelerated a process begun in the 1960s, as film and television integrated, and most of the former movie majors either acquired or were acquired by diversified conglomerates. Besides the Gulf + Western/Paramount, MCA/Universal, and Kinney/Warner affiliations, the Coca Cola Company purchased Columbia in 1982.

The most flamboyant of the new, cross-industry joint ventures involved the founding in 1983 of the first new major film studio since the 1940s, according to industry publicity: TriStar Studios, formed by a partnership between Columbia Pictures, HBO, and the CBS television network. TriStar released fifteen films in its first two years of operation, including such hits as *The Natural* and *Rambo*, all produced by Columbia, reserved for HBO pay television viewing, and finally aired on CBS. Originally owned by the three partners with 25 percent each, with the remaining 25 percent sold publicly, CBS sold its shares to Columbia in 1985. One reason for Columbia's purchase was the prospect of also producing shows for television, which TriStar was prohibited from doing as long as it was partially owned by a network. In 1986, Time Inc. sold its shares to Columbia, subsequently forming its own production house, HBO Pictures. By the end of 1987, TriStar had indeed expanded into production both for network and syndication, in addition to owning the Loew's theater chain. Plans were announced late in 1987 for the merger of TriStar and the Coca Cola Company's entertainment divisions through a stock purchase agreement, thus making TriStar virtually a Coca Cola subsidiary. In addition to Columbia Pictures, Coca Cola also owned, at the end of 1987, Embassy Communications and Merv Griffin Enterprises, both television production houses, and was part owner of RCA-Columbia Home Video and the Weintraub Entertainment Group. In 1988, all of Coca Cola's production ventures, including TriStar, were subsumed under a new subsidiary called Columbia Pictures Entertainment.[36]

Another significant venture was that of the Disney Corporation, whose children-and-family-oriented pay televison service, The Disney Channel, launched in September 1983 and backed by Westinghouse, achieved substantial success. In addition, Disney returned to the broadcast television production business in 1986 with the "Disney Sunday Movie"; by 1987, another show, "Gummi Bears," had been added. Through its subsidiary Touchstone Pictures, which began releasing movies targeted at a more adult audience to theatrical exhibition in 1985, Disney's Touchstone TV group produced the 1987 network show "The Oldest Rookie"; its shows in syndication through subsidiary Buena Vista Television included "Duck Tales" and "Win, Lose, or Draw." In addition, Disney agreed to purchase its first broadcast television station, KHJ Los Angeles, in 1987.

Paramount Pictures, owned by Gulf + Western, made no other foray into pay TV since its Premiere venture, although several lucrative deals with existing services provided a post-theatrical market for its films. Paramount remained heavily involved in cable and broadcast television distribution, however, through its partnership with MCA and Time Inc. in the USA Cable Network, a basic cable service that in July 1984 discussed implementation of a thirty-day exclusive "window" plan similar in concept to Premiere's. This "Partners' Project" would allow USA a thirty-day period of exclusive rights to theatrical films and other programs, after pay cable but before syndication or network run. Neither Paramount nor its parent Gulf + Western owns cable systems, but the company has expanded once again into theater ownership.

Warner Communications, a diversified media company built on the foundations of the former studio, started early in cable, and by 1988 its subsidiary Warner Cable operated 101 systems across the United States. In 1979, it formed Warner Amex Satellite Entertainment Company with American Express as a partner. Warner Amex at one time owned the merged Showtime/The Movie Channel pay TV network, which as the second-largest pay TV effort finally issued a serious challenge to HBO's long-standing dominance. However, suffering from heavy losses in its cable system division and from its Atari subsidiary, Warner sold its interest in The Movie Channel, along with its innovative basic cable services Nickelodeon, MTV, and VH-1, to Viacom in 1986. (Viacom itself is the spun-off former syndication subsidiary of CBS, divested by court order following the establishment of the syndication and financial interest rules in 1970.) *Broadcasting* reported in May 1988 that Warner regretted its move and wanted to get back into cable, as well as the newly profitable first-run syndication market. One step in this direction was the 1987 purchase of part of the Turner Broadcasting System, owner of the Cable News Network and WTBS superstation, in the wake of Ted Turner's disastrous attempt to take over CBS in 1985. Further, in May 1988 Warner made a stock-swap offer for the Lorimar Telepictures Corporation, a leader in the television production and syndication field. In addition, through its 1986 purchase of Chris

Craft Corporation stock, Warner Communications owned 42 percent of five VHF and two UHF television stations.[37]

Universal Pictures, part of MCA/Universal Corporation, in addition to owning 50 percent of the USA Network with Paramount also operated MCA Radio Network and owned one VHF station. MGM/UA, after going through a series of ownership changes in the mid 1980s, exists primarily as a television and movie production company. Turner Broadcasting purchased the MGM film library in 1986, with plans to use the films on Turner cable networks. In the early 1980s, MGM/UA spun off United Artists Communication Corporation, which owned part of TBS, a chain of movie theaters, and twenty-three cable systems. In May 1988, UACC announced plans to merge with United Cable Company, an MSO operating forty-nine cable systems. The new company, United Artists Entertainment Company, represented the third largest MSO in the United States, with 2.3 million subscribers. In a further example of the entertainment industry's wheels within wheels, both United Artists and United Cable were partially owned by TeleCommunications Inc. (TCI), the cable systems operator in first place in the United States with 4.6 million subscribers at the end of 1987. TCI owned 52 percent of United Artists Entertainment.

As for 20th Century-Fox, it was purchased by the Australian media magnate Rupert Murdock's News Corporation in 1985, which owned both Fox Broadcasting and 20th Century-Fox Films. Capitalizing on the new viability of independent broadcast stations, Murdoch formed the Fox Broadcasting Company in 1986, a potential fourth network. Starting out by offering just one night a week of prime-time programming, Fox expanded to two nights that same year and announced in May 1988 that it would offer programs on Monday nights as well by May 1989. Fox's network plans were buttressed by Murdoch's 1986 purchase of Metromedia, a broadcasting and television production company. Fox's stations include KTTV-LA, WNEW-NY, WFLD-Chicago, WTTG-Washington, KRLD-Dallas-Fort Worth, and KRIV in Houston—some of the largest and most successful independent stations in the country.[38]

Ted Turner agreed in mid-1985 to purchase MGM/UA in expectation of splitting up the two companies again by selling United Artists to Kirk Kerkorian, a longtime movie magnate. Turner's acquisition of the film company—coming after his much-publicized attempt at a hostile takeover of the CBS network—seemed calculated to assure a strong source of programs for his expanding cable empire. MGM's library included not only 2,200 MGM films, but also the 750 pre-1948 Warner films purchased in 1956 and 700 RKO features. A substantial number of short subjects and cartoons were also in the collection, along with television series, made-for-TV movies, and specials. In addition, Turner planned to use the MGM production facilities, for both TV and film. The purchase also included MGM/UA's home entertainment and pay TV operations.[39]

Other striking changes have occurred in the broadcasting industry. In addition to Turner's acquistion of MGM and Murdoch's merger of Metromedia and Fox, the ABC network in early 1985 was acquired by Capitol Cities Communications, owner of a full complement of radio and TV stations. ABC, which had ventured into film production in 1981, closed its operations following the merger. Although ABC produced several successful films during the four years of its operation, including *Silkwood*, *Prizzi's Honor*, and *The Flamingo Kid*, ultimately "the complexities of the theatrical marketplace prevented [them] from achieving [their] financial expectations."[40] CBS also closed down its film production operations in November 1985, after six years of operation and a total of twelve films released. The closing represented a net loss of $21.1 million. An even more startling development was the takeover of RCA (and with it, NBC) by the General Electric Corporation, although no major changes were immediately made.[41]

Thus, through cross ownership and economic ties, all of the major film and broadcasting interests without exception have acquired a financial stake in the operations of both media fields, as well as cable. Although the three major networks have withdrawn from the film production business, previous history shows that when time and finances are right they will probably enter it again. The 1980s atmosphere of across-the-board deregulation combined with a sudden burst in technological development of distribution channels removed the artificially maintained barriers to previous integration of the various arms of the entertainment business and caused the fulfillment of tendencies that, but for outside constraints, could have prevailed as early as the late 1920s.

However, distinctions among the different segments of the industry still exist, if only in the minds of those working within them. Conflicts of interests between program producers and cable industry interests, between cable and broadcasters, between producers and networks, still crop up every day in the complex melange of economics, creativity, and regulation that is the American entertainment industry. Indeed, the expansion of distribution channels and production companies has produced its own set of problems. For example, a battle over the so-called "syndicated exclusivity" rules in 1988 pitted a new alliance of broadcasters and Hollywood production houses against cable interests.

Until the late eighties, program syndicators sold properties to independent or local broadcasting systems with only territorial exclusivity: the station had exclusive rights to the program only within a thirty-five-mile radius of its licensed location. However, with the increasing importation of distant broadcast signals on cable systems within a broadcast station's legal territory, this exclusivity became meaningless because local customers could view the same programs on several different cable channels piped in from surrounding cities or on superstations such as WTBS Atlanta, WGN Chicago, or WPIX New York. Broadcasters protested against this situation, and Hollywood program producers supported them since lack of true local-market exclusivity naturally reduced the prices broadcasters were willing to pay for syndicated material. In May 1988, the new Syndex II rules were officially adopted by the FCC, allowing local broadcasters, after purchasing exclusive rights to a program, to notify the local cable operator that henceforth all competing imported signals must be "blacked out" if the cable also carries the local broadcaster's program.

The increasing deregulation of cable during the Reagan years brought to cable the same kind of antitrust suspicions fomerly leveled against the movie business, as cable system operators—the "exhibitors" of the cable business—purchased ownership in program production and distribution companies. In the eyes of some industry observers, cable seems to fall into a gap in regulation. In the Cable Act of 1984, the FCC ruled that a cable system faces effective competition when its market is served by three or more unduplicated broadcast television signals. The Justice Department contends, on the other hand, that cable may be a "natural monopoly" in the local market, making cable television itself the relevant market in which to weigh antitrust considerations, and not the relative local abundance of program suppliers. However, a series of lawsuits resulted from what one former antitrust division attorney called "Federal policy at war with itself": "cable is treated like a utility for antitrust purposes but treated as a competitive industry for regulatory purposes."[42] No antitrust proceedings have been instituted, and the dominant philosophy seems to favor leaving cable regulation to local authorities. Naturally, Hollywood interests resent the ability of cable operators to maintain a state of vertical integration that was denied to them, once again squaring "Hollywood" and "cable" off against each other despite cross ownership and mutual dependency.[43]

Broadcasters, seemingly besieged on all sides by competition, in the late 1980s managed to repeal, at least temporarily, the Fairness Doctrine that guided television news operations for thirty years. The expiration of the financial interest and syndication rules seems not to appear as a major threat to other players in the business, as the networks' share of the television audience continues to decline. Another concern of the advertising-supported networks is the advent of remote-control units for television, and the "ad-zapping" they make so easy for the consumer not entirely enthralled by the fast pace and style of broadcast commercials. Although the Nielsen ratings still count as viewers those who tape a program and watch it later, increasing numbers of viewers use their VCR's fast-forward button to skip over commercials, cutting right to the program; others use commercial breaks to switch from channel to channel, not only avoiding the sales pitch, but also possibly switching to a more amusing program on another network.

However, the greatest growth in any of the segments of the entertainment industry continues to be that of the videocassette market, which benefits the film companies primarily; overall, the proliferation of channels of distribution for a multiplicity of programming affects no one interest group more positively than the producers, whose output can barely keep up with demand. What this will mean for the consumer, or for the forms taken on by individual films or television programs, is hard to predict. For the film industry, or rather for the diversified companies with names carried over from the studios of long ago, the outlook is almost entirely positive. As *The Economist* quoted an unidentified film industry executive in 1983, "When television started in the 1950's, there was a strong view that that was the end of Hollywood. When cable came, we all thought that would kill our sales to the networks. None of these things happened. Every time the market expands, the combination is greater than before. After all, it should be immaterial to Hollywood how people see its product so long as they pay."[44]

NOTES

1. Arguably, at least; several other small towns in mountainous terrain compete for the honor of stringing the first TV cable.

2. Erik Barnouw, *A Tower in Babel* (New York: Oxford University Press, 1966, p. 247), states that in 1923 residents of Dundee, Michigan, erected a community radio antenna and charged customers $1.50 a month for signals relayed by wire.

3. National Cable Television Association, *A Cable Primer* (Washington, D.C.: NCTA, 1979), pp. 30, 31; *Broadcasting/Cablecasting Yearbook 1985* (Washington, D.C.: Broadcasting Publications, 1986), p. 5; Federal Communications Commission, *Carter Mountain Transmission Corp. v. FCC*, Docket 12931, February 16, 1962.

4. NCTA, *A Cable Primer*, p. 32; Craig Leddy, "Cable TV: The Tough Get Going," *Channels of Communication: The Essential 1985 Field Guide to the Electronic Media* (December 1984): 34–35.

5. *Home Box Office v. FCC*, 567 F. 2d 9, Dist. of Columbia Cir., 1977, cert denied, 98 S.Ct. 111, 1977.

6. *Broadcasting/Cablecasting Yearbook 1982* (Washington, D.C.: Broadcasting Publications, 1982); *Cablefile/82* (Denver: Titsch Publishing, 1982).

7. Lawrence B. Hilford, "Deposition taken in *United States of America v. Columbia Pictures Industries, Inc; Getty Oil Company; MCA Inc; Paramount Pictures Corporation; and Twentieth Century Fox Film Corporation*," Civil Action no. 8—Civ. 4438, United States District Court for the Southern District of New York, September 9, 1980.

8. Fred Dawson, "Waiting for Goettel," *Cablevision*, December 1, 1980, pp. 88–96.

9. Jane Mayer, "Hard Bargainer: Show Buyer for HBO Is a Power in Pay TV, a 'Pain' in Hollywood," *Wall Street Journal*, August 15, 1983, p. 1; Pamela G. Hollie, "Hollywood Offers Pay-TV Challenge," *New York Times*, April 29, 1980, sec. D, p. 1; "Hollywood Battles for New Markets," *Dun's Review*, June 1980, p. 75.

10. Tony Schwartz, "Pay Cable Is Fighting for Movies," *New York Times*, August 22, 1981, sec. C, p. 24.

11. Hilford, "Deposition," p. 99.

12. Premiere publicity package, 1980.

13. *Broadcasting*, April 28, 1980, pp. 22, 23; "Time Inc. to Oppose Getty TV-Film Deal," *New York Times*, April 24, 1980, sec. D, p. 4; "Getty's Pay TV Venture Is Sued by Justice Unit," *Wall Street Journal*, August 5, 1980, sec. 5, p. 1; "Hollwood Challenges HBO Clout in Lucrative Cable-Movie Business," *Wall Street Journal*, August 11, 1980, sec. 15, p. 4.

14. Tony Schwartz, "New Pay-TV Service to Offer Box-Office Hits," *New York Times*, May 19, 1980, sec. D, pp. 1, 10.

15. *Wall Street Journal*, November 21, 1980; *New York Times*, November 21, 1980, sec. 4, p. 7.

16. *Wall Street Journal*, January 2, 1981.

17. Don LeDuc, *Cable Television and the FCC* (Philadelphia: Temple University Press, 1973); *Wall Street Journal*, February 18, 1981.

18. *Forbes*, July 16, 1984, pp. 46–47.

19. *Moody's Industrial Manual* (New York: Moody's Investors Service, 1985), pp. 6146, 6198, 5788, 6263, 4140.

20. *Electronic Media*, November 29, 1984, pp. 1, 38.

21. *Forbes*, November 19, 1984, pp. 41–42; *Electronic Media*, September 16, 1985, p. 2; September 2, 1985, pp. 1, 27.

22. *Forbes*, September 19, 1984, pp. 41–42; *The Economist*, July 30, 1983, pp. 72–73; *Publishers Weekly*, February 15, 1985, pp. 36–51.

23. *Electronic Media*, August 12, 1985, pp. 1, 21.

24. Ibid., July 6, 1984, pp. 1, 21.

25. "Forcing Open a New Window," *Channels 1987 Field Guide to the Electronic Environment*, December 1986, p. 82; "Waging the Battle for Ultimate Consumer Comfort," *Channels 1988 Field Guide to the Electronic Environment*, December 1987, p. 121; "At the Crossroads," *Channels 1989 Field Guide to the Electronic Environment*, December 1988, p. 102.

26. "Fox Revamps Saturday, Will Expand with Movies," *Broadcasting*, May 23, 1988.

27. *Electronic Media*, May 16, 1985, pp. 1, 45.

28. Paul Lasking, "Shadowboxing with the Networks," *The Nation*, June 14, 1975, pp. 714–18; *Broadcasting*, January 2, 1984, p. 87.

29. *Wall Street Journal*, December 11, 1979, p. 8; September 30, 1970; September 12, 1978, p. 8; April 14, 1972; April 17, 1972.

30. *Broadcasting*, advertisement, February 18, 1986, p. 22.

31. Ibid., October 15, 1984, p. 47.

32. Ibid., November 18, 1985; *Advertising Age*, March 14, 1983, p. M10.

33. "TV Networks Anxious to Make Their Own Shows," *Broadcasting*, May 2, 1988, pp. 40–41.

34. Ibid., September 3, 1984, p. 42.

35. Ibid., December 31, 1984, p. 39.

36. *Wall Street Journal*, November 14, 1985, sec. 1, p. 7; *Broadcasting*, April 28, 1980, pp. 22–23; *View*, June 1983; *Channels 1988: Field Guide to the Electronic Environment*, December 1987 (chart).

37. *Wall Street Journal*, December 13, 1983; *Channels of Communication;* "Warner Wants Back into Cable," *Broadcasting*, May 9, 1988, p. 33; "Warner Makes Stock-Swap Offer for Lorimar," *Broadcasting*, May 16, 1988, pp. 34–35.

38. *Electronic Media*, October 14, 1985, pp. 1, 23.

39. Ibid., August 12, 1985 p. 22.

40. Ibid.

41. Ibid., November 4, 1985, p. 6; *Wall Street Journal*, November 14, 1985, sec. 1, p. 6.

42. "A Lingering Hint of Antitrust Interest," *Broadcasting*, May 9, 1988, p. 59.

43. "Peace Prospects between Cable and Hollywood Moving Slowly," *Broadcasting*, May 16, 1988, pp. 32-33.

44. *The Economist*, July 30, 1983, p. 73.

Conclusion

Although integration and the blurring of distincitons between film, broadcast, cable, and a host of subsidiary industries seems to be almost complete, the persistence of separate categorization in popular thought, academic disciplines, and even in the thinking of the industry itself requires an explanation. In part, these distinctions are maintained as negotiating tools, much as the concept of live TV worked for the networks in the 1950s, or the public service mandate of radio worked for advertisers in the 1930s. For example, during the 1988 oversight hearings, while the actual companies concerned went about their integrated business, drawing profits from both program production and cable distribution, the heads of the two respective trade associations could bargain as adversaries, complete with stereotyped characterizations and insults. An article reporting on these hearings in *Broadcasting* was titled "Peace Prospects Between Cable and Hollywood Moving Slowly," as if the two heavily interrelated industries represent hostile nations. The report of actual bargaining strategies was interspersed with colorful, exaggerated claims that seem designed to emphasize and exacerbate differences rather than common interests. Jack Valenti, head of the Motion Picture Association of America, thus emphasized the monopoly status of cable by commenting that if consumers dislike their cable systems, they have two choices, "commit suicide or go bowling," while John Malone, an executive committee member of the National Cable Television Association (and president of integrated company TCI) referred to negotiations with Valenti: "Isn't that the traditional Hollywood negotiation style? Insult your mother over lunch while you're concluding a deal, then stick you with the check, too."[1]

Rather than assume that these colorful statements reflect an intentional state of industrial hostility between the two parties and their associates, a look at the actual economic conditions that prevail between the two may present another interpretation. Indeed, on a more serious level of discussion this particular article points out one problem both parties share: the inability to get all their members to agree on a desirable policy about cable regulatory issues. This may reflect the tendency, noted by one participant, that more differences exist between big and small or independent companies in each industry than between the largest, more fully integrated companies on both the so-called "cable" and "Hollywood" sides. Add to this the ongoing trend toward consolidation, especially in cable, by which the largest companies buy up smaller holdings, and the potential differences mount. The largest five cable MSOs currently serve 42 percent of the nation's cable customers, as subscription rates rise dramatically across the country.[2]

Other events during 1988 may indicate a fracture of considerable importance within the entertainment institution in an era of multiple markets and ever-proliferating "mechanical reproduction": the issue of copyright and the stake of individual authorship (or at least "ownership") within the media economy. The writers' strike of 1988 over residual payments for syndicated and foreign distribution opened an area of constant tension significantly underresearched in the academic study of media. The organizations that mediate the relationship of individuals to the larger institution—unions, professional associations, music rights organizations, and the body of copyright law—work throughout this larger structure as a significant force, one that, although left out of the scope of this book, is far from negligible. It is also interesting to note some of the changes in Hollywood that reflect the increased disparity between levels, rather than separate industries, in the media economy. By the late 1980s, more than two-thirds of film production in Hollywood was done by small independents, and many of those films ultimately distributed by the major studios were produced independently. Those that were not relied increasingly on cable and videocassette release to make a profit, avenues not really viable even five years before. Thus small films not part of the mainstream finally have at least a chance to reach an audience, although the economics remain borderline.

In part, of course, the segmentation and characterizations that structure our thinking about the media also reflect historical distinctions which, despite current amalgamation, still live and inform the articulations and assumptions under which these institutions are organized and operate. Some of these have been traced in detail as they evolved

from the early days of network radio; it may well be that many of the
dividing lines employed throughout this book no longer exist, and we
must find new institutional categories to refer to the significant sources
of tension and conflict in the media today. On the other hand, while
the economics of the film production, broadcasting, and cable industries
become increasingly intertwined and interdependent—theatrical films
are financed in part by pre-sale of videocassette and pay TV rights
and by profits from exhibition on cable and television, release patterns
now incorporate these alternate methods as an integral part of theatrical
exhibition—certain structures, such as government regulation, rest on
older conditions, giving rise to the frequent quandaries and contradictions experienced by the FCC in attempting to regulate those portions
of the industries under its control, in all their complexity. Older alliances
and conflicts have shifted, elided, and changed forms, but the terms
in which these relations are portrayed remain behind, perhaps to be
used to obscure current, more pressing, conflicts and compromises. In
the rhetoric surrounding the media industries, the role played earlier
by such obscuring concepts as "service in the public interest," "interconnection," "sponsorship," "live," "free TV," and "natural monopoly"
may be occurring in the very idea of separate and competing segments
of the industry—of "Hollywood" and "broadcasting"—as they have
traditionally been defined.

But at the level of the text (and beyond, to the audience), the
distinction between the products of these interrelated industries still
seems fairly clear: there are films, there are television shows, and even
though more and more films are first experienced on "television"—
via air, wire, or VCR—and some films are made for TV, the distinction
between textual forms remains. Never mind that films are made by
broadcast networks and cable MSOs, that Hollywood produces the bulk
of television programming, and that cable consists for the most part
of the recycled products of these two traditions—a certain set of codes
and conventions operates to signal which type of programming any
particular example represents, codes we recognize both in the texts
themselves and in the contexts within which they are produced and
encountered. In chapter 4, the genesis of one particular radio text was
examined as the intersection of three sets of institutional codes—
broadcasting, advertising, and film—and the development of the characteristic broadcast television discourse discussed briefly. If broadcast
television represents the intersection of the structures of broadcasting
(now incorporating the demands of the advertiser within its institutional
frame) with those of Hollywood, resulting in the segmented, interrupted,
discursive flow of mainstream television, then the permeation of insti-

tutional structures in the 1980s by former "rivals" may well mandate changes in the textual forms and codes of "films" and "television shows" themselves.

By conceiving of the production of media as a whole process in which institutions, formal structures, and reception play a part, media texts can be recontextualized, linked to broader social structures and to the particular historical moment that created them. The result of such a process, it is hoped, may be to demonstrate that these textual forms and structures, to use a phrase of philosopher Michel Foucault, "weren't as necessary as all that"; that far from being organic outgrowths of an inevitable process of development, they result from intentions, choices, and decisions made within a dominant value system to the best interests of an institution.[3] The very putting together, in this study, of the formerly disparately conceived film and broadcasting industries works to point out deficiencies in received history, to clarify as intentional decisions and choices phenomena formerly conceived of as "natural" or inevitable, to reconstitute as struggle and tension the course of events that shaped two of our dominant social institutions, tensions that in turn led to the formation of distinct media discourses. In regarding the space of broadcasting as one over which two institutions fought for the right to occupy and define, aided or defeated by the legislative powers of government, instead of inherently separate domains insulated and defined by technology, the realm of "what is" has been discarded in favor of "what makes it so?" and thus the question has been opened to a wider investigation of culture, media, and society.

NOTES

1. "Peace Prospects Between Cable and Hollywood Moving Slowly," *Broadcasting*, May 16, 1988, pp. 32–33.

2. "Cable's Shrinking World," *Broadcasting*, May 1, 1988, p. 22.

3. Michel Foucault, "Questions of Method: An Interview with Michel Foucault," *Ideology and Consciousness* 8 (1981): 3.

Bibliography

1. Books, Dissertations, Journal Articles, and Documents

Allen, Robert C. *Speaking of Soap Operas*. Chapel Hill: University of North Carolina Press, 1986.

———— and Douglas Gomerey. *Film History: Theory and Practice*. New York: Alfred A. Knopf, 1985.

Archer, Gleason L. *Big Business and Radio*. New York: American Historical Company, Inc. 1939.

————. *A History of Broadcasting to 1926*. New York: American Historical Company, Inc. 1938.

Ayer, Douglas, Roy E. Bates, and Peter J. Herman. "Self Censorship in the Movie Industry: A Historical Perspective on Law and Social Change." In *The American Movie Industry*, edited by Gorham Kindem. Carbondale: Southern Illinois University Press, 1982.

Balio, Tino, ed. *The American Film Industry*. Madison: University of Wisconsin Press, 1985.

Baltin, Will. "Era of Pay-As-You-See TV Just Around the Corner." *Film Daily Yearbook 1952*, p. 723. New York: Film Daily Publications, 1952.

————. "The Exhibitor's Place in Television." *Film Daily Yearbook 1950*, pp. 839–41. New York: Film Daily Publications, 1950.

————. "Television Can Hypo Movie Box Office." *Film Daily Yearbook 1951*, pp. 763–64. New York: Film Daily Publications, 1951.

————. "10 Years of Television." *Film Daily Yearbook 1949*, p. 815. New York: Film Daily Publications, 1949.

Banning, W. P. *Commercial Broadcasting Pioneer: The WEAF Experiment, 1922–1926*. Cambridge: Harvard University Press, 1946.

Barker, David. "Television Production Techniques as Communication." In *Television: The Critical View*, 4th ed. Edited by Horace Newcomb. New York: Oxford University Press, 1987.

Barnouw, Erik. *The Golden Web*. New York: Oxford University Press, 1968.
———. *The Image Empire*. New York: Oxford University Press, 1970.
———. *The Sponsor*. New York: Oxford University Press, 1978.
———. *A Tower in Babel*. New York: Oxford University Press, 1966.
Barthes, Roland. *Image Music Text*. New York: Hill and Wang, 1977.
Bochin, Hal W. "The Rise and Fall of the DuMont Network." In *American Broadcasting*, edited by Lawrence W. Lichty and Malachi C. Topping. New York: Hastings House, 1975.
Boddy, William. "The Studios Move into Prime Time." *Cinema Journal* 24 (Summer 1985): 23–37.
Broadcasting/Cablecasting Yearbook 1985. Washington, D.C.: Broadcasting Publications, 1986.
Broadcast Music Inc. *BMI Television Talks 1957*. New York: Channell Press, 1957.
Brooks, Tim, and Earle Marsh. *The Complete Directory to Prime Time Network TV Shows, 1946-Present*, 3d ed. New York: Ballantine Books, 1985
Browne, Nick. "Political Economy of the Television (Super) Text." In *Television: The Critical View*, 4th ed., edited by Horace Newcomb, pp. 585–99. New York: Oxford University Press, 1987.
Buchsbaum, Jonathan. "Zukor Buys Protection: The Paramount Stock Purchase of 1929." *Cine-tracts*, no. 8 (Summer-Fall 1979).
Budd, Mike, Steve Craig, and Clay Steinman, "Fantasy Island: Marketplace of Desire," *Journal of Communication* (Winter 1983): 67-77.
Buxton, Frank, and Bill Owen. *The Big Broadcast*. New York: Viking Press, 1972.
Cassady, Ralph Jr. "Monopoly in Motion Picture Production and Distribution." In *The American Movie Industry*, edited by Gorham Kindem, pp. 25–68. Carbondale: Southern Illinois University Press, 1982.
Castleman, Harry, and Walter J. Podrazik, *The TV Schedule Book: Four Decades of Network Programming from Sign On to Sign Off*. New York: McGraw-Hill, 1984.
CBS Publicity Package. "Television in a Free World." New York: CBS, Inc., 1955.
Coase, R. H. "The Federal Communications Commission." *Journal of Law and Economics* 2 (October 1959): 1–40.
Codell, Martin, ed. *Radio and Its Future*. New York: Harper, 1930.
Cohen, Stanley, and Jock Young, eds. *The Manufacture of News*. New York: Sage, 1981.
Collins, Richard, James Curran, Nicholas Garnham, Paddy Scannell, Philip Schlesinger, and Colin Sparks, eds. *Media, Culture, and Society: A Critical Reader*. London: Sage, 1986.
Conant, Michael. *Antitrust in the Motion Picture Industry*. Berkeley: University of California Press, 1960.
Cook, David A. "The Birth of the Network: How Westinghouse, General Electric, AT&T and RCA Invented the Concept of Advertiser-Supported Broadcasting." *Quarterly Review of Film Studies* 8 (Summer 1983): 3-8.

Corcoran, Farrel. "Television as Ideological Apparatus: The Power and the Pleasure." *Critical Studies in Mass Communication* (June 1984): 131–45.

Danelian, N. R. *AT&T: The Story of Industrial Conquest.* New York: Vanguard, 1939.

Daugherty, Frank. "He Sells Soap!" *The Christian Science Monitor Weekly*, March 25, 1944, p. 8

Dawson, Fred. "Waiting for Goettel." *Cablevision*, December 1, 1980, pp. 88–96.

Dayan, Daniel. "The Tutor Code of Classical Cinema." In *Movies and Methods,* vol. 1, edited by Bill Nichols. Berkeley: University of California Press, 1976.

deCordova, Richard. "The Transition from Radio to Television." Paper presented at the Society for Cinema Studies annual meeting, New York City, 1985.

Delaney, Glover. "Film Programming: Advantages and Problems." In *BMI TV Talks,* pp. 178–88. New York: BMI Inc., 1959.

DeMille, Cecil B. *The Autobiography of Cecil B. DeMille.* Edited by Donald Hayne. Englewood Cliffs, N.J.: Prentice-Hall, 1959.

DeVany, Arthur S., Ross D. Eckert, Charles J. Meyers, Donald J. O'Hara, and Richard J. Scott. *A Property Systems Approach to the Electromagnetic Spectrum.* San Francisco: Cato Institute, 1979.

Dunlap, Orrin E., Jr. *Communications in Space.* New York: Harper and Row, 1964.

———. *The Future of Television.* New York: Harper and Brothers, 1942.

———. "The Swing to California," *New York Times*, October 17, 1937, p. 12.

Dunning, John. *Tune in Yesterday.* Englewood Cliffs, N.J.: Prentice Hall, 1976.

Eckes, Kerman. "The Kines: The Initial Period, 1948-50." Paper presented at the Society for Cinema Studies annual meeting, New York City, June 13, 1985.

Eco, Umberto. *The Role of the Reader: Explorations in the Semiotics of Texts.* Bloomington: Indiana University Press, 1979.

———. "Towards a Semiotic Inquiry into the Television Message." *Working Papers in Cultural Studies* 3 (Autumn 1972): 103–21.

Ellis, John. *Visible Fictions.* London: Routledge and Kegan Paul, 1982.

Emery, Walter B. *Broadcasting and Government.* East Lansing: Michigan State University Press, 1971.

Everson, William. *American Silent Film.* New York: Oxford University Press, 1978.

Fabian, S. H. "Theater TV: A Year of Growth." In *Film Daily Yearbook 1953,* pp. 703–4. New York: Film Daily Publications, 1953.

Federal Communications Commission. "Balaban & Katz Corp...for Consent to Assignment of License of WBKB-TV...." Docket no. 10047. *Reports* 43, August 27, 1951, pp. 645–49.

———. "Comments of the Joint Committee on Toll Television, Marcus Cohn, Cohn & Marks." *Hearings on Pay Television,* June 6, 1955.

————. *Hearings on Subscription Television,* 85th Cong, 2d sess., January 1958.
————. "In Re Application of Gotham Broadcasting Corporation for Authorization to Conduct Subscription Television Operations. . . ." Memorandum Opinion and Order. *Reports* 45, October 3, 1962, pp. 268–88.
————. "In Re: Application of Paramount Pictures for Renewal of Licenses. . . ." Docket nos. 10031-34. *Reports* 43, August 1, 1952, p. 994.
————. "In Re Applications of New England Theaters Inc., ..." Dockets no. 8557 et al. *Reports* 43, December 15, 1948, pp. 301–18.
————. "In Re: Petition of Zenith Radio Corporation...for Authority to Conduct 'Phonevision' Test on a Limited Commercial Basis." Docket no. 9517. *Reports* 43, February 8, 1950, pp. 459–72.
————. "In the Matter of the Amendment of Part 3 of the Commission's rules and Regulations. . . . to Provide for Subscription Television Service." Docket no. 11279. *Reports* 43, December 8, 1949.
————. "Memorandum Opinion and Order: In Matter of Applications of Paramount Pictures. . . ." *Reports* 43, part 1. August 1, 1952, pp. 992–95; "Memorandum Opinion," August 13, 1952, pp. 998–99.
————. "In the Matter of Request by RKO Phonevision Co. . . ." *Reports* 45, May 21, 1965, pp. 2441–445.
————. *Report of the Federal Commnications Commission on the Investigation of the Telephone Industry in the United States.* 76th Cong, 1st sess., House Document no. 340, 1939.
Federal Radio Commission. *Annual Report, 1927.* Washington, D.C.: Government Printing Office, 1928.
————. *Annual Report, 1928.* Washington, D.C.: Government Printing Office, 1929.
————. *Annual Report 1931.* Washington, D.C.: Government Printing Office, 1932.
————. *Third Annual Report, October 1, 1928 to November 1, 1929.* Washington, D.C.: Government Printing Office, 1929.
Film Daily Yearbook. New York: Daily Publications, 1954. "1953 Film Year," pp. 85–91; "TV Sitting Pretty," pp. 687–92.
Fiske, John, and John Hartley. *Reading Television.* New York: Methuen, 1978.
Flitterman, Sandy. "The *Real* Soap Operas: TV Commercials." In *Regarding Television,* edited by E. Ann Kaplan, pp. 84–96. New York: American Film Institute Monographs, 1984.
Fornatale, Peter, and Joshua Mills. *Radio in the Television Age.* New York: Overlook Press, 1980.
Foucault, Michel. "Questions of Method: An Interview with Michel Foucault." *Ideology and Consciousness* 8 (1981): 1–11.
Fox, Stephen. *The Mirror Makers.* New York: Random House/Vintage, 1983.
Goffman, Erving. *Frame Analysis.* New York: Harper and Row, 1974.
Gomery, Douglas. "Brian's Song: Television, Hollywood, and the Evolution of the Movie Made For Television." In *Television: The Critical View,* 4th ed., edited by Horace Newcomb, pp. 197–220. New York: Oxford University Press, 1987.

————. "The Coming of Sound to American Cinema." Ph.D. diss., University of Wisconsin-Madison, 1975.

————. "Failed Opportunities: The Integration of the U.S. Motion Picture and Television Industries." *Quarterly Review of Film Studies* (Summer 1984): 219-27.

————. "Movies Become Big Business: Publix Theaters and the Chain Store Strategy." In *The American Movie Industry*, edited by Gorham Kindem, pp. 104-16. Cardondale: Southern Illinois University Press, 1982.

————. "Radio, Television, and Film: The State of Study in the 1980's." *Feedback* (Fall 1985): 12-16.

————. "Toward an Economic History of the Cinema: The Coming of Sound to Hollywood." In *The Cinematic Apparatus*, edited by Stephen Heath and Teresa deLauretis. New York: St. Martin's Press, 1982.

Green, Abel, and Joe Laurie Jr. *Show Biz: From Vaude to Video.* New York: Holt, 1951.

Hall, Stuart. "The Determination of News Photographs," *Working Papers in Cultural Studies* no. 3 (Autumn 1972): 53-87.

————. "Encoding and Decoding in the Television Discourse." Occasional Papers, Centre for Cultural Studies, University of Birmingham, 1973.

————. "Encoding/Decoding." In *Culture, Media, Language*, edited by Stuart Hall et al., pp. 128-38. London: Longmans, 1983.

————. "Signification, Representation, Ideology: Althusser and the Post-Structuralist Debates." *Critical Studies in Mass Communication* 2 (June 1985): 91-114.

————. "The Social Production of News: Mugging in the Media." In *The Manufacture of News*, edited by Stanley Cohen and Jock Young. New York: Sage, 1981.

————. "The Toad in the Garden: Thatcherism among the Theorists." In *Marxism and the Interpretation of Culture*, edited by Cary Nelson and Lawrence Grossberg, pp. 35-58. Urbana: University of Illinois Press, 1988.

Hall, Stuart, D. Hobson, A. Lowe, and P. Willis, eds. *Culture, Media, Language.* London: Longmans, 1983.

Halliwell, Leslie. *The Filmgoer's Companion,* 6th ed. New York: Avon, 1978.

————. *Halliwell's Film Guide,* 3d ed. New York: Scribners, 1984.

Halpern, Nathan L. "Theater Television." In *Film Daily Yearbook 1951,* pp. 761-62. New York: Film Daily Publications, 1951.

————. "Theatre TV Ready and Able." In *Film Daily Yearbook 1952,* pp. 747-48. New York: Film Daily Publications, 1952.

————. "Today, Not Tomorrow." In *Film Daily Yearbook 1953,* p. 721. New York: Film Daily Publications, 1953.

Head, Sidney W. *Broadcasting in America.* Boston: Houghton Mifflin, 1956.

Heath, Stephen, and Theresa deLauretis, eds. *The Cinematic Apparatus.* New York: St. Martin's Press, 1982.

Heath, Stephen. *Questions of Cinema.* Bloomington: Indiana University Press, 1985.

Herzel, Leo. "'Public Interest' and the Market in Color Television Regulation." *University of Chicago Law Review* 18 (1951): 802–16.

Hess, Gary N. "An Historical Study of the Du Mont Television Network." Ph.D. diss., Northwestern University, 1960, repr. New York: Arno Press, 1979.

Hettinger, Herman S. *A Decade of Radio Advertising*. Chicago: University of Chicago Press, 1933, repr. New York: Arno Press, 1971.

Hilford, Lawrence B. "Deposition taken in *United States of America v. Columbia Pictures Industries, Inc; Getty Oil Company; MCA Inc; Paramount Pictures Corporation; and Twentieth Century Fox Film Corporation*." Civil Action no. 8-Civ. 4438. United States District Court for the Southern District of New York, September 9, 1980.

Hilmes, Michele. "The Television Apparatus: Direct Address." *Journal of Film and Video* 37 (Fall 1985): 27-36.

Hollie, Pamela G. "Hollywood Offers Pay-TV Challenge." *New York Times*, April 29, 1980, sec. D, p. 1.

Horwitz, Robert B. "The Regulation/Deregulation of American Broadcasting." *Quarterly Review of Film Studies* 8, no. 3 (Summer 1983): 25–38.

Hower, Ralph M. *The History of an Advertising Agency: N. W. Ayer & Son at Work, 1869-1939*. Cambridge: Harvard University Press, 1939.

Huettig, May D. *Economic Control of the Motion Picture Industry*. Philadelphia: University of Pennsylvania Press, 1944.

———. "This Motion Picture Industry Today." In *The American Film Industry*, edited by Tino Balio, p. 233. Madison: University of Wisconsin Press, 1976.

Jacobs, Lea. "The Paramount Case and the Role of the Distributor." *Journal of the University Film and Video Association* 35 (Winter 1983): 44.

Jacobs, Lewis. *The Rise of the American Film*. New York: Columbia University Press, 1939.

Jewell, Richard B. "Hollywood and Radio: Competition and Partnership in the 1930s." *Historical Journal of Film, Radio, and Television* 4, no. 2 (1984): 125–41.

Johnson, Nicholas. "Towers of Babel: The Chaos in Radio Spectrum Utilization and Allocation." *Law and Contemporary Problems* 34 (Summer 1969): 503–34.

Jowett, Garth. *Film: The Democratic Art*. Boston: Little, Brown, 1976.

Judson, Arthur. "How CBS Got Its Start." *American Heritage* (August 1955): 77–81.

Kahn, Frank J., ed. *Documents in American Broadcasting*. New York: Appleton-Century-Crofts. 1968.

Kaplan, E. Ann, ed. *Regarding Television*. New York: AFI Monographs, 1984.

Kindem, Gorham, ed. *The American Movie Industry*. Carbondale: Southern Illinois University Press, 1982.

———. "Hollywood's Conversion to Color: the Technological, Economic and Aesthetic Factors." In *The American Movie Industry*, edited by Gorham

Kindem, pp. 146–61. Carbondale: Southern Illinois University Press, 1982.

Knight, Arthur. *The Liveliest Art.* New York: Macmillan, 1957.

LaBadie, Donald. "TV's Threshold Year." In *Film Daily Yearbook 1955,* pp. 679–81. New York: Film Daily Publications, 1955.

Landry, Robert. *This Fascinating Radio Business.* Indianapolis: Bobbs-Merrill, 1946.

Larsen, Allan D. "Integration and Attempted Integration Between the Motion Picture and Television Industries Through 1956." Ph.D. diss., Ohio State University, 1979.

Lasking, Paul. "Shadowboxing with the Networks." *The Nation,* June 14, 1975, pp. 714–18.

Leddy, Craig. "Cable TV: The Tough Get Going." *Channels of Communication,* December 1984, pp. 34–35.

LeDuc, Don. *Cable Television and the FCC: A Crisis in Media Control.* Philadelphia: Temple University Press, 1973

Levey, Arthur. "Box Office TV Assures Future of Motion Picture Exhibitors." In *Film Daily Yearbook 1952,* pp. 753–55. New York: Film Daily Publications, 1952.

———. "Box Office TV Assures Future of Motion Picture Exhibitors." In *Film Daily Yearbook 1953,* pp. 722–23. New York: Film Daily Publications, 1953.

Levin, Harvey J. "New Technology and the Old Regulation in Radio Spectrum Management." *American Economic Review* 56 (May 1966): 339–49.

Lewis, Howard T. *The Motion Picture Industry.* New York: Van Nostrand, 1933.

Lichty, Lawrence W., and Malachi C. Topping. *American Broadcasting: A Sourcebook on the History of Radio and Television.* New York: Hastings House, 1975.

Lief, Alfred. *"It Floats": The Story of Procter & Gamble.* New York: Rinehart, 1958.

Long, Stewart Lewis. *The Development of the Television Network Monopoly.* New York: Arno Press, 1979.

Lucich, Bernard, "The Lux Radio Theatre." In *American Broadcasting: A Sourcebook on the History of Radio and Television,* edited by Lawrence W. Lichty and Malachi C. Topping, pp. 391–94. New York: Hastings House, 1975.

Lyons, Eugene. *David Sarnoff.* New York: Harper and Row, 1966.

MacDonald, J. Fred. *Don't Touch That Dial!: Radio Programming in American Life, 1920–1960.* Chicago: Nelson-Hall, 1972.

MacGowan, Kenneth R. *Behind The Screen: The History and Techniques of the Motion Picture.* New York: Delacorte Press, 1965.

MacLaurin, W. Rupert. "Patent and Technological Progress: A Study of Television." *Journal of Political Economy* (April 1950): 142.

Mander, Mary. "The Public Debate About Broadcasting in the Twenties: An Interpretative History." *Journal of Broadcasting* 28 (Spring 1984): 167–85.

Marchand, Roland. *Advertising the American Dream.* Berkeley: University of California Press, 1985.

Mattelart, Michele. "Can Industrialized Culture Be a Culture of Difference?: A Reflection on France's Confrontation with the U. S. Model of Serialized Cultural Production." In *Marxism and the Interpretation of Culture*, edited by Carey Nelson and Lawrence Grossberg. Urbana: University of Illinois Press, 1988.

Mayer, Jane. "Hard Bargainer: Show Buyer for HBO Is a Power in Pay TV, a 'Pain' in Hollywood." *Wall Street Journal*, August 15, 1983, p. 1.

McArthur, Colin. *Television and History*. London: British Film Institute, 1978.

McCoy, John Evans, and Harry P. Warner. "Theater Television: What, How, and When." *International Projectionist*, November 1949.

McDonald, E. F., Jr. "Facts About Phonevision." In *Film Daily Yearbook 1951*, pp. 766-67. New York: FDY Publications, 1951.

———. "More Facts About Phonevision." In *Film Daily Yearbook 1952*, pp. 751-53. New York: FDY Publications, 1952.

———. "The Movies' Role in Phonevision." In *Film Daily Yearbook 1949*, pp. 811-13. New York: Film Daily Publications, 1949.

———. "Television Is a Giant." In *Film Daily Yearbook 1950*, pp. 843-44. New York: FDY Publications, 1950.

Mix, Jennie Irene. "Good National Radio Programs Prove What the Public Wants." *Radio Broadcast*, May 1925, pp. 62-65. In *American Broadcasting*, edited by Lawrence W. Lichty and Malachi C. Topping. New York: Hastings House, 1975.

Moody's Industrial Manual 1985. New York: Moody's Investors Service, 1985, pp. 6146, 6198, 5788, 6263, 4140.

Mosco, Vincent. *Broadcasting in the United States; Innovative Challenge and Organizational Control*. New York: Ablex, 1979.

Murdock, Graham. "Large Corporations and the Control of the Communications Industries." In *Culture, Society and the Media*, edited by Michael Gurevitch et al., pp. 118-50. London: Methuen, 1982.

Murray, Lawrence L. "Complacency, Competition, and Cooperation: The Film Industry Responds to the Challenge of Television." *Journal of Popular Film* 6 (Spring 1977): 47-72.

Museum of Broadcasting. *KTLA: West Coast Pioneer*. New York: Museum of Broadcasting, 1985

Musser, Charles. "The Early Cinema of Edwin Porter." *Cinema Journal* 19 (Fall 1979): 23.

National Cable Television Association. *A Cable Primer*. Washington, D.C.: NCTA, 1979.

Nelson, Cary, and Lawrence Grossberg, eds. *Marxism and the Interpretation of Culture*. Urbana: University of Illinois Press, 1988.

Newcomb, Horace. *Television: The Critical View*, 4th ed. New York: Oxford University Press, 1987.

Nichols, Bill. *Movies and Methods*, vol. 2. Berkeley: University of California Press, 1985.

Noll, R.G., M.J. Peck, and J. J. MacGowan. *Economic Aspects of Television Regulation*. Washington, D.C,: Brookings Institution, 1973.

Nye, Russell. *The Unembarrassed Muse*. New York: Dial Press, 1970.

Ostroff, David H. "A History of STV, Inc. and the 1964 California Vote Against Pay Television." *Journal of Broadcasting* 27 (Fall 1983): 371–86.

Paley, William S. "Radio and Entertainment." In *Radio and Its Future*, ed. Martin Codell. New York: Harper Books, 1930.

Pepper, Robert. "The Pre-Freeze TV Stations." In *American Broadcasting: A Sourcebook on the History of Radio and Television*, edited by Lawrence W. Lichty and Malachi C. Topping, pp. 139–55. New York: Hastings House, 1975.

Pfeffer, Jeffrey. "Merger as a Response to Organizational Interdependence." *Administrative Science Quarterly* 17 (September 1972): 382–94.

Raibourne, Paul. "No Man Is an Island." In *Film Daily Yearbook 1949*, pp. 809–10. New York: Film Daily Publications, 1949.

Read, Oliver, and Walter L. Welch. *From Tin Foil to Stereo: The Evolution of the Phonograph*. Indianapolis: Howard Sams, 1959.

Rico, Don, ed. *Pay Television Newletter and Digest*, February 1958.

Ringgold, Gene, and DeWitt Bodeen. *The Films of Cecil B. DeMille*. New York: Citadel Press, 1969.

Robinson, Glen O. "Radio Spectrum Regulation: The Administrative Process and the Problems of Institutional Reform." *Minnesota Law Review* 53 (June 1969): 1179.

Robinson, Thomas Porter. *Radio Networks and the Federal Government*. New York: Columbia University Press, 1943.

Rothafel, Samuel L., and Raymond F. Yates. *Broadcasting: Its New Day*. New York: Century, 1925.

Sarno, Edward F., Jr. "The National Radio Conferences." *Journal of Broadcasting* 13 (Spring 1969): 189–202.

Sarnoff, David. "The Future of Radio and Public Interest, Convenience, and Necessity." Testimony before the FCC, Washington, D.C., June 15, 1936, November 14, 1938.

Sarnoff, Robert W. "Film and Television: A Harmonious Partnership." In *Film Daily Yearbook 1953*, pp. 707–9. New York: Film Daily Publications, 1953.

Schmeckbier, L. F. *The Federal Radio Commission*. Washington, D.C.: Brookings Institution, 1932.

Schnapper, Amy. "The Distribution of Theatrical Feature Films to Television." Ph.D. Diss. University of Wisconsin, Madison, 1975.

Schwartz, Tony. "New Pay-TV Service to Offer Box-Office Hits." *New York Times*, May 19, 1980, sec. D, p. 1.

Schwoch, James. "The Revolution in Radio: Mutual Broadcasting System and a Reconsideration of Radio as a Model for Television History." Paper presented at the Society for Cinema Studies-University Film and Video Association joint conference, Bozeman, Montana, June 1988.

Settel, Irving. *A Pictorial History of Radio*. New York: Citadel Press, 1960.

Shaffer, Helen B. "Movie-TV Competition." *Editorial Research Reports*, January 18, 1957, pp. 45–61.

Shupert, George T. "Paramount's TV Network Plans." In *Film Daily Yearbook 1950*, pp. 844-45. New York: Film Daily Publications, 1950.

Siepmann, Charles A. "An Excerpt from an Interview with Former Senator Clarence Dill." Transcribed from the TV series "Communications and Society." Fall 1968.

————. *Radio's Second Chance.* Boston: Little, Brown, 1946.

————. *Radio, Television, and Society.* New York: Oxford University Press, 1950.

Sklar, Robert. *Movie-Made America.* New York: Vintage Books, 1976.

Smoodin, Eric, "Motion Pictures and Television, 1930-1945." *Journal of the University Film and Video Association* (Summer 1982): 3-18.

Spalding, John W. "1928: Radio Becomes a Mass Advertising Medium." In *American Broadcasting*, edited by Lawrence W. Lichty and Malachi C. Topping, pp. 219-28. New York: Hastings House, 1975.

Staiger, Janet. "Combination and Litigation: Structures of Film Distribution, 1896-1917." *Cinema Journal* 23 (Winter 1983): 41-72.

————. "Mass-Produced Photoplays: Economic and Signifying Practices in the First Years of Hollywood." In *Movies and Methods*, vol. 2, edited by Bill Nichols, pp. 144-61. Berkeley: University of California Press, 1985.

Sterling, Christopher, and John Kitross. *Stay Tuned.* Belmont, Calif: Wadsworth Publishing, 1978.

Stern, Robert H. "Regulatory Influences upon Television's Development: Early Years Under the Federal Radio Commission." *American Journal of Economics and Sociology* 22, no. 3 (1963): 347-62.

————. "Television in the Thirties: Emerging Patterns of Technical Development, Industrial Control and Governmental Concern." *The American Journal of Economics and Sociology* 23, no. 3 (1964): 285-301.

Stewart, Irwin. "The Public Control of Radio." *Air Law Review* 8 (1937): 131-52.

————, ed. *Radio.* Washington, D.C.: The American Academy of Political and Social Science, 1929.

Stuart, Frederic. "The Effects of Television on the Motion Picture Industry, 1948-1960." In *The American Movie Industry*, edited by Gorham Kindem. Carbondale: Southern Illinois University Press, 1982.

Summers, Harrison B., ed. *A Thirty Year History of Programs Carried on National Radio Networks in the United States, 1926-1956.* Columbus: Ohio State University Press, 1958, repr. New York: Arno Press, 1971.

Summers, Robert E., and Harrison B. Summers. *Broadcasting and the Public Interest.* Belmont, Calif: Wadsworth Publishing, 1966.

Thompson, Kristin, and David Bordwell. "Space and Narrative in the Films of Ozu." *Screen* 17 (Summer 1976): 42-43.

Tyler, Poyntz, ed. *Television and Radio.* New York: H. W. Wilson Company, 1961.

U.S. Congress. House. Merchant Marine and Fisheries Committee. *Hearing on Governmental Control of Radio Communications.* Washington, D.C.: Government Printing Office, 1919.

————. *Hearings on HR 13159, A Bill to Further Regulate Radio Communications.* 65th Cong., 3d sess. Washington, D.C.: Government Printing Office, 1918.

U.S. Senate. Senate Resolution no. 2930. *Congressional Record* no. 5735. 65th Cong., 2d sess., 1924.

U.S. Senate. Committee on Interstate and Foreign Commerce. *Hearings before the Committee on Interstate Commerce on Senate Resolution 251.* 76th Cong., 3d sess., April 10 and 11, 1940. Washington, D.C.: Government Printing Office, 1940.

————. *Television Inquiry (Subscription Television): Hearings.* 84th Cong., 2d sess., April 23 and 25, 1956. Washington, D.C.: Government Printing Office, 1956. "Statement of Marcus Cohn," pp. 1217, 1450; "Statement of Paul Raibourne," p. 1081.

————. *Hearings before the Subcommittee on Communications on Amendment of the Communications Act of 1934.* S. 2834. 85th Cong., 2d sess. Washington, D. C.: Government Printing Office, 1958.

————. *Report on Network Broadcasting.* House Report no. 1297. 85th Cong., 2d sess. 1958. Washington, D.C.: Government Printing Office, 1958.

————. *Hearings on Subscription Television.* 85th Cong., 2d sess. Washington, D.C.: Government Printing Office, 1958. "Statement of Leonard Goldenson," January 14, 23, 1958, pp. 370–81; "Statement of Solomon Sagall," pp. 355–67.

Vianello, Robert. "The Power Politics of 'Live' Television." *Journal of Film and Video* 37 (Summer 1985): 26–40.

————. "The Rise of the Telefilm." *Quarterly Review of Film Studies,* (Summer 1984): 200–15.

Wainwright, Loudon S. "First Customers for Pay Television." *Life,* October 14, 1957, p. 63.

Waldrop, Frank C., and Joseph Borkin. *Television: A Struggle For Power.* New York: William Morrow, 1938.

Watt, Kenneth. "One Minute to Go." *Saturday Evening Post,* April 2, 1938, p. 8, April 9, 1938, p. 22.

Wertheim, Arthur Frank. *Radio Comedy.* New York: Oxford University Press, 1979.

Westinghouse Broadcasting Company. "History of Broadcasting and KDKA Radio" (news release, no date). In *American Broadcasting,* edited by Lawrence W. Lichty and Malachi C. Topping, pp. 102–10. New York: Hastings House, 1975.

White, Llewellyn. *The American Radio.* Chicago: University of Chicago Press, 1947.

Whitney, Simon N. "Antitrust Policies and the Motion Picture Industry." In *The American Movie Industry,* edited by Gorham Kindem. Carbondale: Southern Illinois University Press, 1982.

————. "The Impact of Antitrust Laws: Vertical Disintegration in the Motion Picture Industry." *Papers and Proceedings,* American Economic Association, May 1955.

Williams, Raymond. *Television: Technology and Cultural Form*. New York: Schocken, 1977.

Wood, James Playstead. *The Story of Advertising*. New York: Ronald Press, 1958.

2. Periodicals

Only longer and more important articles have been cited above. The following journals and trade periodicals publish primarily or frequently on the film and broadcasting industries. For specific references, see the endnotes following each chapter.

Advertising Age, Billboard, Broadcasting, Business Week, Cablevision, Channels of Communication, Electronic Media, Film Daily Yearbook, Forbes, Fortune, Motion Picture Herald, Moving Picture World (later *Motion Picture World*) *New York Times, Newsweek, Radio Broadcast, Variety,* and *Wall Street Journal*.

3. Radio Programs

Many recordings of old radio programs are available commercially and in research collections. *Radio Soundtracks: A Reference Guide* by Michael Pitts (Metuchen, N. J.: Scarecrow Press, 1986) provides much useful information on those available and a list of sources. The Museum of Broadcasting in New York City and the Library of Congress both contain substantial collections of radio programs. The following is a listing of radio recordings quoted in this text.

"Hollywood Hotel." Aired October 5, 1934. New York: Museum of Broadcasting collection.

"Lux Radio Theatre: Dark Victory." Aired April 4, 1938. Minneapolis: Radio Reruns, 1977.

"Lux Radio Theatre: The Legionnaire and the Lady." Aired June 1, 1936. Audio recording, Museum of Broadcasting, New York.

"Lux Radio Theatre: Poppy." Aired March 7, 1938. Minneapolis: Radio Reruns, 1977.

"Lux Radio Theatre: To Have and Have Not." Aired October 14, 1946. Sandy Hook, N.J.: Radiola, 1971.

"Paramount Movie Parade (The Movie Parade)." No date, circa 1935. New York: Museum of Broadcasting collection.

Index

A Note on the Author

Michele Hilmes is assistant professor and discipline director of communication arts at Spring Hill College, Mobile, Alabama. She has contributed to *Hollywood in the Age of Television* edited by Tino Balio, as well as the *Quarterly Review of Film Studies,* the *Velvet Light Trap,* and other film-related publications.